The Anglo-Saxons and Medieval England

An Enthralling Guide to the People, Culture, and Major Events

Free limited time bonus

Stop for a moment. We have a free bonus set up for you. The problem is this: we forget 90% of everything that we read after 7 days. Crazy fact, right? Here's the solution: we've created a printable, 1-page pdf summary for this book that you're reading now. All you have to do to get your free pdf summary is to go to the following website:

https://livetolearn.lpages.co/enthrallinghistory/

Or, Scan the QR code!

Once you do, it will be intuitive. Enjoy, and thank you!

Table of Contents

Part 1: The Anglo-Saxons

An Enthralling Overview of the People and History of England from the Early Middle Ages to the Battle of Hastings

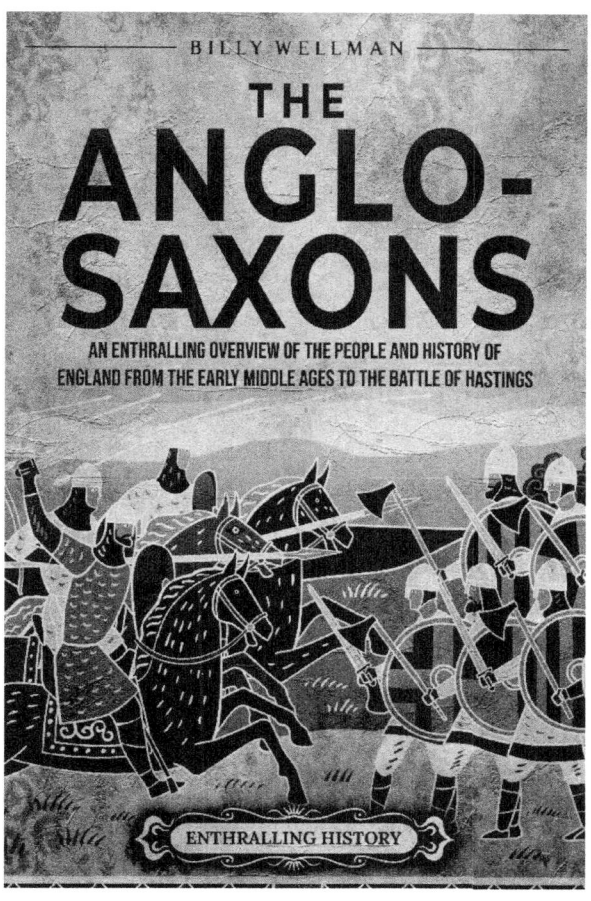

Introduction

Hearing the name "Anglo-Saxon" produces many different sentiments in both casual and curious students of history. Indeed, even though this name is recognizable to most, there have been many changing perceptions and even myths regarding this group of people.

We have a general idea of who the Anglo-Saxons were and where they lived. Most people are aware that the term describes an ethnocultural group that dwelled in the British Isles during the Middle Ages. In fact, until developments in recent scholarship (made possible in part by new archeological discoveries), the generally held belief was that the Anglo-Saxons occupied a place between Rome and William the Conqueror in Britain's history. This concept came from the far more widespread popularity of these two historical benchmarks, but it should not reduce the importance of the Anglo-Saxons in English and European history.

But why exactly? In what ways are the Anglo-Saxons relevant today? Behind the veil of mystery that surrounds the Anglo-Saxons lies the dynamic culture of a unique people. So profoundly did this culture exert its influence during the Early Middle Ages that its legacies can be observed at first glance. To begin with, the group of people we refer to as Anglo-Saxons are responsible for the language this book is written in. Modern English directly descends from the language these people spoke—Old English. They also gave England its name—the land of the Angles—and established the first English kingdoms from which a unified Kingdom of England would arise in the tenth century.

The Anglo-Saxons, once pagan Germanic invaders, were responsible for sowing the social and cultural seeds that shaped England, including conversion to Christianity. Some of the most recognizable and oldest centers of English Christian practices, including Canterbury, York, Rochester, and Winchester, all date back to the age of the Anglo-Saxons. Even the current English administration system can be traced back to the Anglo-Saxons, who reshaped and revived the settlement patterns of post-Roman Britain after the old Roman centers were decimated.

All this, combined with an amazing cultural and material heritage and a compelling history, certainly makes it clear that the Anglo-Saxons are very much relevant.

Still, before we dive deep into the history of the Anglo-Saxons, we must consider an important detail: to whom exactly does this term refer? Problems arise when assigning ethnonyms to groups of people from the past, especially considering that the Early Middle Ages, also referred to as the Dark Ages, are notorious for failing to produce many written records. We will analyze the emergence of the term "Anglo-Saxon" in more detail in the chapters that follow, but we must establish here that the Anglo-Saxons are an identifiable and distinct group that can be adequately studied.

The people whose history we are about to recount did not necessarily refer to themselves as Anglo-Saxons. However, sources first began to use this distinction in the eighth century. King Alfred the Great, one of the most prominent figures from the period, referred to himself as "King of the Anglo-Saxons" in the second half of the ninth century. As we will come to see, the name "Anglo-Saxon" has been used at times to combine many important attributes into one cultural, religious, linguistic, national, social, or ethnic identity. We will explore exactly how these identities were utilized in varying contexts.

This book thus focuses on telling the history of the Anglo-Saxons, the distinct group of people that dominated post-Roman England in the Early Middle Ages until their eventual defeat by William the Conqueror in 1066. In the opening chapters, we will look at Britain under late Roman control, discussing the socio-political and cultural impact the Romans left on the island as they were gradually ousted by migratory barbarians. Then, we will look at the collapse of Roman rule in Britain and the gradual replacement of Roman society by the Anglo-Saxons.

The middle chapters of the book will be concerned with the establishment of Anglo-Saxon society in Britain, including the era of Christianization that was ushered in from the seventh century onward. Christianization came hand-in-hand with the emergence of the first political entities in England, which we can call kingdoms. Over the years, territorial and political differences between these kingdoms increased until the old tribal chiefdoms were replaced by a method of political organization greatly influenced by Christianity.

We will also examine the cultural and socio-economic developments that gave rise to this unique civilization in the British Isles. We will explore the history of the early Anglo-Saxon kingdoms that battled among themselves for dominance before they came across their most dangerous enemy—the Vikings. The complex relationships that would emerge between the Anglo-Saxons and the Vikings would shape the final part of the Anglo-Saxon's history.

The final chapters of the book will cover the Norman Conquest of England and its aftermath. In addition to immediate political consequences, this included the acceptance, gradual modification, and appropriation of the Anglo-Saxon history of England.

Chapter 1: The End of Roman Rule in Britain

In this chapter, we will briefly summarize the history of Roman rule in Britain and discuss the final years of Britannia as a Roman province. After taking hold of Britannia in the late first century AD, the Romans lost control at the beginning of the fifth century AD. Even though Britain lay at the edge of the Roman Empire, it was well integrated by the fourth century AD. The free local Briton population of the island, who were of Celtic origin, were full-fledged citizens of Rome by the time the empire started to experience prolonged periods of domestic and external crises. This chapter will thus examine the nature of Roman control over Britain and the gradual decline of Roman rule on the island.

Roman Britain

Britain, or Britannia as it was called by the Romans, was one of the most unique provinces of the Roman Empire. The first Roman expeditions to Britain were famously organized by Julius Caesar when he crossed the English Channel twice during his conquests of Gaul. These expeditions in 55 and 54 BC achieved little territorial gain. The conquest of Britain did not properly begin until 43 AD under Emperor Claudius.

Even before Caesar, however, the local Briton population of the island was under the Roman sphere of influence, trading heavily with merchants from neighboring Roman provinces. By 77 AD, Wales was conquered. For the rest of the century, Roman legions under General Gnaeus Julius Agricola continued to assert Roman power in the northern part of the island. Eventually, in 122 AD, the northern border of the province was established with the construction of Hadrian's Wall—a defensive structure that stretched the length of the island along the River Tyne. Built to deter invasions from the ever-so-zealous northern Celtic tribes, it marked the extent of direct Roman control over Britain and continued to play its part very well for the next two centuries.

Britannia was one of the farthest-lying provinces of the vast Roman Empire that, at its peak, exerted its influence as far as Mesopotamia. The fact that it was a large island outside of *Mare Nostrum*—"Our Sea" as the Mediterranean was referred to by the Romans—made its control even more remarkable. In terms of utility, Britain was nothing special for Rome, at least in economic terms. It had a terrible climate and was characterized by a lack of arable land in its western and northern parts, which made the practice of large-scale agriculture very difficult. Some of the island's products, such as tin, were highly valuable, but this was not nearly enough to propel Britannia to the status of a profitable Roman province, especially considering the riches with which other distant lands supplied Rome.

Considering Britannia's relative economic unimportance, it might seem strange that it housed a significant portion of the Roman legions as early as the mid-second century. Up to 50,000 Roman soldiers were stationed on the island, a number that constituted about a tenth of the Roman army. These soldiers mainly guarded the western and northernmost frontiers of Britannia, supported by a network of forts.

Nevertheless, the process of Britain's Romanization was slow and gradual. Eventually, Rome achieved its goals there as well as it had elsewhere, primarily because the benefits the Romans brought were immense. The main benefits for the local people were security and interconnectedness with the rest of the "civilized" world, which meant economic and sociocultural integration. Britain became a normal Roman province, and its population rightfully considered themselves Roman.

The Romans' extensive military presence on the island no doubt accelerated their control of Britannia and rendered possible resistance from the locals useless. In fact, there is no record of a large-scale, united revolt against Roman rule in Britain until well into the fourth century. By this time, the Roman Empire was steadily in decline. In just two hundred years, the Romans radically transformed the everyday life of Britannia, and the province seemed to accept its new role as part of the cosmopolitan Roman world.

In 197, fifty years after the establishment of Hadrian's Wall as the province's northern border, Britannia was divided into two administrative units—Upper and Lower Britannia. Then, a hundred years later, under Emperor Diocletian, new administrative divisions were implemented. By 314, the Roman province was made up of four such units. The north, with its capital at York, was reorganized into Britannia Secunda; the west, including the Roman possessions in Wales, was named Britannia Prima, with Cirencester likely its capital; the central-eastern part of the island became Flavia Caesariensis, centered around Lincoln; and, finally, the southern part of Britain was called Maxima Caesariensis, which housed London and was the most socio-economically advanced of the four.

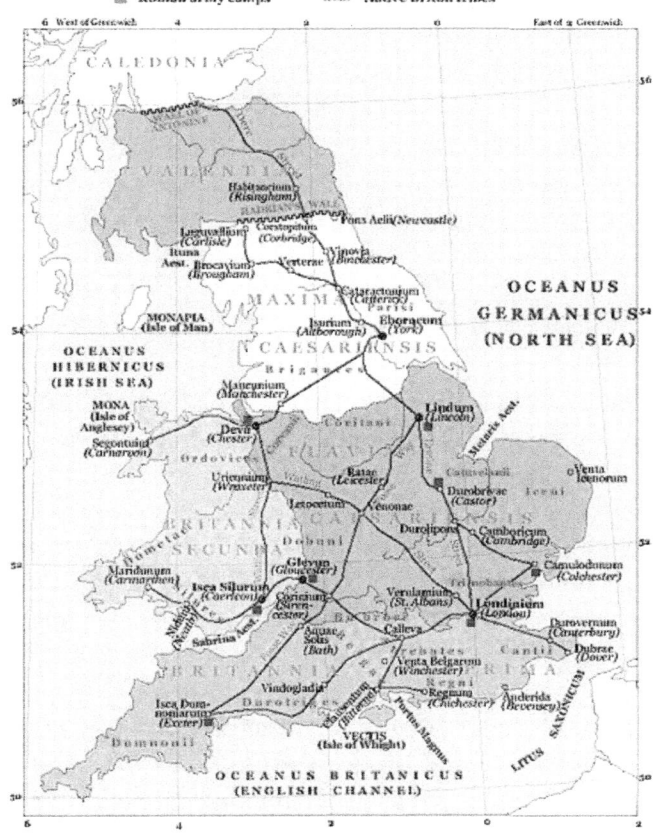

Map of Roman Britain.

The Romans made London the administrative center of the province, building on the importance of the town before their arrival. Here dwelt the *vicarius,* the emperor's representative and the most important Roman administrator on the island. The *vicarius* was responsible for governing the province and reported directly to the emperor. Governors of the four sub-provinces of Britannia, on the other hand, were more involved in day-to-day bureaucracy—the collection of taxes, settling of legal disputes, maintaining public order, and employment of civil servants.

Records indicate that the individuals holding these offices were directly appointed by the central Roman government and were frequently changed to avoid the abuse of power. This was, nevertheless, frequent. Roman bureaucracy was full of power-hungry individuals, and corruption was rampant in Britain, just like in any other Roman province. It was, in fact, far easier to practice corruption in Britain considering there was no efficient way for the emperors to impose their authority on such a remote province. They relied heavily on the goodwill of their appointed governors.

The Romanization of Britain's settlements can be observed both in descriptions of them in primary sources and archeological evidence. After the Roman conquest, different tribes led by their respective chieftains at first continued to dominate and organize in broadly defined areas. These domains of the old tribal chiefdoms were called civitates, and the towns and settlements that fell under their rough borders soon bore the marks of Roman influence.

The relative peace and security the Romans brought indirectly resulted in the continual growth of Britannia's population. This growth accelerated the process of urbanization. The biggest towns were soon organized in a way that was profoundly Roman, with gridded streets and a city center that contained a forum market, public baths, and administrative buildings. The larger towns regularly hosted traders and farmers from the countryside, who came to these centers to pursue business. The Romans also devoted great attention to building walls around the cities, an important feature of Celtic towns even before the arrival of the Romans. Most stone walls were constructed under the supervision of Roman armies in the third century.

The civitates were governed by local councils that worked hand-in-hand with appointed Roman officials to maintain public order and regulate public life. Only certain men were eligible to become members of these councils, referred to as decurions, and the bureaucrats would often reward them for their dedication and distinguishments with promotions.

The countryside of Britain also came to resemble the typical Roman countryside seen in provinces that had been under Roman control for many centuries, such as Italy or Iberia. The decurions usually came from wealthier families that owned land outside of the towns. Archeological evidence has revealed that they most likely lived in estates that greatly resembled Italian villas in all aspects, most importantly in their grandeur or lavishness. Some of these villas, constructed in the third and fourth centuries, were made from imported materials and feature characteristics such as mosaic floors with depictions of Roman mythology. The villas were surrounded by farmland and smaller dwellings, most likely designated to free peasants or slaves who worked for the estates' wealthy owners. Of course, the countryside from the times of Roman Britain also housed small villages and farmsteads, where the lower classes of society lived.

The economy of Roman Britain, as we mentioned earlier, was nothing special. Much like everywhere else, it was heavily tied to urban or rural life and sometimes even regulated with legislation. For example, British towns were full of different craftsmen, such as tailors, carpenters, smiths, and weavers, who had to pass down their professions to their children as part of Roman law. Doctors, lawyers, and teachers, though less numerous, also made up the cities' workforce. Pottery was one of the most important products, not only in domestic markets but also in other Roman provinces.

Finally, the cultural makeup of Roman Britannia was very interesting. Just like in other provinces of the empire, the Roman imperial cult, which venerated the emperors and Rome itself, was integrated into the local religious beliefs of the Britons. Rome had a relatively tolerant relationship with local traditions and belief systems as long as the newly integrated populations respected Roman customs and recognized the superiority of Roman culture. In Britain, for example, the Roman pantheon of gods and the cult of Augustus, the emperor after whom the imperial cult became especially prominent, were venerated. Temples were constructed in Britain's cities, and evidence shows that the population actively followed ritual practices. Over time, the gods in the equally diverse Celtic pantheon were associated with their Roman counterparts. This, combined with the imposition of otherwise all-encompassing Roman civilization, meant that Britons were well-assimilated Roman citizens.

Profound cultural changes would start to take place in Britain in the fourth century as the Roman Empire began to tolerate and eventually accept Christianity as its official religion. For the first few centuries since the advent of Christianity in Roman Judaea, Roman emperors had exercised different rates of tolerance.

The reasons for the initial widespread dislike of Christianity were multifold. First, there was the odd nature of the belief system and its rituals. A more important factor, caused by the relatively rapid and multi-regional growth of the religion, was that it undermined Roman religious, cultural, and political authority. The persecution of Christianity reached its peak with the reign of Diocletian, who, alongside his co-rulers, issued a series of edicts in the early fourth century that severely restricted Christian worship and rights.

In Britain, the most prominent example of persecution was Saint Alban—who is considered the first recorded British Christian martyr. Under Emperor Constantine the Great, however, persecution of Christianity would stop after about 312. According to the legend, Constantine came to believe in the Christian God after witnessing a vision of the cross before an important and difficult battle. After achieving victory, Constantine began discouraging the persecution of Christians and actively promoted the religion, giving Christian clergy the right to peaceful assembly and practice. Thus, we know that three bishops from Britain were present at the Synod of Arles, held in Roman Gaul in 314.

Threats to Roman Britain

By the late third century, Roman Britain essentially included territories in most of modern-day England and the easternmost parts of Wales. Though several Roman generals campaigned in the Scottish Highlands soon after arriving in Britain, the Romans had abandoned their efforts to conquer the northernmost areas of the island (modern-day Scotland), as we mentioned earlier. The forts along Hadrian's Wall were manned at all times. However, this is not to say there was no contact with the Celtic tribes that lived north of the wall. Archeological evidence suggests that the tribes were dependent on the Romans for trade. Excavated settlement sites north of Hadrian's Wall bear many similarities with those in the territories under direct Roman control.

In Wales, the Roman influence was not as long-lasting despite the Romans' extensive campaigns there during the first century. This was partially because of the mountainous terrain of Wales and the lack of good infrastructure, which meant the region was not as interconnected with the rest of Britain. The military garrisons initially stationed in the most western Roman forts in Wales seem to have been abandoned by the fourth century, and there are considerably fewer Roman-style villas in Wales than in England.

Roman control was threatened by barbarians who lived outside of these rough borders. The most well-known enemies of the Romans in Britain were the Picts ("the painted ones"), who dwelled in the Scottish Highlands. The Picts would usually launch their attacks on the richer eastern ports of Roman Britannia.

The Picts are considered the descendants of the older Caledonii people, who lived in northern Britain before the arrival of the Romans. Much as with other tribes, we know very little about the Picts despite the compelling cultural heritage they left, including large stones that contain complex ornamental carvings. These Pictish carved stones were probably used for border demarcations and gravestones and are mostly found in east and central Scotland, dating to about the seventh century.

Roman shores were also subject to raids from Irish Celts, especially from the Scotti, one of the most widely mentioned barbarian tribes in ancient sources. Their culture is somewhat different from that of the other Celtic peoples of Britain, which can be logically attributed to the geographic separation of the islands.

Interestingly, the most feared barbarians that posed a threat to Britain during Roman rule were the seafaring tribes from northern Germany and the Danish peninsula, namely the Saxons, Angles, and Jutes. The Romans identified them all simply as Saxons, a term that would be later used to distinguish between the eventual Anglo-Saxon inhabitants of Britain and the Saxons who lived in continental Europe. After the second century, frequent contact between the Saxons and the Romans resulted in these barbarian societies' advancements in metallurgy, with the use of gold, silver, and bronze in weapons as well as for decorative purposes.

Of course, Britain was not the only province in the Roman Empire that suffered from regular barbarian invasions. This was the case everywhere in the European provinces. The containment of these invasions, most of which were relatively small-scale, was possible if a constant military presence was maintained at the border. This presence depended on multiple things. Firstly, it depended on the treatment of soldiers and the existing infrastructure—if and how soldiers were paid, their living conditions, the maintenance of roads and communications, and the steadiness of supplies to the frontier positions. Secondly, the defense of Rome's borders against the barbarians also depended on those in charge. Rome's history can be analyzed by observing the reigns of different emperors because they made decisions regarding every aspect of Roman life—above all, military affairs.

It was, of course, the unlimited authority of emperors that allowed them to exert such a direct influence on their domains. However, problems would often arise before the next designated emperor obtained the power and authority necessary to be recognized as emperor. In the Roman Empire, the transfer of power from one emperor to the next was notoriously complicated. The practice of the emperors choosing their successors rarely worked, and the vastness of the empire permitted many usurpers to challenge their authority.

In most cases, the usurpers were military leaders who had gained loyalty and support from their troops and had led their forces in the most distant parts of the Roman Empire. Each general was in command of tens of thousands of troops—a number necessary to maintain control in the many provinces of Rome. These generals often promised their soldiers glory and riches in exchange for their support in the fight for the title of emperor. The soldiers, out of loyalty forged after years of command, championed their leaders. Often, there were multiple "usurper emperors" at once, all claiming their authority in different provinces of the empire. This meant that the actual emperor, who had nominally inherited the title from his predecessor, had to defeat them in battle to properly be *the* Emperor of Rome.

In Britain, however, until the late third century, there were fewer problems with poor military maintenance and potential usurpers. This meant that, despite being a frontier province of the Roman Empire, Britain held its own against barbarian incursions. Troops were constantly stationed on the frontiers and enjoyed good conditions in the forts they occupied. The most important British towns were also walled by the third century, different from similar old towns in Gaul, which only began to build significant stone defenses after the reign of Emperor Aurelian (270–275).

The Roman emperors during the second half of the third century, Aurelian, Probus, and Diocletian, were all veteran generals who had gained experience fighting in the east against far more technologically advanced powers. After gaining power, they bolstered the defenses in the most vulnerable Roman provinces.

In Britain, this also meant reinforcing the system of forts and devoting more resources to the Roman garrisons. As the Saxon incursions on the eastern shores of England intensified by the late third century, the Roman authorities upgraded the defensive capabilities of coastal towns and harbors and established new forts between major cities. These measures aimed to not only dissuade barbarians from trying to attack the shores of Britain but also keep the rogue barbarian bands from reaching the heart of the island.

A Roman military commander of Belgian origin, Marcus Carausius, had been made commander of the Roman navy in the English Channel thanks to his proficiency at fighting barbarians. The navy was to defend the shores of northern Gaul and Britannia from the raids of the Saxon and Frank barbarians. Carausius' position was a very powerful one, entrusting him command over thousands of men. In 286, however, Roman Augustus Maximian blamed Carausius for collaborating with the barbarians and abusing his powers. There is no evidence that Maximian's charges against Carausius were justified, but Carausius, in response, declared himself the emperor of Britain and Gaul and openly rebelled against the central imperial authority. Carausius held considerably more sway than Maximian may have had, derived from the fact that Maximian's attack on Carausius' position in 289 was repelled.

Carausius stayed in power in northern Gaul and Britain. He bolstered his defenses and even minted his own coins, paying the imperial soldiers stationed in the territories he controlled. Historians believe this might suggest that he viewed himself as an equal to the Roman Caesars and enjoyed popular support. His army consisted of his old loyal followers, Roman legions in Britain, and bands of barbarian mercenaries.

In 293, Carausius was assassinated by one of his subordinates, Allectus, who declared himself emperor of Britannia and continued to defy central imperial authority in Rome. By that time, however, Western Roman Emperor Constantius Chlorus had had enough with the usurpers and had launched a successful invasion of Gaul, reclaiming much of the territory usurped by Carausius. Allectus and his supporters thus fled to Britain, where they established their defenses and held out against the "real" emperor's forces for three more years, until 296.

Constantius' reassertion of power in northern Gaul and Britain marked the end of the rebellion. After this incident, Emperor Diocletian introduced profound administrative changes to Britain to ensure that a single usurper could not challenge central authority again. Diocletian's measures brought relative stability to Britain for many decades (though, as we mentioned, the island was repeatedly subject to barbarian raids during the fourth century).

Three Usurpers

While 410 is generally considered the end of Roman rule over Britain, the decline of Roman influence on the island was a gradual process. As demonstrated, Roman Britannia faced many internal and external threats from the first to the fourth centuries, but it fared relatively well. The system of defenses established in Britain proved to be effective, and as long as a military presence was maintained, the barbarian invasions could not significantly undermine Roman control in the province.

In the late fourth century, however, the situation in Britannia began to deteriorate—in line with the overall situation in the Western Roman Empire. The empire was battling with migrating barbarian tribes forced to move westward into the territories of the Roman Empire during the Great Migration, as well as with economic crises, overextension, corruption, and civil wars between influential military leaders. All these factors played a role in the decline of Roman rule in Britain. It began when three consecutive usurpers, like Carausius almost a century before, challenged the authority of the imperial power.

In 383, Roman general Magnus Maximus, who had been assigned to Britain three years earlier, instigated the first revolt, declaring himself emperor. It is unclear whether this decision was Maximus' intention or his discontented soldiers pushed him to rebel, having felt disfavored due to the increasing number of foreign soldiers in the Roman armies. Whatever the case, Maximus, using his forces from Britain, quickly asserted himself in northern Gaul, making the city of Augusta Treverorum (modern-day Trier) his center. The same year, he defeated Western Emperor Gratian, who was killed in a skirmish in southeastern France, and marched to Italy to install himself as the "legitimate" emperor in Rome.

However, Maximus was stopped in his tracks by another Roman general, Flavius Bauto, who negotiated with him on behalf of Gratian's twelve-year-old successor, Valentinian II. In the end, Maximus was recognized as the "Augustus" of Gaul and Britannia, a rank that technically made him the equal of Valentinian and Theodosius, the ruler in the east. For the next few years, Maximus, now the recognized and legitimate Augustus of Gaul and Britannia, oversaw the defenses against the barbarians. He might have even campaigned against the Picts in the north.

Still, it appears that Maximus aspired to become Caesar as he tried to seize the opportunity four years later, taking his forces from Britannia and Gaul into northern Italia and attacking the city of Milan. Milan was the capital of the still young Emperor Valentinian II and his mother, Justina, who likely exerted much influence on her son and ruled from behind the scenes. They were forced to flee to the Greek city of Thessalonica, where they pleaded for Eastern Emperor Theodosius' help. Before Theodosius could properly assemble his forces and personally lead them to meet Maximus in battle, Maximus asserted his power in the other Italian cities. He prepared to defend against the impending response from the east at the Save River. The two armies finally met near the town of Siscia, in modern-day Croatia, where Theodosius routed Maximus' men. He captured the usurper and had him executed for treason, thus ending the first major rebellion from Britain in the late fourth century.

Emperor Theodosius I, who reigned as the Eastern Roman Emperor until his death in early 395, is regarded as one of the last great emperors before the fall of Rome in 476. In addition to defeating the usurper Magnum Maximus, he stabilized the mass migration of barbarians into the empire's territories relatively well, integrating many of them peacefully into Roman lands. Immediately after defeating Maximus, he reasserted control over Gaul and Britain and sent legions back to Hadrian's Wall to continue guarding against the barbarian attacks there.

In 392, another usurper, Eugenius, tried to challenge Theodosius' authority, but he ended the revolt two years later. In late 394, however, he began to suffer from a severe disease and died in January of the following year. His ten-year-old son, Honorius, succeeded him as emperor in the West, while his older brother, Arcadius, ruled in the East. As Honorius was too young to rule, Stilicho, the husband of Theodosius' niece, assumed his regency.

During this time, Britain became increasingly isolated from the rest of the empire. The heightened barbarian invasions in the Roman lands made it difficult to establish communications. Stilicho may have at first campaigned in Britain against the Scots and the Picts, but sometime in 401 or 402, he requested the support of the British legions to fight against the barbarians in Gaul.

While barbarian raids in the more exposed parts of Britain continued, the situation became far worse in late 406, when large numbers of migrating barbarians made the crucial decision to cross the Rhine River— the border that separated Roman Gaul from the lands of the Germanic tribes. Barbarians had already migrated into Roman lands in numerous areas, and many were even offered positions in the Roman armies as *foederati* soldiers. However, crossing the Rhine, which most likely occurred on the last day of 406, marked a significant event. In contemporary chronicles, it is referred to as the event that brought about the widespread destruction of Roman towns in Gaul.

Roman legions were unable to stop the barbarians from crossing the river, as it had been frozen throughout winter. The defenses along the Rhine might also have been weakened, with soldiers sent to defend Italy from the more immediate Vandal, Visigothic, and Ostrogothic invasions that threatened the heart of the empire. Whatever the reasons for the crossing, towns such as Mainz, Rheims, Amiens, and many others were plundered by hordes of Alan, Alemanni, Burgundian, Saxon, Sarmatian, and Vandal tribes, putting further pressure on the Western Roman Empire. From this point, it became increasingly clear that it was impossible for Rome to salvage the situation.

The crossing of the Rhine held major importance for Roman Britannia. The citizens were clearly disenchanted by Emperor Honorius' decision to withdraw many soldiers from Britain, believing that the new wave of barbarian invasions also posed a threat to the island. Thus, in early 406, the people of Britain revolted again, electing their own emperor, a distinguished soldier named Marcus. He only lasted as a usurper for a few months before being overthrown in favor of another soldier—Gratian. It was likely the remaining Roman soldiers in Britain organized these rebellions, motivated by the fact that they had not been paid for years by Rome and wanting to take matters into their own hands.

Whatever the case, Gratian was also deposed in early 407, replaced by another man—Flavius Constantinus. Constantinus, or Constantine, was chosen in direct response to the barbarians crossing the Rhine, deduced from his actions after he assumed power in February of 407. Shortly after usurping power, he took the remaining British forces and crossed the English Channel to reach the city of Boulogne. This move was calculated to either directly fight the invading barbarians or reestablish contact with central imperial authority in Rome to pay his army. The second possibility is less likely as Constantine was technically revolting against Rome. It is unlikely the government would have met his demands unless he asserted himself by force.

Constantine's next course of action is even stranger. After arriving in Gaul and asserting himself in Boulogne, he entrusted control of a portion of his army to one of the commanders, Gerontius, and sent him to Spain. After reaching Spain, Gerontius rebelled against his former general, most likely in 409, and later turned back to face him, rousing Gaul's population against him. In an even stranger turn of events, around the same time, Constantine was briefly recognized by Emperor Honorius as co-emperor after he achieved some successes against the barbarians in Gaul.

Britain, on the other hand, was suffering heavily from renewed Saxon, Scot, and Pict attacks in 408–409, finding it increasingly difficult to repel them without a military presence. The British population in the cities, which had not received any help from the empire, decided to expel the Roman administrators—referring, most likely, to those that Constantine had put in place. This also took place in Gaul.

Our knowledge of this unexpected turn of events comes from Greek historian Zosimus, who lived in Constantinople in the late fifth century and wrote about the history of the Roman Empire from the mid-third to early fifth centuries. Zosimus blames this level of disenchantment on Constantine's rather unsuccessful rebellion and his inability to gain widespread support. He writes that the situation in Britannia certainly did not change for good with the rise of Constantine, who largely ignored the island and pushed his own agenda, which ended in complete failure. To complicate matters even more, in 411, after his attempted invasion of Italy, Constantine was captured and executed by Honorius, leading to a complete failure of Roman control in Gaul and Britain for a time.

The barbarian raids in Britain continued, however. According to Zosimus, the British population requested help from none other than Emperor Honorius. As it appears, this request was rejected by the emperor in 410. He was in no position to offer help to the British and told them to organize defenses on their own.

Nevertheless, it is unclear whether this correspondence between the British people and Honorius took place. For one, the cohesiveness of Roman communications at that time was questionable as the empire's administrative apparatus was failing due to increased barbarian invasions. In addition, Britannia was still technically rebelling against Honorius. (The British legions had proclaimed Marcus as their emperor in 406.) They may have thought that financial or military assistance from Rome was the only way to end the barbarian raids and were ready to declare their allegiance to the emperor. Since the description of these events in Zosimus' writings happens in the middle of his account of the ongoing situation in Italy, many historians even believe that he confused Britannia with the Italian province of Brettia.

Still, the year 410 marks the end of Roman control over Britain as Roman forces never again reinforced Britannia. Instead, the Romano-British population of the island had to find ways to adapt to the increasingly challenging circumstances, marking a new era in the history of Britain.

Chapter 2: The Arrival of the Anglo-Saxons in Britain

In 410, the Western Roman Empire was on the verge of collapse. It became increasingly difficult to deal with the waves of migratory barbarians into its territories, and the empire was struggling with an array of internal problems that significantly reduced its ability to rule effectively. As a result, the emperor had stopped caring for the farthest-lying provinces of the empire, unable to provide military and financial support and urging them to stand up for themselves in the face of barbarian threat. After being denied aid, Britain's population realized it was useless to rely on central imperial authority anymore. Britain was left alone and, if it wanted to survive, it had to survive alone. In this chapter, we will discuss the developments in post-Roman Britain, covering the gradual change of the status quo and the arrival of the eventual masters of the island—the Anglo-Saxons.

The Questions in Sub-Roman Britain

In the year 410, the situation in Britain was dire. Roman legions, stationed as garrisons to guard the frontier province, had been mostly withdrawn by the actions of Magnus Maximus in the late fourth century and by Stilicho and Constantine over the past decade. Whatever troops remained in Britain were likely of local Romano-Briton origin. As we mentioned, the population had also turned against the Roman magistrates in the cities. These people would have included civil servants who occupied higher positions in the Roman bureaucracy, though we do not know their names because of a lack of contemporary sources.

All in all, we can only speculate that the underlying theme of the chaotic situation was the following: the population of Britain, the majority of which were assimilated Britons, had rejected the notion of Roman authorities ruling over them, though they did not abandon their ways of life, which were still very Roman. Having decided to act independently, they must reorganize the government. Most importantly, they must also deal with barbarian incursions from all sides, including the Celtic Picts and Scots from the north and the west and the Germanic Saxons by sea.

Our knowledge of the events immediately following Honorius' refusal to help Britain depends largely on sources compiled from the late fifth century, which are profoundly criticized. Essentially, we know the least about the turn of events from the end of Roman rule in Britain to the arrival of the Anglo-Saxons and their rise to dominance, a period of about three or four decades.

The first source that tries to present a chronological account of this period is the work of Gildas, a British Christian monk who lived in the late fifth and early sixth centuries. His work *About the Ruin and Conquest of Britain* is mainly a religious book aimed at chastising the rulers of western Britain in the early sixth century. The historical account Gildas presents comprises one portion of the book and relies heavily on remembered and retold stories available to him. This means that the recounted events closer to the time of Gildas, i.e., the middle sixth century, should be considered more accurate than earlier ones. Other British sources of later times are partially or fully based on his work, so it is important to briefly discuss what we can infer from Gildas' account.

The historical inaccuracies in Gildas' account can be noticed right away, as he begins his story with the overthrow of usurper Magnum Maximus in 388, whom he refers to as the first truly independent ruler of Britain. According to Gildas, the Britons requested help from the imperial government three times after the overthrow of Maximus as the Picts and Scots continued their attacks. Gildas mentions that the Britons were told to, at first, build a turf wall as a defensive measure from the barbarians in the north. After the second appeal, they were told to build a stone wall. It is highly probable that this refers to the Roman-built defenses of the Antonine Wall and Hadrian's Wall and that his account serves to explain the existence of these walls in northern Britain.

It was Hadrian's Wall that was constructed first, beginning in 122. Work on the Antonine Wall, located farther north than Hadrian's Wall, began some twenty years later. Eventually, as we mentioned, the Antonine Wall was abandoned as it proved more difficult for the Romans to maintain, and Hadrian's Wall became the northernmost frontier of Roman Britannia. However, the construction of these defenses is by no means connected to the overthrow of Magnus Maximus or the period that Gildas talks about in his work. Gildas' account also completely omits Constantine's later rebellion, though it is unlikely the source that provided him with the story of Magnus Maximus would have left this out.

What Gildas rightly mentions is that a third appeal for help was made to a Roman general called Agitius, but this also produced no response from the imperial authority. Gildas mentions that, after this, as the Picts and Scots' attacks intensified, an "unlucky tyrant" (*infaustus tyrannus*) of Britain sought advice from his council and invited the Saxons to help against these invasions.

Gildas' account is used by the early eighth-century English monk Bede in his *Ecclesiastical History of the English People*. Bede adapts this history and does not largely diverge from Gildas' narrative, fixing the date of the Saxons' arrival in 447. There is no way of knowing whether this is the date of the first Saxon mercenaries' arrival, but the general chronological order of the story after their arrival in Britain matches Gildas' account.

We also have the account from the *History of the Britons*, which was originally attributed to a Welsh monk named Nennius, who lived in the ninth century. Nennius' story, however, is heavily influenced by the fact that he wrote as a monk under King Merfyn of the Welsh Kingdom of Gwynedd. Many details might have been changed accordingly. Evidence about the events of early fifth-century Britain can also be found in the *Anglo-Saxon Chronicle*, compiled in the later ninth century. Still, the identification of exact dates is very difficult.

Vortigern, Hengist, and Horsa

From these accounts, we can derive the basic outline of the early post-Roman history of Britain. After Britain's inability to gain support from the failing Roman Empire, the raiding Celtic tribes, especially from the north, put increasing pressure on the Romano-Briton population. This persisted for some time before those who still held authority in the former Roman province, be it a council or the "unlucky tyrant" referred to by Gildas, called for help from the next best option—the Saxons. The Britons decided to invite Saxon mercenaries to fight off the Pict and Scot raiders, which led to more and more Saxon fighters arriving in Britain.

But who exactly was in charge of Britain after the expulsion of Roman magistrates? This is a question that needs to be answered before we discuss the rate and degree of Saxon migration to Britain.

Even though Britannia was no longer connected to the central imperial authority in Rome, its way of life and social organization was still very much Roman. The Britons still regarded themselves as rightful members of Roman civilization. The expulsion of imperial authorities was simply a sign of protest to the emperor who cared little for his subjects, not a complete rejection of Rome.

One aspect of social life that had been present in Britain from the time of the Romans was the local councils, which were established to govern the Britain civitates more effectively. In Zosimus' account of Honorius' alleged response to the plea of the Britons, the emperor seemed to address the cities of Britain. This indicates that the local governance system was still prominent in 410. There is little reason to suspect that it would be completely abandoned afterward.

Similarly, there is a high chance that those who had supposedly asked the emperor for help were members of the higher classes, perhaps the landed nobility whose estates, located outside of the walled cities, were more threatened by the barbarian invasions. It is also likely that this circle of local administrators and nobles governed Britain in the absence of a clear ruler after the revolt in 406.

However, desperate times call for desperate measures, and the Britons likely searched for individual figures to lead them out of their desperation in the early fifth century. In times of great crisis, the Roman Republic itself would grant almost unrestricted power to a single individual—the dictator—who would be elected for a certain term by the Senate to deal with the crisis. It is thus likely that the "unlucky tyrant," who, according to Gildas, resorted to calling the Saxons for aid against the Picts and the Scots, was a real historical figure.

In Gildas' account, this figure is aided by a council, which might refer to one of the local councils from the original organization of Roman civitates in Britain. Still, as Gildas refers to him as *tyrannus*, it seems he was not elected to this position. The fact that Gildas refers to him as "unlucky" likely signifies that after his decision, Britain was swarmed by the immigrating Saxons and forced to go to war. Thus, we can infer from

Gildas' account that, though a single man held considerable power in immediate post-Roman Britain, the old local council organization was still very prominent.

Bede, the author of the *Ecclesiastical History of the English People*, expands on Gildas' account of the tyrant. He identifies him as a man named Vortigern, which translates from Celtic as "high king." This does not necessarily mean Vortigern was the king who ruled over all the territories in former Roman Britannia. Nevertheless, he held some power and influence in early fifth-century Britain. Crucially, Bede also mentions the names of the first invited Saxon leaders, brothers Hengist and Horsa. According to Bede, they were the first chieftains of the Saxon barbarians who eventually also fought against the Britons, Vortigern included.

Illustration of Bede.

Later sources expand on this account, saying that the chieftain brothers landed near Ebbsfleet in Kent. The small force they brought was successful at first in defeating the Picts and was paid by the Britons. After witnessing their success, Vortigern believed that the strategy was working and asked the brothers to bring back more of their tribesmen to settle in Kent and fight. Seeing the chaotic situation in Britain, Hengist and Horsa sent word back to their homeland, noting that the Britons were still very disorganized and requested more reinforcements. According to the chronicles, they intended to betray their employers.

The Saxon soldiers brought their families and settled in southeastern Britain. Nennius writes that Vortigern fell in love with Hengist's daughter, who had come to Britain. Blinded with love, the British ruler told Hengist that he would do anything in exchange for his daughter's hand. The Saxon chieftain requested control of Kent, which was granted to him in due time.

Sometime after this, conflict broke out between the Saxons and the Britons, the exact reasons for which are unknown. Gildas says that the first part of the conflict culminated in the Battle of Mount Badon, an exceptionally bloody battle in which the Britons achieved victory and beat the Saxons back to Kent, establishing a truce.

There is a lot to unpack in this account of Vortigern, Hengist, and Horsa. First, though all early chronicles mention Hengist and Horsa as the first Saxon leaders who crossed the English Channel to fight as mercenaries for the Britons, historians hold the consensus that they were not real figures. The details about them do not appear in Gildas' account, the earliest compilation of retold and remembered stories by his contemporaries. Bede's and Nennius' accounts, as well as the *Anglo-Saxon Chronicle*, say that Hengist and Horsa trace their genealogy to Woden, or Odin—the most revered god in Norse mythology and an important deity in early Germanic pagan beliefs. Their names, "Hengist" and "Horsa," are also Old English for "stallion" and "horse."

The combination of all these factors, including their alliterative names, mythical genealogy, and the lack of historical evidence from closer to their time, makes it unclear whether they really existed. For that matter, the same can be said about Vortigern. Still, it is far more probable one powerful individual among the Britons invited the Saxons to come and fight as mercenaries against the Picts and the Scots immediately after the collapse of the Roman order.

We can reasonably infer from all these accounts, however, that by the late fifth century, profound changes had already begun to take place in post-Roman Britain. The local Romano-Briton population had called for aid from the Germanic Saxons, who had begun coming in increasing numbers and settling in Kent. By the time of Gildas, a conflict between the Saxons and the Britons had already broken out and been resolved.

Reconstructing the Anglo-Saxon Settlement

Since the textual evidence we have of immediate post-Roman Britain is not enough to reconstruct the history of the Saxons' arrival, we must look at material evidence that dates back to the fifth century to confirm these sometimes-conflicting accounts. From this evidence, we can deduce that a significant cultural and linguistic shift took place in Britain in the mid-fifth century that, in a way, supports the narratives of the chroniclers we discussed.

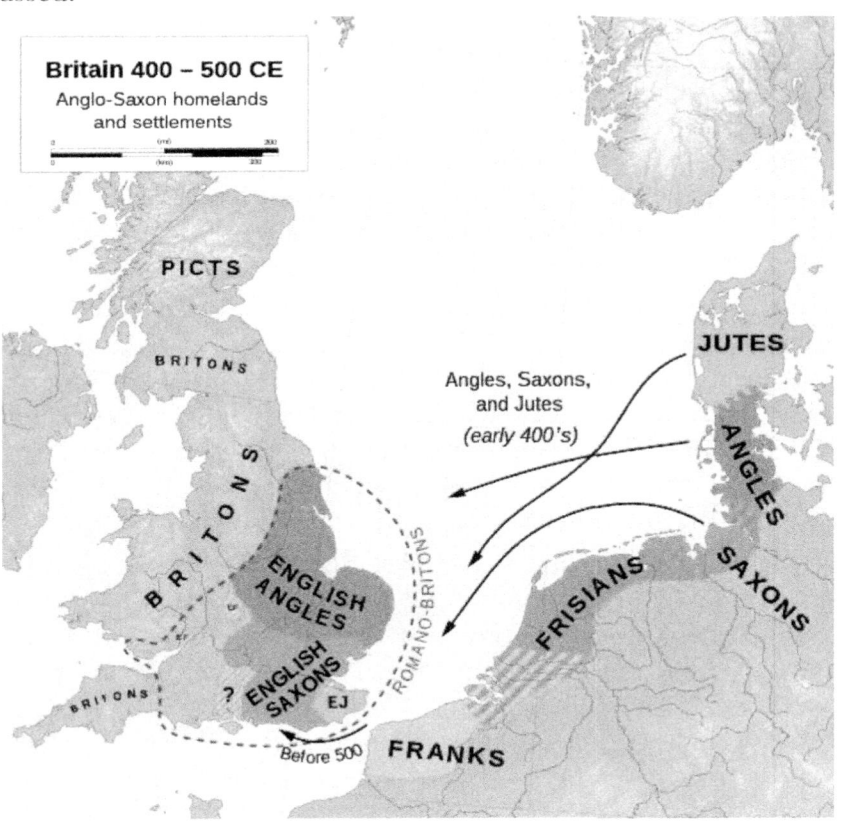

Patterns of Anglo-Saxon migration to England.
mbartelsm, CC BY-SA 3.0 <https://creativecommons.org/licenses/by-sa/3.0>, via Wikimedia Commons; https://commons.wikimedia.org/wiki/File:Anglo-Saxon_Homelands_and_Settlements.svg

By the time of the decline of Roman rule, most of the British population spoke two languages—a Brittonic version of Latin or British

Celtic. Latin was obviously brought to the island by the Romans and was the de-facto language of the province just as it was in the empire. British Celtic, on the other hand, was the original language of the Britons, who maintained a strong link to their Celtic origins and did not give up speaking the language even as they were conquered and dominated by a completely different civilization. This can be explained by the relative tolerance the Romans showed toward the cultures and languages of the people they conquered, as we discussed earlier.

In post-Roman Britain, it appears that language played a vital role in identifying the ethnic or cultural makeup of the society. The primarily Saxon, Angle, and Jute immigrants that began arriving in Britain in the fifth century brought their own dialects of Germanic languages. These dialects eventually merged into Old English, an ancestor of the modern English language used to write this book. In the following few centuries, as the influence of these Germanic migrants grew, Old English appears to have become the dominant language in eastern, southern, and central Britain, while British Celtic was driven to the edges of the old Roman province.

By the eighth century, Celtic was spoken in Wales, Ireland, and Scotland—the areas less affected by the Anglo-Saxon migration. It was also spoken in the most southwestern areas of Britain—most famously in Cornwall, where Cornish (a version of Celtic) continued to be prominently spoken until the eighteenth century despite centuries of Anglicization. Celtic also persevered in northwestern France in the region of Brittany, where many Britons migrated after the arrival of the Saxons.

Though Old English has some Celtic influences, it has few words of Celtic origin. This is a unique phenomenon. While the Germanic tribes penetrated deep into the territories of the Roman Empire—for example, into Gaul, Iberia, Italia, and even North Africa—they largely adopted local languages. Thus, key questions arise when examining the emergence of Old English as the dominant language of post-Roman Britain. Was it the result of a decisive military takeover and the forceful assertion of a completely new order that might have included, for example, the prohibition of British Celtic? Or, did it result from the emergence of an Old English-speaking elite whose language became more prestigious for commoners to speak over time, at the expense of their native languages?

The idea of the Anglo-Saxons' military domination is partially supported by the accounts of Gildas and Bede, which mention conflicts breaking out between the immigrants and the locals soon after the collapse of Roman rule in Britain.

The second hypothesis is somewhat supported by textual evidence. The *Anglo-Saxon Chronicle* mentions that the early Saxons killed many local British leaders in their encounters in the second half of the fifth century. According to Nennius' *History of the Britons*, Hengist invited Vortigern and other British leaders to a feast to celebrate peace, where Hengist had instructed his men to hide knives in their attire and kill the unsuspecting Britons. Many British leaders (who, if Nennius is correct, were the remaining nobility) were slain. Vortigern, who was spared, was forced to give up control of eastern and central British lands to the Saxons. This account is repeated in Geoffrey of Monmouth's *History of the Kings of Britain*, though the reliability of this source is also doubted. Still, it appears that the Saxons somehow eliminated the high-ranking local British nobility and asserted themselves in their place.

According to this theory, this resulted in a dramatic shift in the political order. Many Britons would have been influenced to adopt the language of the Saxons, as it may have given them more advantages or been required by the new leadership. Nevertheless, the language shift that took place in post-Roman Britain was gradual, as every language shift is. It must have taken place over several generations as the Anglo-Saxon domination of England became more prominent.

Archeological evidence supports the general claim that the Anglo-Saxon settlement occurred in Britain from east to west. The clearest evidence of this is the distribution of Anglo-Saxon burial sites, which are distinguishable from Romano-British sites. For example, Mucking, an archeological site located in southeastern Essex, contains a large cemetery where both Romano-British and Anglo-Saxon-style burial sites have been discovered, and the latter are more numerous.

Mucking is believed to have been a British settlement before it was abandoned and inhabited by the Anglo-Saxons, possibly even earlier than the traditional date of their migration to Britain in the 420s or 430s. The proximity of this site to other Romano-British settlements and the diffusion of Saxon graves with local graves suggests that the Germanic inhabitants of the place may have been *foederati* soldiers in the late fourth or early fifth century. Mucking also contains more than two hundred Saxon-style buildings, called *Grubenhaus*, a type of small pit-house. Generally, the earliest Anglo-Saxon sites have been discovered in the eastern parts of England, all the way north to the River Humber. This also partially confirms the account of their settlement patterns in the late fifth and early sixth centuries.

The fact that the earliest Anglo-Saxons were mercenaries can be quite reasonably reconfirmed by the discovery of belt fittings that bear ornamental carvings, including animal carvings that resemble Germanic styles. They have been found in an array of sites, such as Mucking, the late Roman burial sites at Winchester, and even France.

Though these belt fittings are reminiscent of the Germanic style and taste, they were most likely used by both Saxon and local Romano-British soldiers. Late Roman pottery also bears a Germanic style, so much so that the pots have been attributed to a distinct Romano-Saxon style, indicating a high degree of contact between the two cultures. It is apparent that Roman Britannia started to produce pots with Germanic decorations as early as the late fourth century. This indicates a demand for such goods, pointing to the close relationship the late Roman Britannia had with the Saxon culture.

Thus, there is linguistic, cultural, and material evidence of Saxon presence in Britain by the mid-fifth century that supports contemporary literary sources. People of Germanic origin populated parts of eastern Britain, especially the region of Kent, and very likely arrived there as *foederati* mercenaries. It appears that they lived somewhat separate from the rest of the local British society. In time, more Saxons migrated to the shores of Britain and, whether through warfare, domination of the Briton elites, or cultural assimilation, asserted their control over the local population. What came next was a profound transformation of the social, cultural, and political landscape of post-Roman Britain. By the mid-sixth century, the Anglo-Saxons were master of Britain.

Chapter 3: The Birth of Anglo-Saxon England

In this chapter, we will look at the period following the Anglo-Saxon settlement in post-Roman Britain, which includes profound socio-political transformations. As we saw in the previous chapter, the events following the Anglo-Saxons' arrival in Britain that caused them to become the dominant force by the middle of the sixth century are shrouded in mystery. But, by the late sixth century, when Pope Gregory I decided to send a mission to Britain, the Anglo-Saxons had already established their state-like formations, based fundamentally on their native tribal structures. As we will see, the transformation from these forms of social and political organization to a better-developed kingship was aided by the introduction of Christianity, a similarity that Anglo-Saxon England shared with Early Middle Ages Western Europe.

Origins of Anglo-Saxon Kingdoms

In whatever way the Saxon immigrants came to dominate the local Romano-Briton population, it would take them centuries to form what could be referred to as "kingdoms." This was due to fundamental differences between the socio-cultural organizations of the Romano-Briton civilization and the Saxons' Germanic way of life.

At the time of the Great Migration, the social organization of the Saxons, Angles, and Jutes was still in the form of tribal chiefdoms. These chiefdoms had a strict hierarchy, with a successful military leader, or chieftain, at the top. A chieftain would hold almost undisputed authority and executive power, though he would often consult with a council of elders or experienced warriors for advice on important matters. He would often oversee not only his tribal village but also several other surrounding villages, mostly based on his military power. Thus, the chieftain's status, though based on kinship and mostly hereditary, would sometimes be the subject of contention between the different tribes or communities that made up a chiefdom.

Each community that served the chieftain would be bound to him by a series of aspects, most prominently sacred oaths with which they swore their loyalty. This was rooted in their pagan belief systems. Chieftains also collected different types of tribute as a testament to their subordinates' loyalty.

Overall, the social organization of Germanic chiefdoms was very different from that of the Romano-Briton civilization, which was far more based on clearly defined socio-economic roles, centrally appointed bureaucracy for administration, and distinctions between urban and rural classes.

As the Anglo-Saxons and Jutes began arriving in Britain in large numbers by the end of the fifth century, they continued to practice their native forms of social organization and patterns of settlement, which included the formation of small chiefdoms. This is not to say that their communities excluded the local Romano-Britons, however, or that they did not take over the existing settlement patterns.

One of the major pieces of evidence for this is the adoption and modification of topographical names. This is apparent in Kent, for example, which would emerge as one of the major kingdoms in later Anglo-Saxon England. The name was derived from its old Latin name, *Cantium,* with its center at the old Latin *Durovernum Cantiacorum*, which means "stronghold of the *Cantiaci* (Kentish) people." Eventually, the Anglo-Saxons would adopt and modify the name into Old English as *Cantwaraburg,* from which stems the modern name of Canterbury.

Romano-Briton political units, whether civitates, sub-provinces, or small communities, were largely preserved by the Anglo-Saxons in different areas, as well. One example is the Kingdom of Northumbria, which achieved its relatively stable form of social and political organization in the seventh century. Its boundaries closely resemble those of the late Roman administrative unit, Britannia Secunda, introduced by the reforms of Diocletian. Of course, Northumbria is a reference to a geographic demarcation—north of the Humber River. This referencing system was increasingly used in the Middle Anglo-Saxon period, from the late seventh century onward. The city of York, the center of the Roman sub-province, retained its importance in the later Anglo-Saxon kingdom, as well.

The Anglo-Saxon tribal chiefdoms varied in size and importance, and the emerging kingdoms absorbed many of them to form larger political units. In addition to Bede's *Ecclesiastical History*, we know of them from the Tribal Hidage—a unique list compiled during the seventh to the ninth centuries that mentions the names of thirty-five tribes and assigns "hides" to each one of them. A hide was an old English unit of measurement for land. After the Norman Conquest of 1066, it appears to have been 120 acres, but it was most likely a much smaller unit during the Anglo-Saxon period. In any case, the Tribal Hidage was most likely compiled by a powerful leader to accept tributes from his subordinates based on their size and productive capacity. It is thus likely that larger or more powerful chiefdoms asserted their dominance over the smaller and weaker tribes, exacting tribute in exchange for protection, among other reasons.

We should also consider the social, rather than spatial, organization that led to large-scale political transformation. Bede, for example, clearly refers to the larger kingdoms that existed during his time by the name of their peoples instead of their lands—the Mercians, for example. This suggests that social relationships that stemmed from the old values of hierarchical kinship remained just as important as the distribution of different tribes in certain territories. The smaller tribes or chiefdoms that made up the larger kingdoms thus continued to recognize and acknowledge their leader, or "king," in exchange for his protection. This is not unique to the Anglo-Saxons. It was the prevalent form of socio-political organization in Early Middle Ages Europe, where the prominence and power of war chieftains and their chiefdoms led to the rise of clear political boundaries.

Though military power was most important, after a while the "royal" lineage of a single family would have accumulated enough support and legitimacy to press its claims to control of a certain territory. Those who inhabited this territory would often support the claimant, even if his authority was temporarily challenged by a usurper from a rival faction or chiefdom.

Thus, the origins of kingship in Anglo-Saxon England lay in fundamental relationships between tribal communities and distinguished war leaders who accrued support, power, wealth, and prestige over time, eventually inheriting the position based on the successes of their predecessors. The importance of this inherently tribal understanding of social relations is affirmed when we trace the etymology of the word "king" (*cyning* in Old English), which derives from "kin" (*cynn*).

Reconstructing the exact relationships between the early Anglo-Saxon chiefdoms is very difficult, not only because of the lack of evidence but also because such relationships are always complex. There is no reason to suspect that the emigrating Angles, Saxons, and Jutes were mostly peaceful with each other. They were different peoples with different leaders who, as we will see later, settled in different parts of Britain with different interests.

A tribal leader could gain power that would raise his prestige as a chieftain in many ways, not just through warfare and military domination of a rival chiefdom or tribe. In a small area that was populated with rival small-scale chiefdoms, conflicts over resources, above all, were bound to happen. Chieftains might also strengthen their position through intermarriages between the tribes' elite, which would improve relations between the two. They could also simply negotiate the patronage of a smaller or weaker tribe if it was in need.

Kingship thus emerged from the merging of small tribes and chiefdoms, which could happen for various reasons. As in other parts of the world, kingship in Anglo-Saxon England had multiple tiers. The notion of "over-kingship," something that Bede identifies by the word *imperium* (rule of the emperor) instead of the word *regnum* (rule of the king), certainly existed. Naturally, some kings were more powerful and prominent and exerted their influence over others. This was a larger-scale version of the domination of one chieftain over the others but was much less rare and much more unstable.

For example, Bede refers to King Ethelbert of Kent as the third figure to exert "over-kingship" over the other lesser kingdoms in southern England. Before him, Bede mentions King Ælle of the South Saxons and King Ceawlin of the West Saxons, who reigned in the late fifth to early and late sixth centuries, respectively. Bede again says that these figures were kings of different peoples—South Saxons and West Saxons— suggesting that the territorial boundaries between them were not yet firmly in place.

In conclusion, based on the material and textual evidence of fifth, sixth, and early seventh-century Britain, several things can be assumed about the emergence of kingship in Anglo-Saxon Britain. The first Anglo-Saxon kings of Britain emerged from a complex network of tribal interrelations that favored chiefdoms with prominent chieftains as their leaders. Early chieftains emerged either through military dominance or negotiations and alliances between different chiefdoms, resulting in a fluid political system. Some chiefdoms integrated local civil and social structures into their rule to bolster their legitimacy and gain more power.

Everything from the deaths of prominent leaders to the outcomes of battles and inter-tribal "royal" marriages may have contributed to shifts in power between the chiefdoms of Britain early on, which we must imagine were frequent. Undoubtedly, some chiefdoms declined soon after gaining power, while others persisted thanks to the intricacies they developed to maintain loyalty and support, such as the payment of tributes and military service.

After these relationships became more permanent and rooted over decades, we can more reliably call a former chieftain, who had perhaps inherited leadership, a king. And, as it appears, by the late sixth century, these developments were already well underway when the papal mission arrived in the domains of the Anglo-Saxons to spread Christianity.

Early Anglo-Saxon Society

A term often used to refer to the organization of Anglo-Saxon rule in England from the sixth century is "heptarchy," or the "rule of the seven." This term implies that seven dominant kingdoms existed in Anglo-Saxon England, whose dominance became especially prominent during the seventh century.

When we describe the political organization of Early Middle Ages England as a heptarchy, it is important to understand that the dynamics between the kingdoms were constantly evolving. It is likely that clear differences between the kingdoms, such as established borders, did not exist and were always fluctuating.

The seven kingdoms of the heptarchy included Wessex, Sussex, Essex, Kent, East Anglia, Mercia, and Northumbria. Wessex, East Anglia, Mercia, and Northumbria would eventually overpower the other three, though their rise and decline is a complex matter we will discuss later.

The kingdoms of the Anglo-Saxon heptarchy.

Importantly, these kingdoms can best be distinguished by the ethnocultural groups that dominated them. The Saxon migrants of Britain mostly organized themselves in Wessex, Sussex, and Essex, evident in the naming of their domains. The Angles, on the other hand, settled in the northern and central-eastern parts of the island in Northumbria, East Anglia, and Mercia. Kent, which included the areas first settled by the "Saxon" warriors invited by the Romano-Briton rulers, was most prominently inhabited by the Jutes.

These Germanic groups were technically different when we consider their ethnic and cultural characteristics. They had all dwelled in different regions of continental Europe, concentrated separately in northern Germany and Jutland. However, they still shared many similarities, especially in the eyes of the Romano-Britons, who conveniently called them all Saxons when they first arrived as pseudo-*foederati* soldiers. At least, they were far more different from the locals and their mix of Celtic and Roman culture than from each other.

Thus, when these Germanic groups eventually replaced the Romano-Britons as masters of Britain, they needed a term to distinguish themselves from their counterparts that still inhabited northern Germany and Jutland. Since their Germanic dialects had coalesced to the point that a distinct language—Old English—had been developed, it was logical that the most obvious distinction should be linguistic. Thus, they used the term "Anglo-Saxon" to refer to the Germanic inhabitants of Britain, as opposed to "Saxon," which referred to the continental group. By the eighth century, when the term began to be used extensively in this context, the Angle, Saxon, and Jute tribes that had originally migrated to Britain had assimilated with and dominated the local Britons.

Some rulers of the kingdoms of the heptarchy would also be considered over-kings, as their domains contained several sub-kingdoms or sub-provinces, each with less powerful rulers but a clearly stated identity. Such polities included, most importantly, Bernicia and Deira, which covered most of the Kingdom of Northumbria; Lindsey and Middle Anglia, part of the Kingdom of Mercia; and Hwicce and Gewisse in the Kingdom of Wessex.

The arrival of Anglo-Saxons and the gradual establishment of their domains profoundly affected more than just the political situation of post-Roman Britain. The immigrants brought a unique culture and way of life that was integrated with the remnants of the Romano-Briton culture, giving birth to a completely new society. While some social structures and lifestyles were maintained or modified, others—especially the belief systems and overall culture of the region—were profoundly shaken up.

The imposition of Anglo-Saxon rule and the subsequent growth of chiefdoms into kingdoms meant that they must reorganize socially and economically, above all. The old tribal Anglo-Saxon lifestyle, based on warfare and sustained by constant plundering and raiding, could not be maintained for long. Better and more reliable sources of income were necessary if the chieftains, now princes and kings, were to maintain their power and keep the political status quo. Many of them decided to revive the agriculture-based economy of Roman Britain, some with more success than others.

The main producers of agricultural goods—and thus the contributors to the economy—were no longer servile peasants who worked for a small group of elites on their lavish estates, however. Instead, the main practitioners of agriculture were the ceorls, free members of the lowest social class in the Anglo-Saxon kingdoms. The ceorls, or churls, were essentially free peasants, practicing communal agriculture while also paying regular tax to the nobles. This class of free peasantry was maintained until the advent of feudal manorialism in Europe, when the ceorls' freedoms were gradually reduced by the landed nobility in the High Middle Ages. By the late seventh century, for example, Anglo-Saxon nobles began to possess substantial estates housing several peasant families, which were occasionally taxed a fixed amount in exchange for protection by the nobility.

The granting of lands by kings was more common with distinguished members of society, such as good warriors, loyal nobles, or bishops. Again, this was done to increase the kings' influence and power. They hoped to not only build good relationships with their subordinates and guarantee their support in the future but also buy services for themselves. Esteemed warriors, for example, were granted sizeable estates by kings so that they would fight for them and their descendants.

The domestic economy began to increase as the social and political roles in Anglo-Saxon England became more fixed. With it came the development of early industries and the rise of exports by local merchants, who mostly traded with the Franks across the English Channel. The relative establishment of borders between the different kingdoms made the defense and oversight of trade routes and networks more feasible, increasing domestic exchange and the production of goods such as pottery, metals, and woolen cloth. These goods were also exported to foreign markets in the early stages of development.

As Early Middle Ages Europe recovered from the complete socio-economic collapse that had followed the fall of the Western Roman Empire, global trading networks were also being re-established, and Anglo-Saxon kingdoms were part of it. Archeological evidence points to the existence of exotic goods like silks and lavish vessels from Byzantium, elephant ivory, and Arabian incense in Early Anglo-Saxon England.

The Anglo-Saxons' connection with European civilizations is evidenced by the presence of Byzantine gold coins dated to the seventh century. Early Anglo-Saxon gold coinage was also developed by then, influenced by the Frankish Merovingian style, with depictions of rulers' busts on one side and symbols, such as crosses, on the other. The earliest Anglo-Saxon coins were minted at major trading sites, referred to as wics, such as in London, York, or Ipswich. Wics would increasingly develop in coastal areas from the middle of the seventh century.

At this stage, coins minted in Anglo-Saxon England did not correspond to European standards, especially the fixed rates and regulated minting present in the Byzantine Empire. Still, the fact that the Anglo-Saxons switched from a gold to a silver-based economy in the late seventh century and began minting their own silver coins indicates some level of cohesion with continental societies, like the Franks, who probably influenced this shift.

From Briton Christianity to Anglo-Saxon Paganism

Importantly, Roman Britain had been Christian before the Anglo-Saxons' migration in the fifth century, though the role of Christianity had certainly diminished with the arrival of Anglo-Saxon paganism as the major belief system. One must imagine that this religious distinction was one of the biggest differences between the local Romano-Britons and the Anglo-Saxons. It could have been one of the main drivers of conflict between the two groups, in whatever form that transpired.

Before the end of Roman rule in Britain in the early fifth century, British bishops had been actively involved in the religious affairs of the empire, attending several councils during the fourth century. While they were not present at the First Council of Nicaea in 325, which came to regulate many of the doctrinal issues of early Christianity, they were present at Arles in 314, at Serdica in 343, and at Ariminum in 359. This is even more impressive considering that Britain had been one of the last provinces where Roman rule was consolidated and was farthest from the birthplace of Christianity. The remoteness of the region meant that the local polytheistic Celtic belief system was a major competitor to Christianity.

Despite the smaller size of the Church in late Roman Britain, some religious figures stood out. A theologian from the British Isles in the late fourth to early fifth centuries, Pelagius was a prominent figure of the early Church, alongside such contemporaries as Augustine of Hippo. At this time, many of the central questions in Christianity were still being identified and clarified, and there were several different versions of the religion.

Pelagius was active in the decades after the establishment of the Nicene Creed that sought to introduce doctrinal universality and resolve many of the issues of the Church in the early fourth century. He was the proponent of a theological understanding of Christianity called Pelagianism. Pelagius, alongside his disciple Celestius, argued against the belief that humans were inherently sinful, tainted by original sin, and instead believed that God had granted humans a degree of free will to choose between good or evil, including the capacity to sin. For these views, he was condemned by several consecutive councils held in Africa. (He had moved there to escape from his original dwelling in Rome, which was sacked in 410.)

Pelagius' principal opponent was St. Augustine of Hippo, who eventually became one of the most important theologians of Christianity. In 418, Pelagianism was declared heretical, and Pelagius was excommunicated from the Church, though a version of this belief system continued to be prominent in some regions, including post-Roman Britain.

In fact, in the late 420s, Bishop Germanus of Auxxere from Gaul was sent to Britain to deal with the rising prominence of Pelagianism in the British clergy. (Germanus also led the Britons in a successful battle against the barbarians.) The *Life of Saint Germanus,* which recounts the story of his visit to Britain, provides insights into post-Roman Britain's socio-political situation near the beginning of the Anglo-Saxon migration.

In short, there is good evidence that Christianity had been firmly established in Roman Britain by the time of the pagan Anglo-Saxons' arrival. Although the importance of Christianity would gradually decline from the middle of the fifth to the end of the sixth century, Christian communities nevertheless persevered in parts of post-Roman Britain, especially in the western part of the island.

During this period characterized by the Germanic societies' rise in prominence, it is logical that their belief system became the most important. Anglo-Saxon paganism is a religion we know little about, partially due to the lack of any written sources composed by its followers. What we know of the pagan beliefs and practices of Anglo-Saxons comes from the later writings of Christian authors such as Bede—who, of course, held quite negative views of them.

The Anglo-Saxons certainly did not use the word "pagan" to describe their religious belief system. This was a Latin pejorative word used by Early Middle Ages writers to express their disapproval of the un-Christian religion. Sometimes, pagans were also called "heathens" in early Anglo-Saxon Old English, a word that has retained its negative connotation. Interestingly, the Anglo-Saxons would themselves refer to the Viking invaders of Britain in the eighth and ninth centuries as heathens.

Anglo-Saxon paganism was a polytheistic belief system. Though the practice of paganism had several distinctions based on the regional distribution of Germanic tribes, its overarching system was shared by the Germanic peoples. It shared many similarities with other Germanic beliefs that would eventually develop into systems we know far more about, like the Norse mythology of Scandinavian peoples. For example, the pagan Anglo-Saxon deity of whom we have the most evidence is Woden, who shared many similarities with Odin, the chief deity in the Norse pantheon. Many places throughout England seem to bear his name, such as the village of Woodnesborough, or "Woden's Borough," and Wansdyke, or "Woden's Dyke," a defensive structure in western England. Woden is also mentioned as the ancestor of the royal families of Kent, Mercia, East Anglia, and Wessex, which can be explained as an attempt to legitimize royal rule.

In addition to a pantheon of gods and goddesses, the Anglo-Saxons also believed in other deities and supernatural beings, such as spirits and ghosts. Their rituals—like animal sacrifice, which was very prominent— were directed by priests and generally sought divine favor or luck from the deities.

We have every reason to suspect that aspects of the pagan Anglo-Saxon belief system were closely interlinked with everyday life, including areas such as agriculture, military affairs, and laws. Some characteristics of Anglo-Saxon society and other early Germanic societies, such as the role of storytelling and general assembly, can also be explained by the important role of pagan priests and religious practices.

In turn, as Anglo-Saxon chieftains began to increase their power after coming to post-Roman Britain, transforming their domains into "kingdoms," it is possible they were challenged by the priestly class. While the "political" leaders of the early Anglo-Saxon society were tribal chieftains who held military power, the priests held the same role in the "socio-cultural" context. If this is true, conversion to Christianity would have offered the tribal leaders and chieftains the ability to gain more influence in religious affairs. They could exert control over the Christian clergy, thus bringing an aspect of Anglo-Saxon social life further under their power. Therefore, it is necessary to view the emergence of Anglo-Saxon kingship as inherently interconnected with their Christianization.

Christianity and Anglo-Saxons

The conversion of Anglo-Saxons to Christianity marks a turning point in their history. It held paramount importance not only for the local population and the kings but also for the rest of the Christian world, which had experienced many setbacks with the fall of the Western Roman Empire. The migrating hordes of pagan barbarians that had overwhelmed the socio-political structures of the empire had also undermined Christianity in the fifth century.

The declining prominence of Christianity as a religion in provinces such as Gaul, Iberia, and Britannia, and to a lesser extent in North Africa and Italia, led to the development of another set of problems. Many practices previously kept by Christian clergy, like record-keeping or education, continued to decline, leading to a vacuum of knowledge in post-Roman Western Europe after 476. For example, it would take a long time for the tradition of learning, previously heavily tied to Christianity, to reemerge as a widespread aspect of European public life in the Late Middle Ages.

More importantly, Christianity had also been a source of legitimacy for late Roman rulers. Since the late fourth century, the Roman emperors had been Christians, a status that had become synonymous with Roman emperorship. This became apparent in the political chaos that ensued after 476. The barbarian invaders, as in England, had begun assimilating local populations. They began to call themselves kings, introducing a completely different culture and way of life that dominated the old Roman civilization and traditions. Overall, this was a decentralized process.

Who were the local populations to look up to in such times of crisis? Some pointed to the emperor in Constantinople. Despite the fall of Rome, the Eastern Roman (Byzantine) Empire had persevered, still the largest and the most powerful political entity in the known world in the fifth century. It was "Roman" by all means, with a Christian emperor and way of life characteristic of the Roman Empire.

The self-proclaimed "kings" of the Franks, Visigoths, Vandals, Ostrogoths, Burgundians, and other former barbarian peoples recognized the importance of the Eastern Roman Emperor. They also began to adopt some of the practices and titles of the old Western emperors to legitimize their rule. Some, like King Theodoric the Great of the Ostrogothic Kingdom, waged wars on neighboring rulers to strengthen their positions as the most prominent kings in post-Roman Europe. Nevertheless, these barbarian kings were never recognized by Byzantium as legitimate rulers, let alone as equals of the emperor in Constantinople.

Eastern writers denounced their kingship and lamented the days when the western half of the empire had been as strong. Many imagined a world in which the Eastern Roman Empire reestablished control over the lost provinces in Europe. This was perhaps best achieved by Emperor Justinian in the middle of the sixth century when he reconquered parts of Italy, North Africa, and Iberia for a time.

However, perhaps it was clear from the beginning that there was no way for the Eastern Roman Empire to exercise control over the old provinces of the West. The scale of the socio-political turmoil was way too large for that to have been possible. The barbarian invasions had disrupted communication channels between the East and the West, where, as we mentioned, any remnant of central administration had disappeared by the late fifth century. All in all, as the future of Europe and the old territories of the Western Roman Empire seemed uncertain, the Eastern Roman Empire could not afford to resolve the turmoil of the West.

Still, an individual or institution needed to reimpose order to keep the emerging barbarian kingdoms in check and provide a solution to the chaos that had ensued after the fall of Rome. And, in due time, the Roman Catholic Church would take this mantle. It had suffered just as much with the fall of the Western Roman Empire. It was largely deprived of its wealth and material resources, but it had managed to retain its prestige. Christianity was still the religion in most of post-Roman Europe, which was now essentially governed by pagan kings.

From the sixth century, early popes of the Roman Church tried to leverage this situation by offering Christianity to barbarian kings as a source of legitimacy and a way of identifying with the old power of the empire. This resonated deeply with the people. One by one, barbarian kings accepted this opportunity, converting to Christianity. The conversion of a leader would prompt his subjects to also convert, resulting in a ripple effect that continued in Western Europe for about two centuries until most barbarian kingdoms were, at least in name, Christian.

Of course, it would take generations before the old pagan ways of life would be abandoned and a Christian society characteristic of the Middle Ages would become firmly established. Nevertheless, by the late seventh century, most of the old Western Roman Empire in Europe, including Italia, Gaul, Iberia, and Britannia, was under the control of Christian rulers. The Roman Church slowly became as important as it had been during the late Roman Empire. This became even more pronounced with the reign of Charlemagne.

Again, it is in Venerable Bede's *Ecclesiastical History of the English People* that we find the story of the conversion of the Anglo-Saxons. Even though he provides a rather simplistic account of the conversion, historians consider the general outline of his story correct.

The first Anglo-Saxon king to convert was King Ethelbert of Kent, sometime in the late sixth century. He had married a Merovingian Frankish princess, Bertha, daughter of Charibert I, who was a Christian. At the time, Canterbury was a prominent center in the Kingdom of Kent. It seems that after the arrival of Bertha, King Ethelbert allowed a Frankish bishop to restore an old chapel there. This points to King Ethelbert's already tolerant attitude toward freedom of worship.

It is possible that Ethelbert and his court requested that the pope send a Christian mission to their domains. At the time, the Roman Church was headed by Pope Gregory I, who became known as Gregory the Great for his efforts and very successful papacy. Pope Gregory endorsed many missionary activities early on, to the extent that the early Roman Church largely owed its renewed prevalence in post-Roman Europe to him.

Obvious political circumstances would have made the Gregorian mission to the Anglo-Saxons, and especially to the court of King Ethelbert, a logical decision. First, Gregory wrote extensively to Frankish kings to aid the mission by sending monks and priests from their domains to accompany Augustine, a monk from Rome whom Gregory had chosen to lead the mission in 595. By involving the Franks, Gregory knew Ethelbert would be more inclined to receive it positively. (His wife was of Frankish origin and the Franks exerted great influence over Kent both economically and culturally.) Besides, Ethelbert had already allowed Bertha and a Frankish chaplain to practice Christianity in Canterbury.

Most importantly, the conversion of Kent would have been a big step toward the conversion of other Anglo-Saxon kingdoms, as at the time Kent was the most prominent of them. In any case, after departing Rome and suffering a series of initial setbacks, the Gregorian mission landed in Kent in 597.

Bede's account of the conversion of the Anglo-Saxons is very optimistic and biased. His depiction of the events that followed the conversion of Ethelbert, which most likely took place in 597, describes an eager population and a chain reaction of conversion of other kingdoms that only ended in the 660s. Though Bede equates the conversion of a leader to the conversion of the rest of his subjects, this notion is only partially true even when applied to societies with a strong relationship between the leader and his subjects, such as the Anglo-Saxons.

Ethelbert's conversion was not solely motivated by religious reasons; clear political motivations were behind this move. It also appears that Ethelbert did not actively force his subjects to convert and only loosely promoted Christianity. Though some members of his court followed through and converted, it is unlikely that most of the Anglo-Saxon population accepted Christianity in the next few years. Pope Gregory's letter to the Church in Alexandria, dating to 598, mentions that ten thousand Anglo-Saxons had been converted. Also, by the year 601, the mission that had been firmly established at Canterbury reported back to Rome, asking for additional resources to expand Christianity outside of Kent. This suggests that the missionaries might have faced difficulties.

The Christianization of Anglo-Saxon England took generations. King Caedwalla of Wessex, for example, referred to as the last pagan Anglo-Saxon king, did not convert until 688, and his baptism took place in Rome. Moreover, active campaigns against paganism were likely directed by the kings only in the late seventh century.

Before that, it appears that pagan and Christian kings alternated in Anglo-Saxon kingdoms. A king would convert to Christianity, but his successor would revert to paganism, halting the spread of the religion. For example, after the death of Saberht of Essex, a nephew of Ethelbert who was baptized in the latter's court in 604, his successors—Sexred and Sæwred —continued to promote paganism from 613 onward. Paganism would persist in Essex until the middle of the seventh century before King Sigebehrt was convinced by King Oswiu of Northumbria to adopt Christianity in 653.

Overall, this might have been the reason that communication between the Church in Britain and the papacy also declined between the late 620s and the late 650s. The situation was chaotic, with individual kings trying to assert their dominance over the Christian bishops who would gain prominence during the reigns of previous kings, and so on. External reasons, like relations with the Christian Franks, might have also influenced the maneuverings of the Anglo-Saxons throughout the seventh century.

Complications also came from the type of Christianity adopted by the Anglo-Saxon rulers and their subjects, as the Gregorian mission to Kent does not appear to be the only Christian influence, especially in the eastern and northern Anglo-Saxon domains. Wessex, Northumbria, and Mercia were all influenced by Christian missionaries coming from Scotland and Ireland. It was not until the Synod of Whitby in 664 that the rulers of the heptarchy came together to erase the differences in their respective Christian worship.

If we consider the fact that Roman Britons had practiced Christianity well before the Gregorian mission, it is also likely that many people who appeared to have been Christian to Bede, Augustine, and other early Christian figures were Britons and not Anglo-Saxons.

Thus, in the 660s, the papacy appointed Greek Theodore as the head of the Church in Canterbury to unify the differences between Scottish, British, and Anglo-Saxon Christianity that had been promoted by the papal missionaries. The Church in Anglo-Saxon England clearly needed to be reorganized. Theodore's efforts, which included actions like reorganizing the existing English dioceses and redistributing resources to different bishoprics, culminated in the clarification of doctrine at the Synod of Whitby, held in the Kingdom of Northumbria. As he wrote the *Ecclesiastic History* in 731, Bede regarded Theodore's reforms as essentially the golden era of Anglo-Saxon Christianity.

Anglo-Saxon rulers, just like other barbarian kings in Europe after the fall of Rome, were attracted to Christianity to exploit the political positives that it brought. Besides being a way to identify with the great Romans as an essential element of the *Romanitas*, or "Romanness," Christianity also brought a mysticism that reconfirmed the powers of the kings in different aspects.

From early on, Christianity in Anglo-Saxon England helped restructure religious life around the royal family and the king and away from the powerful pagan priests. It managed to achieve this effect in an entirely aesthetic manner, as well. Kingship became grander, increasingly resembling the lavishness of the old Roman emperors who were exalted during their lifetimes—the best of whom were perceived to possess qualities that put them above others in the social hierarchy. The royal regalia of Anglo-Saxon kings became more precious and pronounced, sometimes even excessive, made from imported luxurious materials such as silk and containing more and more jewelry. Whereas before they had been fellow tribal chieftains who had risen to prominence, the kings were now distinguished by their majestic nature.

Though it would be a while before Anglo-Saxon society would accept the idea that kingship was divinely ordained, the adoption of Christianity was certainly a calculated step toward consolidating the power of the Anglo-Saxon kings, who needed to be perceived as "kings." Christianity brought officials that would be very useful in this endeavor. Clergymen were literate and therefore knowledgeable, not only about religious matters but also about history, society, culture, and laws. Forging close relations with the Christian clergy thus meant forging close relations with people who could be of great use in the courts. This relationship thus became intertwined early on and had practical effects.

As Anglo-Saxons converted in increasing numbers and as Christianity became more entrenched in society, maintaining patronage over the clergy emerged as an expensive endeavor, one that only the richest of the nobility could sustain. Despite its costs, which included granting hides of land and numerous resources to the Church, the benefits of patronage were immense for the rulers. Kings who appointed bishops loyal to them were now essentially in charge of the territories under these respective bishoprics or dioceses. Appointment of loyal bishops in what would otherwise be considered "foreign" lands was, in fact, one of the ways kings increased their influence over their rivals. Over time, the ability to appoint religious officials to oversee territories became synonymous with kingship. As a result, lesser kingdoms, such as the Hwicce, were completely absorbed by larger kingdoms.

Overall, Christianity acted as a facilitator in governance and an accelerator of political cohesion in an unstable environment. The Anglo-Saxon rulers' adoption of Christianity was a conscious effort to reinvent and elevate early kingship to a new level.

By the middle of the eighth century, paganism had essentially been eliminated as a prevalent social and cultural force in the Anglo-Saxon kingdoms. The Anglo-Saxon Church, at first divided according to the political influences of separate leaders, now adhered to the principles and doctrines promoted by the Roman Church and administered by two archbishops: of Canterbury, since 669, and of York, since 735.

The result was a completely different political landscape, with fewer and larger kingdoms of the heptarchy having eliminated the smaller distinctions based on tribal lineage. In addition to the homogeneity introduced by Christianity, a common "English" language had also fully developed from the old dialects of the Angles, Saxons, and Jutes, providing the basis for a shared sense of identity. Still, despite this, the political rivalries between the largest kingdoms were all but over.

Chapter 4: Mercian Supremacy

In this chapter, we will look at the period of Anglo-Saxon history that follows their Christianization. This era, lasting from the early eighth to the middle of the ninth century, is often differentiated as the time of "Mercian Supremacy"—a term coined in the early twentieth century. This is because the Kingdom of Mercia emerged as the most dominant kingdom in Britain for about a century and a half. Mercia's supremacy, spearheaded by the succession of its powerful kings Ethelbald and Offa, was manifested in the political, economic, and cultural domination of its neighbors. When we consider the factors that made Mercia the most powerful kingdom of the Anglo-Saxons in the eighth century, it is important to think about how close Mercia came to politically unifying Anglo-Saxon England. The developments in this period would lay further foundations for the notion of a united kingdom of England.

Rise of Mercia

An obvious peculiarity to note when discussing Mercian dominance throughout the eighth century is the lack of written documents produced in Mercia. In fact, most of what we know of the reigns of kings Æthelbald (Ethelbald) and Offa are from sources written in other kingdoms—for example, the works of a Benedictine monk named Boniface, who was from Wessex. Mercian rulers seem to only have commissioned charters. Later rulers, like Alfred the Great of Wessex, refer to the law codes produced in this period in Mercia, though there is a lack of archeological and textual evidence to confirm this.

Even though we know that Mercia was the strongest political and economic force in Britain at this time, the lack of documents suggests that the structural organization of Mercian power was very different from other dominant kingdoms of the time. Additionally, any such material could have easily been destroyed later, especially during the Viking invasions, which hit Mercia especially hard.

However, there is no reason to suspect that foreign chronicles had an active agenda against the Mercian kings or that their writings had an inherent bias. Still, their perspectives, especially when classifying the rulers' decisions, would have starkly differed from the accounts of those who operated closer to the royal courts of Mercia in the eighth century.

When we talk about the domination of Mercia throughout the eighth century, we should not forget that the kingdom had also been relatively strong in the previous hundred years. Its rulers were overkings of smaller kingdoms of central England and sometimes dominated parts of the south. King Penda, for example, who reigned until his death in 655, repeatedly waged successful wars against the Northumbrians, East Anglians, and West Saxons. During his reign, Mercian control over the Midlands became firmly established, and his influence spilled over to his successors. At this time, the Mercians also asserted their power over the kingdom of Hwicce and even occupied southeastern parts of England, such as London and Surrey. Thus, by the late seventh century, it can be said that Mercia was already positioned to dominate its rivals, though not to the extent that it would later.

The nature of Mercian dominance in the eighth century, therefore, stems mostly from two factors. First was the Christianization of Anglo-Saxon domains, tied in with the strengthening of kingship. The second factor was the longevity of two of its consecutive rulers —Ethelbald and Offa. In fact, the two are among the longest-ruling kings in Anglo-Saxon history. In comparison, there were more than ten Northumbrian kings in the same period.

Thanks to the influence of Christian clergy and territorial advances that former Mercian kings had made before their reigns, Ethelbald and Offa built upon the foundations presented to them and made Mercia the supreme Anglo-Saxon kingdom in Britain. They utilized their vast resources to introduce better methods of exercising royal authority on a grander scale and thus came in touching distance of creating the first "English" state—though this was most likely never their intention.

Ethelbald became king of the Mercians in 716, succeeding his cousin, Ceolred, to the throne. Ethelbald had been in exile during Ceolred's reign (perhaps by Ceolred himself) for unknown reasons. The story of his accession is recounted in the *Life of Saint Guthlac*, written by an author named Felix for King Ælfwald of East Anglia, who reigned from 713 to 749. The author mentions that the exiled Ethelbald was in contact with Guthlac, a former Mercian nobleman who had retired from public life and was living as a Hermit in Crowland, in modern-day Lincolnshire. Guthlac had prophesized about Ethelbald becoming king, though he died two years before his prophecy was fulfilled. Exactly how Ethelbald took over the throne of Mercia is unclear, but his contact with Guthlac and the mention of him in an East Anglian source suggest that he was a favored candidate.

Whatever the exact story behind Ethelbald's accession, he appears to have become the most powerful ruler south of the Humber River over the next fifteen years, especially after the death of the kings of Wessex and Kent in 725 and 726. The Ismere Diploma, a charter issued by Ethelbald in 736 that records a grant of land to one of his subjects, attributes the titles "King of the Mercians and the South English" and *Rex Britanniæ*, "King of Britain," to Ethelbald. Though "King of Britain" should be considered a typical exaggeration, the other title is consistent with the account in *Ecclesiastical History*, where Bede calls Ethelbald the "overking south of the Humber." It is unclear if "south English" refers to all the peoples south of the Humber or just those considered Angles (inhabitants of Mercia and East Anglia), but it signifies the powerful position Ethelbald enjoyed during this time.

By the middle 730s, the Kingdom of Mercia under Ethelbald controlled significant territories south of the Humber and had considerable influence over their political affairs. For example, Ethelbald appears as the overking of Hwicce, southwest of the Mercian heartlands, which was ruled by a local royal dynasty subject to Ethelbald's rule. Mercian charters of the time mention this relationship. Other documents contain information about religious lands further to the east, in the areas around London, being exempt from taxes, which suggests the extent of Ethelbald's power there.

The influence of Ethelbald's rule further south—in the Kingdom of Kent, for example—was less pronounced. It can only be inferred from the fact that the three successive archbishops of Canterbury in the middle of the eighth century were Mercian. Kentish kings of the time appear to have granted lands without Ethelbald's direct involvement, suggesting that the extent of his political influence there was limited to religious institutions.

Ethelbald was also the overlord of London, sponsoring the activities of the Church there, and it was during his reign that the city finally fell out of the political influence of the kings of Essex.

Ethelbald's relationships with the kings of Wessex and Northumbria appear to have been more complicated, perhaps due to the relative strength of these kingdoms compared to Kent, East Anglia, or Essex. There is evidence he campaigned against Wessex as early as 733 and again in 740 against the new King Cuthred. Three years later, however, Cuthred and Ethelbald waged a common offensive against the Britons of Wales, suggesting that either Cuthred was subordinated by Mercia or the Britons were simply a faction they saw as a common enemy.

Thus, Bede's account of Ethelbald's over-kingship of the "English south of the Humber" should not be taken as the manifestation of a true hegemon. Anglo-Saxon kingship, though profoundly transformed by the introduction to Christianity, was still in its early stages of development. Likewise, communication channels were simply not developed enough to make Ethelbald the clear authority in the eyes of the southern English.

Despite this, the influence he had—especially over the dominions of the Hwicce, East Anglia and Essex—was certainly more than that of previous rulers, making it worthy of highlighting, even by a writer from a rival Northumbrian court.

Ethelbald also campaigned against Northumbria on two occasions, in 737 and 740. Though his offensives gained him little influence north of the Humber, it highlights that he was trying to exploit the weakness of Northumbria while King Eadberht was away fighting the Picts in the north. Some have also suggested that Ethelbald allied with the Picts to undermine Northumbrian dominance north of his realm. Whatever the case, Mercian military and political dominance during the reign of Ethelbald was confined south of the Humber.

Ethelbald's rule was controversial, to say the least. There is contrasting evidence about the nature of his relationship with the Church or even his "unchristian" conduct. Boniface accused Ethelbald of not respecting the principle of monogamy and of being an adulterer, for example, in addition to his exploitative and harsh treatment of the religious clergy. The first of these accusations might be explained by the prevalence of pagan or pre-Christian tendencies among Anglo-Saxon rulers, whose moral compass might not have been fully fixed to the new standards. His alleged harsh treatment of monks and bishops, on the other hand, might indicate that he viewed his influence over religious affairs as a political advantage.

His unpopularity is also supported by his cause of death in 757— murder. The Mercian king was murdered treacherously for unclear reasons. The fact that he was briefly succeeded by a nobleman named Beornred suggests a possible conspiracy, especially since Beornred's rule was cut short by Offa, who defeated the contender either in the same year or the following.

King Offa of the Mercians

Offa's reign, which lasted for thirty-nine years, is only similar to his predecessor Ethelbald's in the territorial extent of his power. His rule was concentrated in the Mercian Midlands and included London, which had emerged as a significant trading hub for early medieval merchants. Offa exerted more direct control over his subjects in Hwicce and Essex, often placing Mercian nobles in positions of power in these kingdoms and contributing to their political decline.

Unlike Ethelbald, he perceived himself simply as "King of the Mercians" and did not adopt superlative titles that claimed over-kingship of other kingdoms. The official charters he issued never attribute another title to him, unlike Ethelbald's. This might suggest that in his day, Mercian Supremacy was already seen as something normal and the territories he controlled were viewed as an enlarged Mercian kingdom, not a combination of smaller realms. Thus, there is no evidence that he intended to unify a nation of Anglo-Saxon or English people. Instead, he seems to have been motivated primarily by the pragmatic political goals of expanding power.

Much like Ethelbald, he confined the extent of his ambitions to the territories south of the Humber and did not pursue significant military gains in Northumbria. However, the fact that his daughter was married off to King Æthelred of Northumbria suggests he was not completely uninvolved.

King Offa of Mercia on a silver penny.

Where Offa and Ethelbald significantly differ is their perception of Christian kingship and the perception of their status through other actions.

Offa maintained regular correspondence with Charlemagne of the Carolingian Empire. However, his relationship with the Frankish Carolingian ruler was complicated, as evidenced by the letters they exchanged. Offa was indeed the most powerful king in Britain at the time, much respected by his contemporaries, including his rivals. However, in his correspondence with Charlemagne, he appears overly ambitious, and his ambitions are checked by the Carolingian emperor, who clearly did not view him as an equal.

Charlemagne was, for example, insulted when Offa asked for his daughter Bertha to be married to Offa's son Ecgfrith. Offa's request was a reciprocal proposition, as Charlemagne's court had requested for Offa's daughter to marry Charles, the son of the emperor. Insulted, Charlemagne issued a trade embargo on Mercian merchants in his lands. Offa reciprocated with an embargo on Frankish merchants trading on Mercian soil. Despite this, the two rulers maintained their relationship, lifting the trade embargoes by the late eighth century. Charlemagne even sent gifts to the Mercian king. At the very least, Charlemagne saw Offa as a respectable figure and a potential ally, whereas Offa was influenced by Charlemagne's grandeur and status.

Frankish influence on Mercia during the reign of Offa can be clearly observed in certain aspects. In the history of Medieval Europe, Christian kingship became the most prominent form during Charlemagne's reign. Charlemagne maintained very close relations with the papacy and pushed his image as a Christian monarch of Europe in the pattern of the old Roman emperors—manifested by his crowning as emperor in 800 by Pope Leo III. From his reign onward, the connection between royal authority and Christianity became more important throughout Europe. And Offa's Mercia was by no means an exception.

Offa began to emulate some of the royal practices of Charlemagne's court. For example, in 787, he anointed his son, Ecgfrith, as his co-ruler and intended successor, something that was done by Charlemagne and previous Frankish kings. Ecgfrith's anointing was carried out by a Christian bishop, essentially making him a legitimate successor and amplifying the relationship between the Church and royal authority. The assertion of kingship and transmission of power was thus made into a sacred ritual, resembling a Christian rite. Furthermore, Offa welcomed continental bishops into his court and promoted their missionary activities throughout his realm. The missionaries held a religious council after being received at Canterbury, which was attended by King Offa.

Offa was also strictly monogamous, something that constituted a conscious break from his pagan or Germanic identity. In fact, the image of his wife Cynethryth as the queen of the kingdom was also very prominent in eighth-century Mercia. In the official charters, she is mentioned as the "Queen of the Mercians," and archeological evidence includes coins minted in her name. All this suggests a close interrelation between the status of the queen and her public image as such. It was yet another manifestation of Christian kingship: the king had one wife who was the queen of the kingdom and supported the king by being involved in the affairs of the court. Monogamy provided legitimacy, a sense of civility and Christianity, and a sustainable lifestyle for Offa—something to be emulated by future Anglo-Saxon monarchs.

King Offa died in 796 from natural causes. Ironically, though he had tried to guarantee a safe and fruitful reign for his son Ecgfrith by involving him in court affairs during his lifetime, Ecgfrith's reign lasted for only a few months. He also died unexpectedly in December of 796. Alcuin of York, a contemporary teacher from Northumbria and a disciple of Archbishop Ecbert, mentions in his letters that King Offa had dedicated his life to preparing Ecgfrith to be the next king, only for God to decide his heir's fate.

Cenwulf, a cousin of Ecgfrith from another branch of the family, became king in late 796, inheriting a large kingdom in dire need of a strong ruler to maintain stability. As time would tell, Cenwulf was such a leader, ruling until 821 and retaining Mercia's influence as the largest and most powerful of the Anglo-Saxon kingdoms. During his reign, the role of the king of Essex diminished. In the charters issued by Cenwulf, the king of Essex eventually appears as an ealdorman—a former local king who had become a vassal of a greater king (eventually, the word *earl* would come to replace *ealdorman*).

In addition to Essex, Cenwulf reasserted Mercian rulership over East Anglia and Kent, which had most likely broken free from Mercian control after the unexpected succession of 796. King Eadberht III had gained influence in Kent, driving out the Mercian-appointed Archbishop of Æthelhard and sacking Canterbury. Interestingly, when declaring war on Kent, Cenwulf sought a judgment from Pope Leo III, who had excommunicated Eadberht, to show that his war on Kent was justifiable and Christian.

Despite Cenwulf's early victories, however, the early ninth century would prove difficult. The main problem Cenwulf had to deal with was the succession of Wessex. The heir, Ecgberht, who had been forced into exile by King Offa, returned to Wessex and defied Mercian domination. To reimpose his authority, Cenwulf launched an invasion against Ecgberht but did not achieve his goals. Wessex retained its independence.

Most of the pressing political problems Mercia encountered during the period of its dominance were linked to having to constantly assert control over its subjects through military means. And, though Mercian was among the first of the Anglo-Saxon kingdoms to consistently militarily dominate its neighbors, it would struggle to keep its gains permanent.

A New Society

There is much more to the era of Mercian domination than successful military conquests and political power. In fact, it can be argued that if it were not for the development of these aspects, the advances made by kings Ethelbald and Offa would not have been sustainable. The period of

Mercian Supremacy encompasses socio-economic and cultural transformations that shaped the appearance of Anglo-Saxon life in the eighth century and became its staple for the next centuries.

The main economic factor that drove Mercia's dominance in this period was the drastic development of a network of cities that engaged in trade, known as emporia, mostly located on the eastern coast of England. During the first half of the eighth century, the emporia of Anglo-Saxon England, including London, York, Southampton, and Ipswich, began to expand. Archeological evidence suggests that economic activity in these areas peaked during the eighth century, and this was tied to population growth.

Increasing numbers of arrivals in these cities expanded and modified their layout to accommodate new infrastructural, civilian, and military projects. New roads and bridges were constructed to connect new settlements in areas around London and York to the old city centers. This led to the establishment of new small-scale factories and an increase in trade with continental Europe, especially with northern France and the Low Countries, which were Christianized Frankish domains by the ninth century. Ipswich, a town in what had been East Anglia before its submission to Mercia, developed industries such as pottery making, widely known throughout the Anglo-Saxon realms for its great style and quality.

Historians debate about whether the growth of these cities was stimulated by the policies of Mercian rulers or whether the rulers were simply lucky to rule during an era of growth. However, it is unlikely that an expansion of this scale in such a short time could have persisted organically without the involvement of authoritative figures to provide resources.

Traces of the involvement of "state officials" in the emporia's economic affairs can be observed as early as the late seventh century in Kent. As seen in the royal charters, these individuals were tax or tariff collectors for the Crown. Most likely, these royal servants taxed those who used the roads or entered Anglo-Saxon ports from abroad, as was the practice in continental Europe at the time.

In fact, this practice was most likely adopted from the Franks: under Charlemagne, Frankish traders were protected by the Crown if they were disadvantaged or oppressed in foreign lands. The close relationship between Frankish and Anglo-Saxon merchants can be seen from the incident when Charlemagne and Offa decided to issue embargoes on goods sold by Mercian or Frankish merchants.

In addition to kings, the Church, including local churches and monasteries, may have also contributed to this growth, as they benefitted heavily from the increase in trade, local production, and access to new trade routes. Many such institutions were exempt from taxes or tariffs under Mercian rule in exchange for promoting trade and the exchange of goods on a local level. For instance, the Church needed certain imported goods to conduct its religious ceremonies and rites, like olive oil or wine, which could only be imported from the continent.

Monasteries, which were often secluded from urban areas until small settlements inevitably popped up around them, were linked with the emporia through a network of administrative-type buildings. Located in remote areas of the country along trade routes, these sites include archeological evidence in the form of numerous coins and different local or foreign goods. These production sites likely served as both repositories of goods and administrative centers that further monitored trade and regulated supply and demand between different areas.

The centers of the Anglo-Saxon urban economy were also well supported by a growing rural economy, made possible by advancements in agriculture beginning in the seventh century. Food and raw materials would be supplied to the emporia through the production sites of these rural settlements, which were otherwise outside of the network of the main Anglo-Saxon trade routes.

Among the agricultural advancements of the time was a shift from subsistence farming toward a more diversified farming output. Seventh-century farms began cultivating crops that were also more profitable and supplied the markets of the emporia with their products. This also led to more organized farmlands, with clear demarcations. Archeological evidence also suggests the abandonment of old settlements when the yield no longer satisfied the required levels due to the exhaustion of the land. Historians believe that a large-scale move from such lands to richer soils explains the otherwise unclear abandonment of old settlements like Mucking in Essex, which had been inhabited for several thousand years before. Such changes caused a noticeable increase in rural agricultural production.

Changes to the structure of the Anglo-Saxon economy were heavily tied to the social and cultural changes taking place on a large scale throughout the eighth century. These changes were caused by the Christianization of the Anglo-Saxons, whose rulers were at least nominally Christian by the late seventh century. As Mercia rose to power, Christianity became even more entrenched in Anglo-Saxon society. It was slowly transforming from a society that had been Christianized to a society that was Christian.

This was partially because Christianity tapped into the everyday lives of ordinary people. It regulated most aspects of life from early on due to its many ceremonies and rituals. Though the same can be said of the pagan belief system, which was also based on frequent rituals, Christianity allowed for much less variation from individual to individual. Paganism was comparably a very individualistic religion.

Anglo-Saxon Christianity in the Eighth Century

The growing prominence of Christianity resulted in the development of a very effective network of churches, monasteries, bishoprics, and dioceses throughout Anglo-Saxon realms. The Anglo-Saxon elite, comprised of power-hungry aristocrats, began to exploit these developments in different ways, believing it was possible to gain more power and wealth with the help of Christianity. Exerting influence on the Church put the elites in a powerful position to influence the people, who listened to the friars and bishops and saw them as their spiritual guides throughout life. The Church and the ruling class of the Anglo-Saxons thus began to develop a symbiotic relationship early on. From the late seventh century, various churches and monasteries, which had acquired lands from the nobility, were freed from burdens to increase their influence.

Respecting this complex, mutually beneficial relationship was important. This can be seen from the history of King Ethelbald, who, as monk Boniface writes, greatly exploited the monks in Mercia during his reign. In 749, Ethelbald appears to have fixed his relationship with the Church, exempting it from taxation everywhere throughout his kingdom and granting it the right to enjoy the products from the cultivated lands in its possession. Such privileges, in addition to the monasteries' increased role in domestic trade, accelerated the growth of the Church's power. By the dawn of the eighth century, the Church had been greatly enriched from all these advantages.

Monasteries founded throughout Anglo-Saxon realms from the late seventh century featured a diverse range of influences from neighboring cultures, including Irish, Frankish, and even Italian traditions. This resulted in a diverse range of monastic daily life patterns. Many monasteries were large and in remote areas secluded from the public, but this was not always the case.

In Old English, the word *minster* was used to refer to all Christian communities, disregarding their size or type of organization—a word with the same etymology as the Latin *monasterium*. Though the word was eventually replaced by the term "monastery," it was later used as a title for particular churches throughout England. Among the prominent churches that feature the Old English name are the famous Westminster Abbey in London and the York Minster in Yorkshire. Minsters were endowed with rights by special royal charters.

English minsters had several critics by the mid-eighth century. The Venerable Bede, for example, writing in a letter to Bishop Ecgberht of York in 734, passionately criticizes the practices of monks in Northumbrian monasteries. He mentions corrupt nobles who gained royal charters to establish monasteries but knew nothing of the monastic tradition or Christian ways of life. Bede says that these individuals did not actively pursue Christian lifestyles, breaking many sacred rules such as celibacy and using the privileges that came with the charters to enrich themselves and accumulate wealth that could be passed down to future generations.

Essentially, Bede's criticism lay in the belief that monastic life must be entirely ecclesiastical, practiced solely by the clergy and not pursued by secular figures such as the nobility. He felt that the socio-political elites of the Anglo-Saxon community were encroaching on ecclesiastical life with their influences and undermining its independence.

Bede was not alone in his criticism, as the monk Boniface made similar accusations in his 747 letter to Archbishop Cuthbert of Canterbury. In it, he suggested the archbishop introduce the same reforms to the Anglo-Saxon Church that had been introduced in the Frankish Church. One of the necessary reforms was for laymen to be stripped of control over monasteries, Boniface asserted. He also mentioned that changes should be made in the behavior and appearance of the clergy. For example, bishops should dress in more modest attire.

These criticisms would be addressed the same year at the Council of Clovesho—a special synod that had first convened five years earlier. The Council of 747 was attended by the clergy from the Archdiocese of Canterbury and King Ethelbald of Mercia. After much discussion and deliberation, the synod proclaimed a series of canons that must be observed in monasteries, addressing apparent shortcomings among the members of the clergy such as instances of debauchery and drunkenness or arrogance and luxurious lifestyles. The council also sought to introduce clearer boundaries for the involvement of laymen—most importantly, of Anglo-Saxon nobility—in the religious affairs of monasteries. The council suggested that local bishops investigate local monasteries under the control of wealthy aristocrats to solve the possible problems addressed by Bede and Boniface in their letters.

It appears the council aimed to better define the borders between secular and ecclesiastical life while not publicly condemning the aristocracy for exploiting Christianity for personal gain or issuing extreme punishments such as excommunication. As we can see from the council's proceedings, the Anglo-Saxon Church of the eighth century was certainly in a bittersweet rivalry with the Anglo-Saxon political elites. It recognized that the quick spread of Christianity was largely due to the Anglo-Saxon nobility's involvement, but it was also critical of the nobility for not upholding high standards of ecclesiastical life in the monasteries under their domains.

Criticism directed at the heavy involvement of secular leaders in religious institutions was rooted in truth. However, the Anglo-Saxon Church had its own problems with the constantly shifting political climate and the association of certain religious institutions with certain rulers. Kings Ethelbald, Offa, and Cenwulf would often provide patronage to monasteries and other religious institutions located in conquered territories. This would bring these institutions under the king's direct influence, serving their agenda when it came to, for example, spreading the political power of Mercians over their newly acquired subjects. Ninth-century Kentish monasteries, for example, though nominally under the control of the Archbishopric of Canterbury, were mechanisms for Mercian kings to gain firm political control. The clergy that operated in these institutions were by no means exclusively loyal to the Church, leading to the outbreak of many disputes.

Even though the nobility's involvement in religious affairs during the eighth century brought many problems and criticisms, it is difficult to deny the nobility's material contributions to the development of a unique intellectual and artistic culture. Contact with the Frankish Church was vital in this regard. During the reign of Charlemagne, the English clergy often visited the Frankish court. From there, they brought back different texts and encouraged scholarship in English monasteries.

Developments in intellectual and artistic fields went hand-in-hand for the Anglo-Saxon Church. Insular art, sometimes referred to as Hiberno-Saxon art, is an amazing combination of Anglo-Saxon and Celtic-Irish Christian elements, leading to a style of religious art that was far different from that on the continent. The influence of Irish Christianity is especially evident in Northumbria due to the kingdom's close ties with the Celtic people from Ireland and Scotland.

There are many examples of insular-style religious manuscripts produced in Anglo-Saxon kingdoms during this period. The *Lindisfarne Gospels*, made in Northumbria in the late seventh century, is a Gospel book that bears elaborate, lavish decorations and a distinct style. It features the portraits of the four evangelists and other decorations, such as those on the carpet pages before the beginning of each gospel. This and other manuscripts, such as the earliest surviving Gospel book, the *Book of Durrow*, and the 236-page *Lichfield Gospels*, clearly demonstrate the peak of artistic influences on Anglo-Saxon art in the late seventh to early eighth centuries. These influences persisted until about the tenth century when they were perhaps disrupted by the Viking invasions.

Folio from the Lindisfarne Gospels.
https://commons.wikimedia.org/wiki/File:LindisfarneFol27rIncipitMatt.jpg

The Hiberno-Saxon insular style is also prominent south of the Humber in the realms controlled by Mercia during the eighth century, even though Celtic Christianity had been less prominent in these areas in previous centuries. Here, however, alongside insular elements, Anglo-Saxon art adopts continental influences, drawing heavily from classical and Italian styles. These influences appear clearly in works such as the *Vespasian Psalter*, an illuminated psalter produced at Canterbury in the first half of the eighth century, or the *Stockholm Codex Aureus*, a Gospel book also produced at Canterbury that contains purple parchment decorations resembling old imperial style manuscripts. These books, alongside other works such as the *Book of Nunnaminster*, bear a distinct artistic style deemed "Tiberius style."

Illuminated books weren't the only type of art produced in Anglo-Saxon England during this period. In the eighth century, a unique style of sculpture developed on both sides of the Humber River. Archeological evidence has found a diverse array of such sculptures in Mercia, dated to the late eighth century, that feature a combination of Anglo-Saxon, insular, and classical artistic styles.

The relationship that developed between the Anglo-Saxon Church and the laity was complex and multifaceted. Since the life of a commoner was a Christian one, the Church had the authority and knowledge not only to give general instructions but also to carry out activities to meet the spiritual needs of the laity. Among these were the typical Christian activities of communion, confession, and baptism, for example, as well as other rites such as preaching on Sundays.

Monasteries or other religious institutions were often faced with a range of problems with providing such services to the laity. The most obvious one was that the liturgies were often conducted in Latin, which was unintelligible to most laypeople. Thus, most probably did not understand the meaning behind the passages of the Bible read aloud by the priests. This problem existed among members of the clergy, as well, as many priests in smaller or rural monasteries had simply memorized the Latin phrases of the Mass and could not reliably read or understand Latin. This was one of the problems mentioned during the Council of Clovesho in 747, where it was suggested that the Mass be spoken in Old English in some areas instead of Latin. However, this change was never implemented by the clergy. The council generally encouraged better contact between the laity and members of the clergy for the laypeople to be more actively and passionately involved in spiritual activities.

In conclusion, in addition to large-scale changes in the political climate of Anglo-Saxon England throughout the eighth century, profound social, economic, and cultural changes were also taking place. Mercian domination was supported by an increase in economic activity and a better reorganization of social structures that accelerated growth and interconnectivity. Increased political, economic, and cultural contacts with other societies, most prominently with the Franks under Charlemagne, resulted in the introduction of new influences in all aspects of life. For most of the century and a short period afterward, Mercian kings were greatly respected. They had dominated their rivals on a previously unseen scale. In addition to economic stability, their supremacy was also upheld thanks to their complex relationship with religious structures, which ultimately served as a means of further increasing royal influence in distant lands.

Culturally, Anglo-Saxon England during the era of Mercian Supremacy saw the entrenchment of Christianity as the undisputed major religion and socio-cultural force. The Church established itself as a more respectable and powerful institution, gaining more structure and stability during the reign of the Mercian kings. It also spearheaded the development of a unique Anglo-Saxon art style as it sought to combine influences from neighboring cultures into something wholly distinct.

The Mercian kings had not united all Anglo-Saxons into a single kingdom and did not appear to have intended to. Most of the time, they acted out of pragmatic material interests, but in so doing managed to achieve great power and exert great influence over their rivals. But, as new forces appeared in Anglo-Saxon England in the ninth century, the era of Mercian Supremacy swiftly came to an end.

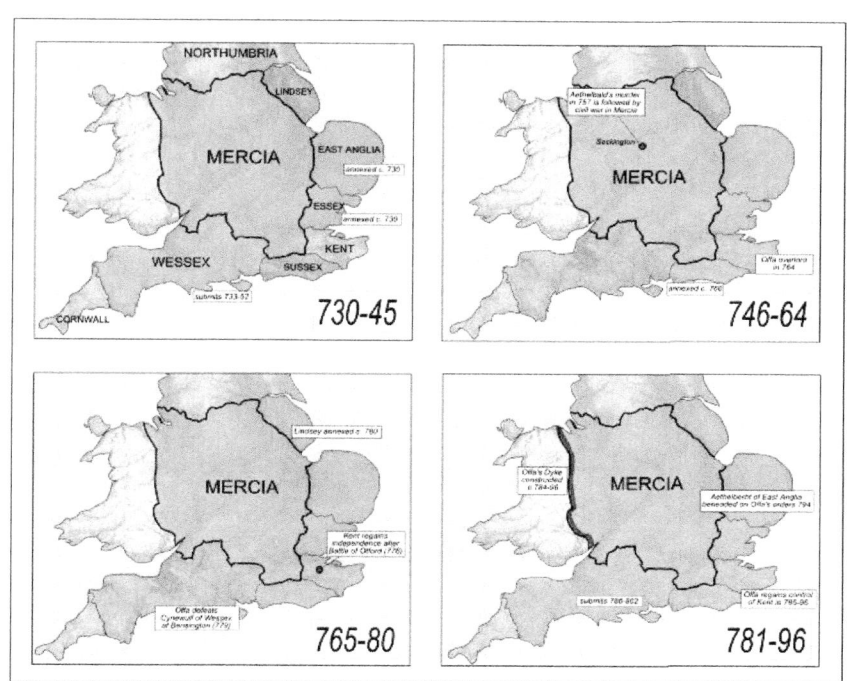

Illustration of Mercia's expansion of power.

Hel-hama, CC BY-SA 3.0 <https://creativecommons.org/licenses/by-sa/3.0>, via Wikimedia Commons; https://commons.wikimedia.org/wiki/File:Mercian_Supremacy_x_4.svg

Chapter 5: Anglo-Saxons and the Viking Age

In this chapter, we will look at the events of the ninth century that profoundly transformed the social, cultural, and political landscape of Anglo-Saxon England. This period marked the gradual decline of Mercian Supremacy in Britain as the most prominent Anglo-Saxon kingdom. In its stead, the Kingdom of Wessex rose, checking the former Mercian power before establishing supremacy over its rivals. More importantly, however, the ninth century saw the Anglo-Saxon kingdoms confronted with their biggest threat yet—the Vikings. Though the story of the Viking invasion of Britain has become widely known, the Vikings are much more than pragmatic and bloody military raids. The arrival of the Vikings marked a turning point for Anglo-Saxon kingdoms, forcing them to reconsider their differences and adopt new strategies to fight off a common enemy. This chapter will thus look at the history of the Anglo-Saxons during the Viking Age to uncover the challenges they would face hundreds of years after the first infamous Viking raid.

The Vikings

The Vikings would first come to raid the Anglo-Saxons in 793, landing at the northeastern settlement of Lindisfarne, then part of the Kingdom of Northumbria. There, they pillaged the monastery and decimated the locals. The violent, ruthless nature of the sudden attack on a religious institution by pagan foreigners caused a shock in the Anglo-Saxon realms and beyond. The Anglo-Saxons had been in contact with people from

Scandinavia since migrating to Britain but had never before engaged in warfare with them.

Alcuin of York, a former Northumbrian scholar who had already joined Charlemagne's court when the raid in Lindisfarne took place, expressed in his letters the horror he had felt from what he deemed a barbaric attack that had desecrated Christianity. He sought to justify the destructive raid as a God-sent punishment for the wicked and unchristian way of life of many Northumbrians and warned that he feared the attack had not been the last one. Alcuin was right—the Vikings came back to Northumbria the next year and continued to frequent northern monasteries, plundering Tynemouth and Hartness by the end of the eighth century. Yet, Alcuin could never imagine the scale of the Viking invasion that was to come to England decades after the first raid at Lindisfarne. The Vikings had not yet become the greatest threat to the Anglo-Saxons.

Northumbria wasn't the only place where the Vikings would make their presence known in the period of about three hundred years known as the Viking Age. Scandinavian Norsemen raided, colonized, conquered, and traded with people across Europe. They established close relations with the Franks, who were becoming the most dominant force in Europe at the time, and reached the Atlantic coast of Iberia and raided some Mediterranean cities. Their ruthless attack on northern France eventually gained them recognition by the Frankish king, as well as a substantial piece of land called Normandy. They established a presence in the Faroes, eastern Ireland, and other smaller islands of the British Isles. Further west, they reached places nobody in Europe had even heard of, founding colonies in Iceland and Greenland and even journeying as far as North America and making landfall at Newfoundland.

Masters of seafaring, the Vikings would also utilize the vast network of major rivers in Eastern Europe to reach major wealthy civilizations of the Near East—the Byzantine Empire and the Muslim world of the Middle East—and travel through the domains of the Kievan Rus and the Black and the Caspian seas. The Vikings would be revered by these peoples for their brilliant military skill and tradesmanship, emerging as some of the most dominant and compelling actors in Europe until the eleventh century.

The image we have of the Vikings as ruthless, ale-consuming warriors with horned helmets comes from contemporary Christian sources that inevitably depict them as pagans and heathens and are appalled by their savagery. The Christian world—before the Vikings themselves would accept the religion—was certainly a victim of their warmongering for a long time, but it would be unfair to only mention the Vikings in this context. In fact, much Viking activity during the Viking Age was concerned with exploration, colonization, and trade, not just military conquest, piracy, and raiding.

The dramatic expansion of Viking influence from the late eighth century has been explained by a few factors. One possible explanation is their comparably tough living conditions in Scandinavia. A potential population boom during the early eighth century would have forced the Scandinavians to search for new areas to settle in as their land became incapable of meeting their increased demand for food. Their decision to begin raiding seems logical from this perspective.

Another explanation for the quick ushering in of the Viking Age credits technological breakthroughs as the main catalysts behind the Vikings going out to sea. Developments in shipbuilding techniques and improvements in navigation were crucial factors in the distinct Viking identity. New ship designs allowed them greater maneuverability, giving them the option to navigate through European rivers, as well as durability and speed.

In addition to these theories, the economic explanation also stands out. The economic recovery and growth of eighth-century Europe after the fall of Rome in 476 could have served as a motivation for Scandinavians to exploit new trade routes and wealthier cities in northern and western Europe. More expensive trade goods were circulating during this period, and the growing Anglo-Saxon, Frankish, Slavic, or even Muslim trading centers seemed like good targets for the Vikings. Scandinavia was first exposed to the trade routes in the northern and eastern parts of Europe, eventually reaching the richer cultures of the Mediterranean basin, such as the Byzantine Empire.

In addition to goods, traders and merchants from different states also exchanged information—a commodity that was just as useful in many cases. They brought news of the places they had visited, including stories about their wealth and political and military weaknesses, crises, or local conflicts. It is not unlikely that one motivation of the Vikings was to exploit these opportunities by launching raids in lands they considered chaotic or unstable, such as the realms of the Anglo-Saxons.

As we have already partially mentioned, the earliest attacks of the Vikings in Anglo-Saxon England were not directed at the richer trade centers, such as the emporia in London or Ipswich. Instead, the initial targets of Viking raids were poorly defended religious institutions, such as monasteries. In the previous chapter, we touched on the material wealth that was present in Christian churches and monasteries of the time, thanks to either patronage from the local elites or to the churches functioning as local centers of trade. In other words, they constituted prime targets that held decent wealth but were also relatively easy to plunder. Although contemporary Christian writers present Viking raids as targeted pagan attacks on Christianity, this was not a tangible motivation of the Vikings.

The End of Mercian Supremacy

In the previous chapter, we talked about the strength of the Anglo-Saxon Kingdom of Mercia during the eighth century. The reigns of Ethelbald and Offa made Mercia ambitious and powerful, but the prosperity of their time would gradually end as Mercia entered its period of decline in the early ninth century. Offa's successor, Cenwulf, can be considered the last great Mercian king, ruling until the year 821, but his rule faced many challenges early on. Imposing over-kingship on lesser kingdoms had always proven to have been a burdensome task for any monarch, but more problems began to arise in the early ninth century. As we mentioned, Cenwulf faced much opposition from the lesser kingdoms, most prominently from Wessex, which rebelled soon after the death of Offa and refused to submit to the Mercians. By the year 825, there were already clear signs of Mercia's declining political power in England.

All in all, the following developments in the Anglo-Saxon realms during the ninth century coincided with an increasing amount of Viking activity in England. The Vikings posed a significant threat to the Anglo-Saxons at a time when they were among their weakest—immediately as the Kingdom of Mercia was losing its control and influence.

The events of the ninth century are mentioned mostly in the *Anglo-Saxon Chronicle*, which presents Wessex's viewpoint on the developments that led to the decline of Mercia. The *Chronicle* mentions that the East Anglians approached Ecgberht of Wessex for help against the Mercians after the passing of Mercian King Ceolwulf—Cenwulf's brother—in 823. At this point, Mercia was plunged into a succession crisis. The armies of Ecgberht decisively defeated the Mercians at the Battle of Ellendon in 825, near the modern town of Swindon, forcing the kingdom to give up its hopes of over-kingship of East Anglia and Kent.

In fact, from 825 onward, Mercian invasions into these lesser kingdoms would no longer result in submission to Mercian rule. We know this from the coins minted in late 820s East Anglia, which bore the name of its local king instead of a Mercian one. Though Mercian kings continued to grant royal charters to some of the religious institutions in East Anglia in the next decades, the real extent of their power and influence was limited compared to a hundred years earlier.

Despite these shortcomings, the Kingdom of Mercia was a strong Anglo-Saxon kingdom during the middle of the ninth century. Certainly, the ambitions of Mercian kings never ceased, as seen in renewed invasions of Wales to extend Mercian influence there, as well as royal marriages with other Anglo-Saxon kingdoms, such as one between Mercian King Burgred and West Saxon princess Æthelswith in 853. Still, Mercia was only a shadow of its former self by this time.

Meanwhile, the Kingdom of Wessex was slowly assuming its position as the new potential power among the Anglo-Saxons. There, King Ecgberht founded a ruling dynasty in 802. With East Anglia's request to help against Mercia, Wessex became more concerned with spreading its influence in Anglo-Saxon realms, as it had primarily waged wars in the west against the Celts during the first two decades of the ninth century. The victory against the Mercians seemed to turn the tide in Wessex's favor.

King Ecgberht proved to be an ambitious ruler. Following his victory, he launched an offensive into Kent, deposing a Mercian-appointed sub-king, which gave him virtual control over southern Anglo-Saxon domains. Then, in 829, according to the *Anglo-Saxon Chronicle*, Ecgberht campaigned against the Mercian King Wiglaf, who was unrelated to the royal line of Mercian kings, and decisively defeated him.

The *Chronicle* mentions that a few years later the Northumbrians also submitted to the West Saxon king at Dore in modern-day Sheffield, granting King Ecgberht the title of *Bretwalda*—which roughly translates to "overking" of Britain, or "Britain-wide" ruler. This title only appears in the *Anglo-Saxon Chronicle* and most likely serves to glorify the achievements of King Ecgberht and his successful undermining of Mercian Supremacy during his reign. Though it is unlikely that Ecgberht was a Britain-wide ruler, the use of the title suggests that he nevertheless held considerable power by 830.

Ecgberht's over-kingship of Mercia and Northumbria was brief and not exactly profound. This is affirmed even though coins were minted in the name of King Ecgberht as "King of the Mercians." Wiglaf returned in 830 and reclaimed the Mercian throne, either forcefully or, more likely, through negotiation with Ecgberht. On the other hand, the Northumbrian King Eanred's submission to Ecgberht at Dore appears to have been voluntary in exchange for tribute—though this is not mentioned in the *Chronicle*. What we can reasonably infer is that Wessex would be overstretched if it tried to impose its dominance over such vast lands in the north as Mercia and especially Northumbria.

In comparison, the West Saxon over-kingship of Kent, Sussex, and Essex was much more expressed. These areas stayed under the influence of Wessex even as Viking raids intensified throughout the ninth century. They enjoyed a great deal of security, especially compared to Mercia and Northumbria, which took the brunt of the Viking invasion. Stable control of these areas was linked to another crucial factor in the succession of West Saxon kings after Ecgberht: the line of succession was direct, culminating in the accession of King Alfred the Great and, eventually, his grandson Æthelstan, who became the first King of the English in 927. The unbroken chain of succession is a testament to the extent of the strength of the Kingdom of Wessex compared to the more fragile Mercia.

It is interesting to examine other political and social factors that provided stability for the emerging Kingdom of Wessex, soon to become the most dominant of the Anglo-Saxon kingdoms. One of the main reasons for the success and longevity of West Saxon rule was the coherence of the kingdom's political and administrative structures and the distribution of royal offices. Importantly, the ealdormen in the Kingdom of Wessex were royally appointed officials who exercised authority in certain areas. Differently from Mercia, where divisions between administrative regions appear to have been less clear, the administrative divisions of Wessex were far more coherent. These units in the Kingdom of Wessex, be they shires or other divisions, seemed to have been introduced by the central government. They were centered on prominent urban areas rather than on the old, roughly defined dwelling areas of local peoples. For example, the region of Dorset, administered by a royally appointed ealdorman, was centered on the city of Dorchester.

The structural coherence of the West Saxon governance was supported by a wide range of sub-offices with clearly defined responsibilities organized in a strict hierarchical fashion. The royally appointed office of the minister is a prominent example. Though the *ministri* were present with limited responsibilities under Mercian rule, they appeared to be involved in a wide range of affairs during the era of Wessex. This can be seen from their frequent mentions in the royal charters. A typical West Saxon minister did not have the same range of power as modern-day ministers. Instead, these individuals held different positions, ranging from managing royal estates to being stewards or simple cupbearers for the king. Despite this, they were very close to the king, something that was naturally considered prestigious. Someone distinguished as a minister in the eyes of the king would have had the opportunity to advance in the hierarchy of royal officials, perhaps even rising to the rank of an ealdorman and holding considerable power.

Anglo-Saxon Society in the Ninth Century

The decline of Mercian power was also accelerated by the changing socio-economic conditions of the Anglo-Saxon kingdoms throughout the ninth century. Archeological evidence suggests significant economic developments south and north of the Humber.

In Northumbria, for example, there is evidence that the currency was progressively debased, perhaps a conscious choice by the Northumbrian kings to affect the kingdom's economy. There are increasingly more base-metal Northumbrian coins found from the middle of the ninth century. This suggests the decision was directed toward making it easier to complete simple transactions between commoners. Northumbrian coins from this period have been found in East Anglia, for example, suggesting that locals preferred to use such coins for everyday transactions.

In other Anglo-Saxon kingdoms, however, a general economic decline was marked by a drastic reduction in the volume of circulating currency. And though the evidence we have of coin usage in this period is insufficient to explain the economic decline, the changing level of coins in circulation does suggest a shift in the nature of their usage.

Archeological evidence also reveals a general decline in the social and economic activities in the most prominent Anglo-Saxon emporia. It appears that few new buildings were constructed in the most active economic areas of these cities from the late eighth century onward, suggesting a halt in economic growth. There is also evidence of less maintenance of these centers, resulting in the worsening condition of infrastructure.

Curiously, the ninth-century emporia appear to have decreased their manufacturing in industries such as textile-making, weapons crafting, pottery-making, and metalworking. Some trading sites, such as Lundenwic in modern-day London, which had been a community with a bustling social and economic life during the era of Mercian Supremacy, entered a period of decline in the late eighth century.

In addition to a smaller scale of activities, this decline was marked by the emporia shrinking in size. The diminishing power of the emporia also adversely affected other types of settlements that had been actively involved in the economic system of Anglo-Saxon kingdoms about a century earlier. Many smaller in-land trading posts and productive repositories that connected rural areas and urban centers either stagnated or were fully abandoned.

The existence of an external threat is one possible explanation for this shift in the socio-economic activity of ninth-century Anglo-Saxon emporia. Perhaps, the increased Viking activity in this period forced the inhabitants of these wealthy sites to become more conservative, hold onto their goods, or even entirely relocate. There is evidence of Viking activity in the southern Anglo-Saxon realms. The *Chronicle* describes the 842 Viking attack on London, for example, as very brutal, and London was targeted many times by the invaders in the middle of the ninth century.

This hypothesis can also be supported by the discovery of a ditch constructed in northern Lundenwic during this time. It is possible that the ditch was a defensive structure to keep the invaders in check. The increased presence of the Vikings in this period might have hindered the arrival of foreign merchants, who were afraid of Viking piracy and did not dare to cross the English Channel. Royal charters dating back to the later years of King Offa's reign mention the need to protect the waters of Kent and Sussex, for example, and even Charlemagne had decided to build a fleet to keep the northern shores of his vast empire safe from piracy. Thus, we know that external threat had existed for quite some time.

However, this explanation is only partial, as it appears that the decline of the emporia from their once-great status had already begun by the time the Vikings began to increasingly visit the Anglo-Saxon shores. There were most likely other reasons, as well. A change in environmental conditions is another factor that could have forced the inhabitants of productive sites to relocate to other centers, for example. There is also evidence of new settlements becoming magnets of urban growth in the later ninth and early tenth centuries. These settlements could have evolved as economic rivals to the emporia, which were so interconnected and dependent on each other that one's decline could have accelerated the decline of the others.

Despite this general trend of decline, however, some urban sites continued to flourish during the ninth century. This is most notable in Canterbury, an important British center since Roman times and both the royal seat and the archbishopric see since the early seventh century. Archeological evidence and royal charters reveal the intricate urban design of the walled city, with a high level of infrastructural maintenance and even local regulations for constructing new buildings—they needed to be a certain distance apart to allow for rainwater to effectively disperse. Canterbury was a densely populated city in this period, containing multiple burgages—plots of land rented out by the nobility or the king. Thus, the inhabitants of Canterbury enjoyed some of the highest quality properties of all the Anglo-Saxon urban areas.

The city also had a bustling life full of public areas such as marketplaces, as well as fraternities and guilds, each having a different purpose and organizational structure. Some of these guilds were concerned with maintaining public properties and the image of the city, while others focused on serving specific parts of the city's population, such as merchants or laborers. The city's mints were also among the most active throughout the Anglo-Saxon kingdoms, and a high volume of silver and gold coins suggests the increased wealth of Canterbury. All in all, when we consider the demise of emporia during this period, the economic might of Canterbury appears much more imposing.

Important developments were also taking place in the Church. The Church had accrued much material wealth thanks to donations from its early patrons and the social conditions that had allowed the religious institutions to prosper, at least economically. By the late ninth century, however, the Anglo-Saxon Church appears to have entered a crisis of learning, marked by a decrease in intellectual activity and ability. This constitutes the second characteristic of post-Mercian Anglo-Saxon society.

Life of King Alfred, produced by a Welsh biographer of the later West Saxon king, describes that the intellectual tradition that guaranteed the pursuit of knowledge had disappeared by the time Alfred became king. Latin had become a language that even the clergy themselves could not properly understand, let alone freely speak and translate into vernacular English. The knowledge of this fact was widespread, and the disrepute of the Anglo-Saxon Church was even alluded to by foreign bishops, who criticized the lack of important aspects of Church life such as regular synods, among other shortcomings.

In short, contemporary commentators allude to the fact that despite the existence of many wealthy religious institutions, they rarely followed a strict, disciplined Christian monastic life. Archeological evidence supports written sources—only a handful of manuscripts produced in the middle of the ninth century have been discovered. In the royal and legal charters, historians have identified the worsening quality of the Latin language and script. There is evidence of lessened activities in the scriptoriums of different monasteries, including in Christ Church at Canterbury.

In addition, an increasing number of royal documents produced in vernacular also suggest the gradual replacement of Latin with Old English. This is interesting considering the boom of social and economic activities in Canterbury. Again, the decline of Latin in Canterbury during the mid to late ninth century can be explained by the increasing Viking threat, which had forced many people to seek refuge inside the well-fortified walled city. This urban growth may have dramatically increased the prominence of Old English and caused a reciprocal decline in the use of Latin.

The situation might have been less severe in the western Anglo-Saxon domains, such as Wessex or the West Midlands of Mercia, where the tradition for learning and mastery of Latin maintained high standards during the middle of the ninth century. This is perhaps thanks to the continental influences present in these areas. For example, King Æthelwulf of Wessex had a foreign scribe in his court from Frankia, and the documents produced during his reign show a high-level mastery of Latin. Still, the situation was sufficiently bad enough that King Alfred envisioned a revival of learning and monasticism in his kingdom when he became king.

The Great Heathen Army

The Anglo-Saxon Chronicle does not mention that Viking attacks on Anglo-Saxon realms occurred from the very late eighth century to the middle of the ninth century. In fact, the *Chronicle* says nothing of Viking activity between 795 (two years after the attack on Lindisfarne) and 835, the date of its account of the Viking raid on Sheppey in southern England. For the next decade and a half, Viking raids were generally smaller, containing a force of thirty to forty ships each, at best. The *Chronicle* records battles throughout the 830s and 840s at Southampton, Hingston Down, and the River Parret, for example, providing few new details about the Vikings or the battles themselves.

It is in the invasion of 851 when the Vikings are described as having a considerably larger force of about 350 ships. This invasion, directed at Canterbury and London, seems to be the largest-recorded single Viking raid, and its scale can be confirmed by descriptions of Viking attacks in other contemporary sources. The Franks, for example, whose shores were just as exposed to Viking activity, recorded in the 840s that Viking raids contained hundreds of ships.

The nature of Viking activity appears to have changed around this time, as well. After their attack in 851, the Vikings did not go home for winter and instead stayed at Thanet, terrorizing the local population for a few months before deciding to set sail. Written sources claim that other Viking bands had acted similarly in Ireland, where the Vikings had emerged as frequent visitors around the same time.

Despite the increasing scale of Viking attacks year after year, the Anglo-Saxons resisted the foreigners with great success. The *Chronicle* (which we should remember is a source compiled in a West Saxon court) records that the kings of Wessex defeated the invaders on multiple occasions. For instance, King Æthelwulf of Wessex repelled the 851 invasion, accompanied by his son, Æthelbald.

It appears that the Vikings would strike a coastal area of England and proceed to overwhelm the local defenses for a time, but the response from Anglo-Saxon armies would be timely, eventually forcing the Vikings to retreat. We can infer from the way the *Chronicle* speaks of the Vikings during the first half of the ninth century that it saw them as a recurring threat that could nevertheless be contained.

A new era of Viking invasions began in 865 with the arrival of what the *Anglo-Saxon Chronicle* calls the "Great Heathen Army," an army composed of a confederation of Danish, Swedish, and Norwegian Vikings. Though the exact size of this army is unclear, it probably contained no more than a few thousand raiders, most of them experienced warriors.

The Great Heathen Army landed in East Anglia, overrunning defenses and rampaging northward through the Anglo-Saxon countryside, reaching York by 866. To the horror of the Anglo-Saxons, the army was later reinforced by another force, dramatically increasing the danger they posed to the locals.

What differentiated the Great Heathen Army from previous Viking raids was that it intended from the very beginning to conquer and occupy the Anglo-Saxon lands instead of simply pillaging and raiding. Such clearly defined goals made cooperation among different Viking groups within the army possible. On the whole, it was a common practice for different Viking warbands to come together for raids, split the booty, and separate after the end of their attacks. In fact, achieving a force of this size, one worthy of being deemed "great," certainly suggests that despite the different Viking groups within the army, it was still very efficient and successful.

It is also unclear who exactly was in charge of the Great Heathen Army. According to legend, it was led by the three sons of the legendary Viking Ragnar Lodbrok, one of the most prominent Viking leaders of the Viking Age until that point. The legend tells that Ragnar's sons—Ivar the Boneless, Halfdan Ragnarsson, and Ubba—had joined their forces to avenge the death of their father at the hands of King Ælla of Northumbria, who had captured and executed Ragnar during a previous raid into his territory. The Nordic sources that mention the invasion also depict Ragnar as a half-mythical figure and a pioneer of Viking expansion and exploration, so they should not be considered historically accurate. Nevertheless, the fact that the Great Heathen Army was comprised of prominent Viking figures each leading their bands serves to emphasize its unique nature.

Having landed in East Anglia, the Vikings proceeded to make peace with the locals, who gave the invaders supplies and horses as made their way north toward York. The *Chronicle* mentions that the Kingdom of Northumbria was a prime target for the Vikings because of the political chaos of its succession crisis. At the time, the crown was contested between King Ælla and his brother Osberht. When we also consider the Nordic sources' statement that Ragnar's sons had wished to avenge the death of their father, it is clear the Vikings planned to attack Northumbria from the beginning and would have known of the difficulties the kingdom was facing.

By late 866, the Vikings had decisively defeated the Northumbrians, killing both Ælla and Osberht in battle and establishing themselves at York. For the next few months, they continued to ravage the Northumbrian countryside, imposing their rule on the local population and forcing them to pay *danegeld*—different kinds of tribute the locals would pay to the Vikings in exchange for peace, protection, or to dissuade their future attacks. Though the term was not used until later centuries, some Anglo-Saxons, including Northumbrians, had already been giving tribute to the Vikings by the time the Great Heathen Army landed in

England.

After Northumbria, the next target for the Vikings was the Kingdom of Mercia, the largest Anglo-Saxon kingdom south of the Humber River, possessing thousands of acres of valuable farmland that was ripe for pillaging. The Vikings stayed at Nottingham for the winter of 867-868, where a combined Mercian-West Saxon army tried to check them. Despite the combined effort, however, the Vikings held off the Anglo-Saxons once again. It is likely that after the battle of Nottingham, the Vikings negotiated a peace agreement with the Mercians, probably in exchange for tribute, and left the kingdom alone for a few years.

The *Chronicle* remarks that the Great Heathen Army stayed in Northumbria throughout the winter but turned south and attacked East Anglia in 869. There, they resided in the town of Thetford, where King Edmund of East Anglia attacked them. The Vikings held out throughout the winter, emerging victorious in the battle against Edmund, killing the king.

East Anglia is the first Anglo-Saxon kingdom in the *Chronicle* that is said to have been entirely conquered by the Vikings one year after their initial attack in the winter of 869. The fact that East Anglia was small and one of the richest Anglo-Saxon realms at the time might have motivated the Vikings to take full control of it quickly. The *Chronicle* laments the perishing of the kingdom at the hands of the Vikings, a sentiment that seems cohesive with the public attitude at the time. Edmund would soon be venerated as a martyr, killed at the hands of the ruthless pagans.

Viking activity resumed in the second part of 871 when new bands of Vikings arrived from Scandinavia as reinforcements. They joined the main force at Northumbria and launched another attack on Mercia. This time, the Vikings targeted locations further south, reaching cities such as London and Lincolnshire by 872. Where possible, they tried to avoid confrontation with the Mercian army, instead choosing to overwinter in areas where they could sustain themselves solely by raiding.

This constant pillaging greatly affected the social and economic stability in Mercia. Mercian farmers and citizens lived in constant fear of the Vikings and could not properly access the farmlands in the countryside. The Vikings also posed a threat to some of the cultural centers of Mercia, such as when they targeted St. Wystan's Church at Repton, a site that held great material and spiritual importance for Mercian kings. St. Wystan's was where the royal Mercian mausoleum was located, and the strategic location of the site allowed the Vikings to exert firm control over the Mercian heartlands. The Vikings fortified their position at Repton, and archeological evidence suggests that they built defensive ditches and stayed in the town for a long time, even burying their dead there.

The *Chronicle* mentions that during this period, the Vikings forced King Burgred of Mercia into exile. The year 874 is considered the last year of his reign. Burgred traveled to Rome, probably on a pilgrimage, and died and was buried there. In his place, the Vikings installed a puppet king named Ceolwulf II, with whom they maintained a close relationship. The *Chronicle* says Ceolwulf was an "unwise" king who had sworn an "oath of loyalty" to the Vikings. Even though the Chronicle is a biased source, the dethronement of Burgred in favor of Ceolwulf indicates the influence the invaders had on the Mercian throne. Despite this, it is unlikely Ceolwulf was considered a fully illegitimate king, as he continued to issue royal charters for the five years he ruled, and the nobility and clergy who had also served under Burgred often acted as witnesses for his royal grants.

So, despite the Vikings installing a king they favored, it would be an exaggeration to say that they also put their own people in positions of power in the Mercian court. It seems more likely that Mercia was in a state of severe disarray and the local elites were unable or unwilling to resist the Vikings as long as they maintained their positions of power.

In his *Life of King Alfred*, Asser remarks that the Great Heathen Army split up sometime after their conquest of Mercia. One part of the army returned north to Northumbria and launched an invasion of the Picts in Scotland from there. The other part remained in the Anglo-Saxon realms, moving from place to place to maintain a strong hold on the conquered territories. It seems that the Vikings were content with having destabilized the Anglo-Saxons enough to make a united resistance very difficult; they still enjoyed the booty from constantly raiding the lands.

One kingdom the Vikings repeatedly tried to subdue was the Kingdom of Wessex, which, by 877, had done a relatively good job of keeping the Vikings at arm's length. The Great Heathen Army had raided West Saxon territories on several different occasions since its arrival in 865, but the responses from the kings of Wessex were swift.

Throughout the first years of the 870s, West Saxon kings Æthelred and Alfred were forced to make peace with the Vikings after suffering several defeats at their hands, first at Reading and Basing in January, and later at Wilton in April. These defeats forced the West Saxons to rethink their strategies, and King Alfred finally reached an agreement with the invaders in late 871. He also relocated further south to Winchester and proceeded to build a new force to drive the heathens out of England. Alfred was forced to make peace with the Vikings five years later when the invaders returned after having conquered Mercia. He was forced to give up more lands in the northern territories, and the Vikings essentially gained control of a large part of the northern, central, and eastern territories of Britain.

Alfred the Great

By 877, the Great Heathen Army had defeated the Anglo-Saxon kingdoms of East Anglia, Northumbria, and Mercia. The Vikings had established themselves comfortably in these lands, where any remnant of political leadership had dwindled throughout the 870s. The invaders had successfully installed a puppet king over the western half of Mercia, whereas they possessed the rich Midlands and the eastern territories, including London. Only the Kingdom of Wessex remained a valid Anglo-Saxon rival to the Vikings, and West Saxon kings had never managed to fight the Vikings on their terms.

As we mentioned earlier, a prominent Viking strategy was to quickly storm a poorly defended town, where they would organize their defenses. They would force the royal armies to approach them for negotiations and try to extort as much as possible. If the king refused to negotiate, the Vikings would either pillage the countryside until they had decimated the local population to force the hand of the king or simply relocate to another such town and repeat the process. Both kings of Wessex in this period, Æthelred and Alfred, had fallen victim to this Viking strategy. They had been unable to catch the Vikings off-guard, as the Vikings simply would not take a battle that would be unfavorable for them.

In 876, the part of the Viking army that was south of the Humber proceeded to thus take control of Wareham, in the southernmost part of Wessex, on the English Channel. There, they reached an agreement with Wessex about the exchange of hostages and maintenance of peace but quickly broke the agreement and relocated to Exeter. After this, the Vikings returned to Mercia, where, as we mentioned, they essentially divided the kingdom in two before returning to Wessex.

In January of 878, the Vikings launched a surprise attack on the royal stronghold of Chippenham. They overwhelmed the West Saxons here as well, forcing Alfred to flee with a small band of followers further north to

Somerset, taking refuge in the remote village of Athelney. In the marshlands of Somerset, he set up his fortifications and planned to retaliate. From this remote area, Alfred began mounting a true resistance to the Viking invasion. The *Anglo-Saxon Chronicle* mentions that alone, against all odds, the king started to recruit local militia from Somerset, Wiltshire, and Hampshire during May of 878.

In late May of 878, King Alfred and his force were ready to strike. The king chose not to take the fight directly to Chippenham, where the Vikings, led by their warlord Guthrum, had fortified. Instead, as he gathered his recruits, Alfred drew the Vikings out and engaged in the decisive Battle of Edington with a few thousand men. The *Chronicle* does not mention the details of the battle, but it ended in a West Saxon victory, with the Vikings slaughtered on the battlefield. Alfred pursued the Vikings to the stronghold and laid siege, cutting off supply lines and forcing the Vikings to surrender two weeks later.

As part of the peace agreement, Guthrum converted to Christianity, and the Vikings swore an oath to leave West Saxon lands. Ultimately, Guthrum and some of his men were baptized, and the Viking leader and King Alfred of Wessex agreed on a treaty that fixed the borders between the newly conquered Viking realms in central, northern, and eastern England and the areas under the leadership of Wessex in the south.

Alfred did not have to deal with the Vikings again until the 890s, when a different army raided the areas around Fulham. This time, however, Alfred quickly defeated the invaders and drove them out "by the grace of God." Thus, by the end of the ninth century, the great Viking invasion of Anglo-Saxon England was over.

King Alfred is not only one of the most central Anglo-Saxon figures but also among the most celebrated characters of early Medieval Europe. In popular culture, his image is that of the defeater of the Vikings and the "savior" of England. Alfred was, in fact, the Anglo-Saxon leader who dealt the decisive blow to the Great Heathen Army. Thanks to his efforts, the Vikings were driven back after more than a decade of rampaging through Anglo-Saxon lands. Still, it is perhaps misleading to think of Alfred as the person who defeated "the" Vikings, as they would launch many more invasions into Anglo-Saxon realms in later decades.

King Alfred was arguably also not the person who "saved" England. This is simply because there was no united "England" to save from a foreign invasion at the time. King Alfred's actions were primarily directed at defending his own Kingdom of Wessex, and he did not liberate the English lands that had been under Viking influence since the late ninth century. Even the final agreement he made with Guthrum stated that Alfred would mutually recognize Viking overlordship in these lands, which would eventually be known as the Danelaw ("the land with the Danish laws").

Still, King Alfred is not known as "the Great" for no reason. Though he did not decisively defeat the Vikings or "save" England, he was still the king who laid the foundations for creating a united kingdom out of the Anglo-Saxon realms. In fact, it can be argued that King Alfred's greatest contributions came after his victory at Edington—namely, the steps he took in nation-building that resulted in a united Kingdom of England a few generations later. Thus, it is just as crucial to examine the nature of Alfred's reign after the victory at Edington to truly see the magnificence that earned him a worthy title.

Map of Britain in 886.
https://commons.wikimedia.org/wiki/File:Britain_886.jpg

King Alfred is the Anglo-Saxon king about whom we know the most, by a wide margin. There were many high-quality documents produced during his reign or about his reign, including the *Life of King Alfred* and the *Anglo-Saxon Chronicle*, which provide us with valuable insights into his life.

And, though there is a lack of contemporary royal charters issued in Alfred's name, this is made up for by the fact that Alfred composed a law code for the first time among the Anglo-Saxons in over a hundred years. In addition, many other translated books were produced during Alfred's reign. These were composed by members of Alfred's court, religious figures under Alfred's patronage, or, in rare cases, Alfred himself. The king himself adapted several texts from Latin to Old English, such as St. Augustine's *Soliloquies*—a text that remains central to Christian philosophy today.

The fact that so many written texts linked directly to the king have survived signals different aspects of Alfred's reign. The first advantage is that it is possible to reconstruct Alfred's reign with great accuracy with the help of so many sources. This includes depictions of Alfred's personality and character, allowing us more insight into his life and the decisions that he made.

The survival of these texts also indicates that Alfred took great care of his public image as a Christian king who promoted learning and encouraged the production of new knowledge among his subjects. As we have said, this would have given him more authority in the eyes of the public. As Anglo-Saxon kings were being defeated by the Vikings, Alfred needed all the support he could get from his subjects by presenting himself as a strong king. His new law codex is a significant achievement in this regard, seeking to legitimize his rule through written text and force the profound transformation of West Saxon (or Anglo-Saxon society).

The production of such a large volume of texts also suggests that Alfred sought to be represented as the antithesis of the pagan Vikings who were the main adversary of his time. People would rather side with a king like Alfred who, unlike the Vikings, promoted learning and writing. Whatever the reasons, Alfred was certainly a monarch who cared about his public image and acted to reinforce it however he could.

Charlemagne had been the pioneer in such a transformation of the nature of kingship a hundred years earlier, and his successors had continued to assume and enforce this new understanding. The Frankish emperor may have been the main inspiration for King Alfred, especially when we consider that he needed to legitimize his rule.

Another reason King Alfred emerged as an example of what a king should be like came from the succession difficulties that had plagued the throne of Wessex since the middle of the ninth century. In fact, it was unlikely from the beginning that Alfred would become king, as he was the youngest of the four sons of King Æthelwulf. Wessex had been plunged into a succession crisis when Prince Æthelbald had assumed authority in 856 after his father, King Æthelwulf, had gone on a pilgrimage. As a result, the kingdom had been divided for many years, and all three of Alfred's brothers had emerged as kings. Wessex needed stability and a strong king, and Alfred could have been the key.

It is also very interesting to examine the early years of Alfred before he became king, as they can provide valuable insights into the formation of the future ruler's mind and way of life. Some historians have suggested that Alfred's upbringing might have played a big role in his religiosity and love for learning. As the youngest son, Alfred was likely expected to have a clerical career in the future, which was very common in medieval families where the oldest son would normally inherit the family possessions. Alfred's biography mentions that the king was interested in religious life from a very young age and always attended various ceremonies, such as daily and weekly sermons.

From a young age, the personality of the future king was already directed toward being engaged in activities that were normally neglected by the nobility. At their core, the Anglo-Saxon elites were descendants of old war chieftains and a society that valued violence and sex as prime virtues. According to the biography, Alfred struggled with this dichotomy of Christian life on the one hand and a more primal drive for glory (that included sin) on the other. In his later writings, Alfred asserted that he had been tempted during his youth by several different sins, noting that persevering had been very difficult. He stressed the difficulty of maintaining a healthy balance between the primal urges of the body and the more virtuous undertakings of the mind. A deep reading of Alfred's struggles identifies him not only as a Christian man who strived to be ideal but also as a righteous, Stoic-like man who tried to guide his way with morals.

Interestingly, young Alfred had visited Rome with his brother Æthelred in the year 853, sent there by their father, King Æthelwulf. The *Chronicle* mentions that Alfred was blessed as a future king by Pope Leo IV, and the story of their meeting is confirmed in other written sources. However, the *Chronicle* likely exaggerates when it asserts that the pope specifically blessed Alfred as a future king. Papal letters to King Æthelwulf mention Alfred as a "spiritual son" of the pope who was treated as a real "Roman consul," decorated with lavish garments and accessories.

Nevertheless, this meeting obviously would have helped push Alfred's agenda to present himself as a legitimate, Christian king during Wessex's chaotic political situation in the latter half of the ninth century. Alfred's visit to Rome is thus significant considering his future claims and behavior. It also provides insights into the earliest influences on young Alfred, as the confirmation of kingship by the pope was a profoundly Frankish Carolingian practice.

Whatever the case, Alfred's upbringing and early life played a very important role in the formation of his character, manifested in the policies he promoted throughout his reign. A prime example of this is his love of learning and belief that education was the long-term solution to Wessex's problems. Alfred recognized that education and literacy, together with true monastic tradition, had generally declined in the Anglo-Saxon kingdoms, as we noted earlier. Thus, to reverse this trend, Alfred decided to recruit distinguished scholars and monks to his court. Asser, his biographer from Wales, was among such recruits.

Alfred recognized that despite the importance of Latin as the primary language for learning in Europe at the time, its mastery in Anglo-Saxon lands was very low. He thus directed his reforms at making it easier, as well as necessary, for secular people to study and understand Latin. Translations of many important texts from Latin to Old English served this purpose.

Alfred believed that wisdom, curiosity, and knowledge were ideals that must be pursued by all individuals, including the nobility, who had largely neglected education in exchange for being involved in warfare, for example. He believed there were certain things all men must know, and he made this clear to the nobility.

The king used different tactics to encourage education among the West Saxon elites, even threatening to remove them from their privileged positions if they did not comply with his demands. This is not to say that he neglected all other aspects of the nobles' lives, such as their military skill and knowledge of warfare. We will see later that Alfred himself passed vital military reforms. Instead, he wanted knowledgeable people in his court because he believed it would allow him to make better decisions in all fields, including warfare. The way he saw it, the Crown had no use for uneducated and illiterate servants. Surely enough, in a few decades, an educated court would become a staple of monarchies throughout Europe.

There is no better example of Alfred's contributions to Christian kingship than his legal code. It served as an amalgamation of three legal codes that had come before his time—those of King Æthelbert of Kent, King Ine of Wessex, and King Offa of Mercia. From these previous documents, Alfred took the laws he believed to have been the most important and in need of repetition or clarification. Strictly speaking, there is little additional legal material in Alfred's code, but what it does not lack is Christian and Mosaic undertones.

This is especially apparent in the prologue, where it seems Alfred summarized the essence of the legal traditions of the Abrahamic religions. Providing an overview of Christian law-making at the beginning of the book heavily suggests that Alfred saw his code as a continuation of the tradition—as an essential part of what Christianity stood for. Thus, Alfred the Great's legal code serves as the primary example of an Anglo-Saxon king emphasizing the elements of Christian kingship. Though many had tried to impose this concept, few had succeeded to the level of Alfred's.

Alfred's reforms concerned more than the social and cultural aspects of West Saxon life in the late ninth century. His economic and military reforms were just as vital in making Wessex the newest most dominant Anglo-Saxon kingdom in Britain. These reforms must also be viewed relative to the political context: Alfred knew that his realm was in danger from the Great Heathen Army, and many of the changes were directed at combatting the immediate challenges the Vikings posed to Wessex's security and strength.

His monetary reform was implemented in 875, three years before he defeated the Vikings at Edington. The new West Saxon coinage, minted in Alfred's name throughout "greater Wessex," including London, had a fixed weight and a new design featuring classical Roman influences. What is more impressive is that the coinage reform was carried out with King Ceolwulf of Mercia—and it appears that Alfred was perceived as the "senior" king in this relationship. Many coins bear his name with the title of *Rex Anglorum*— "King of the Angles," or perhaps "King of the English," whereas Ceolwulf is simply mentioned as *rex*.

The fact that these coins were minted in non-traditionally West Saxon territories, such as London, suggests the increasing influence of Wessex over its neighbors by the middle of the 870s. A shared monetary system was key for Mercia and Wessex's economic and social integration, providing a great foundation for an eventual political union between the two kingdoms. The reform was very possibly Alfred's conscious attempt to expand his notion of universal kingship among the Anglo-Saxons. Imposing such an influence on the once-great state of Mercia, now torn by war and spared by Vikings, was the first move in asserting the new dominance of Wessex.

Alfred would gain more influence after the death of King Ceolwulf of Mercia, who was succeeded by an ealdorman named Æthelred in the late 870s. Æthelred ruled over the western part of Mercia still under Anglo-Saxon control but never enjoyed the title of "king," instead recognizing the overlordship of King Alfred. It appears that the two leaders had a mutual understanding, something that can be better seen after Æthelred married Alfred's daughter in the late 880s. Æthelred accepted Alfred as a superior political figure partially because the Vikings had weakened the Mercian position and partially because of Alfred's conscious efforts to transform the existing political relationship.

In addition to measures that altered the Anglo-Saxon economy by accelerating integration between Mercia and Wessex, Alfred took steps to significantly reform the Anglo-Saxon military. These changes were implemented in the face of the looming Viking threat that had identified clear shortcomings in the Anglo-Saxon strategies.

As we have mentioned, the Viking force's primary tactic was to avoid direct confrontation with the Anglo-Saxon armies. Often, the two sides would negotiate for the peaceful retreat of the Vikings in exchange for a sum of money or tribute, but the Vikings would often break these agreements and launch raids on other places. Thus, rather than their skill and ferocity in warfare, it was the adoption of smart tactics and the knowledge of their enemy's weaknesses—in this case, the inability of Anglo-Saxon kings to quickly muster up armies—that gave the Great Heathen Army a big advantage. It was less due to a discrepancy in the quality of the military, as Anglo-Saxon armies could defeat the Vikings when they intercepted them and forced an open battle.

Recognizing this problem, Alfred decided to split his army into two parts, creating a permanent standing force that could be mobilized much more quickly. The other half of the original army stayed in their homes and were not on active duty, but they could be mobilized if the Vikings attacked their residence or areas close by. If these pockets of local resistance could hold up the Vikings, the standing army could quickly provide support and ensure Anglo-Saxon victory.

Once the soldiers in the standing force had served for a certain amount of time, they would be replaced by soldiers who had stayed at home. This measure ensured not only a quick response to decentralized Viking attacks but also that the soldiers would always be fresh and ready for battle. Although communication problems rendered it difficult to coordinate when the standing army would be relieved, the West Saxon forces eventually adapted to the new system.

The final important reform Alfred implemented in the late 870s was the establishment of a network of defensive fortifications, known as burhs, at strategic locations throughout Wessex. The construction of defensive fortifications was nothing new for Britain, begun during the time of the Romans. In fact, some of Alfred's burhs were based on these older structures while others were placed in areas previously disregarded. The goal was to effectively cover all of Alfred's domains and dissuade concentrated Viking attacks in the future. Many fortifications were constructed on royal roads or at convenient locations on rivers to ensure that they restricted free Viking movement.

The burhs eventually grew, transforming the areas around them with new settlements. In a few centuries, many of them would become full-fledged towns with specialized industries and character, whereas others retained purely strategic importance. This reform, too, faced many difficulties. The most obvious was the costs of building and maintenance. A later document titled *Burghal Hidage* mentions that tens of thousands of men were needed to keep the system up and running. Evidence also suggests that Alfred did not complete the construction of several burh sites. Considering these challenges, it is even more impressive that the burh system built by Alfred persevered through time, expanded upon by future West Saxon kings.

All in all, King Alfred the Great of Wessex remains one of the most central figures of Anglo-Saxon history. He emerged as a leader against the Viking invasion and saved what remained of Anglo-Saxon kingdoms south of the Humber. His contributions to Anglo-Saxon resistance against the Great Heathen Army are certainly worthy of praise, and so are his policies as king. They are even more impressive when we consider that Alfred was acting primarily to preserve and protect his own kingdom. His later decisions, however, suggest that Alfred had a vision for the future of Anglo-Saxon kingship—a future he believed lay in integration, with Wessex as the leader. In fact, only two generations later, Alfred's grandson, Æthelstan would bear the title "King of the English" and be recognized as the first king of a united kingdom of England. Alfred was also instrumental in bringing back the tradition and love of learning to Medieval England. It is thanks to his efforts that we know so much about the history of the Anglo-Saxons.

Chapter 6: The Making of England

In this chapter, we will examine the fate of the Anglo-Saxons after the end of the Great Heathen Army invasion in the late ninth century. Previously, we looked at the reign of King Alfred of Wessex—the man commonly considered to have ended the Viking invasion of Anglo-Saxon England. His reforms not only kept the invaders in check but also laid the foundation for the future Kingdom of England. We also mentioned that Alfred's actions were not directed toward this unification, and the same can be said about his successors. As we will come to see, however, the decisions made by the succeeding rulers of Wessex would result in the creation of a unified Anglo-Saxons state. Below, we will take a closer look at the reigns of West Saxon kings such as Edward and Æthelstan and examine their actions within the wider perspective of early English nation-building. Given the unstable political circumstances of the age, examining the processes that led to Anglo-Saxon unification is even more compelling.

After Alfred

King Alfred died in October 899, succeeded by his son Edward, who would come to bear the title "the Elder." During his reign, Alfred was already referred to as the king of the Anglo-Saxons, and for good reason. Alfred's reign had brought much-needed stability to the Kingdom of Wessex, which had emerged as the most dominant of the remaining Anglo-Saxon kingdoms. However, this did not necessarily mean that his successors would likewise be recognized as over-kings.

In fact, the chaotic landscape of early tenth-century England added more complications to the existing power dynamics between the Anglo-

Saxon kingdoms and the Vikings, who had firmly established themselves in eastern and northern England (the Danelaw). The Vikings had controlled territories both north and south of the Humber for decades before their possessions were recognized by Alfred. Since their invasion in 865, they had come to dominate the kingdoms of Northumbria and East Anglia and had emerged as overlords over much of Mercia. Their advance further south had only been stopped thanks to Alfred.

The Vikings' replacement of Anglo-Saxon political organization in the Danelaw remains obscure. In fact, the whole circumstance looked a lot like the arrival of the Anglo-Saxons in post-Roman Britain in the fifth century. Archeological findings from the time, the names of settlements, and genetic evidence clearly point to the increasing presence of the Vikings in these lands. It is unclear, however, whether an increasing number of Scandinavians, who were not necessarily warrior-explorers like traditional Vikings, continued to come to the Danelaw during the early ninth century. It is also possible that the Vikings who conquered these lands emerged as the new elite, replacing the existing Anglo-Saxon nobility through continued tribute collection.

There is also confusion about naming the territories conquered by the Vikings "the Danelaw." The first use of the term appears in eleventh-century sources, and it is unlikely it was used as a conscious distinction between different ethnic groups that made up Viking armies. "Danelaw" or "law of the Danes" suggests that for Anglo-Saxons, the Vikings were Danes, though the Great Heathen Army had contained warrior bands from different parts of Scandinavia. Thus, attributing a simpler term to a combination of Viking ethnicities, nationalities, or cultural identities (that were very similar, nevertheless) is not necessarily accurate. Still, the use of the term reflects the prominence of Scandinavian overlords in these lands.

We don't know how centralized the leadership of the Danelaw was or how connected this Viking realm was to Scandinavia. We can gather from contemporary West Saxon sources and archeological evidence that some form of cohesion existed among the different Viking warrior bands that had settled in the Danelaw. After the initial invasion of the Great Heathen Army, these warrior bands had most likely separated, drawn to different cities that they took over, like York, Nottingham, or Leicester. The *Anglo-Saxon Chronicle* mentions that the Danes had worked the lands they had conquered since the middle of the 870s, suggesting that the Vikings had intended to stay in this part of England. Having their authority over those lands recognized by Alfred in the 880s, the Vikings most likely did not feel the need to significantly alter their political organization in the Danelaw.

The Anglo-Saxons had remained in rough control of the northern part of Northumbria since the kingdom's conquest by the original wave of the Great Heathen Army, but they did not hold any considerable power. The southern lands of Northumbria were directly under the rule of the Vikings, who installed client kings in the northern part of the old kingdom to efficiently impose their rule on their subjects.

The situation was just as chaotic south of the Humber. East Anglia had been completely absorbed by the Vikings, whereas Sussex and Essex had been taken over by the Kingdom of Wessex. A significant part of Mercia had also been conquered by the Vikings, but the western half of the kingdom, commonly referred to as "English Mercia," remained under Anglo-Saxon rule and was politically dominated by Alfred throughout the later years of his reign.

All in all, these were the two significant axes of power in early tenth-century England: the Vikings, who ruled the lands of the Danelaw, and the Anglo-Saxon kingdoms of Wessex and Mercia, with West Saxon leadership. The political conflicts of the early tenth century mainly took place between these two powers.

The Kingdom of Wessex faced a succession struggle after the death of King Alfred in 899. Yes, his son Edward became king, but he was challenged by a person who had a rather serious claim to the West Saxon throne —Æthelwold, the younger son of King Æthelred and a nephew of King Alfred. Æthelwold had been an infant when his father died fighting the Vikings in 871, leading to the crown passing to his brother, Alfred. And though the *Chronicle* depicts a rather simple story of the transfer of power from Alfred to Edward, the events of the first years of the tenth century are very intriguing to examine.

It appears that Æthelwold, having come of age and perhaps aware of the fact that Alfred did not necessarily favor Edward as his successor, openly challenged Edward for the throne of Wessex. He had considerable support both inside Wessex and beyond its borders, though the *Chronicle,* written in the court of the eventual victor—Edward—mentions that Æthelwold's uprising was only an early rebellion swiftly dealt with by Edward.

In reality, Æthelwold sought military assistance from the Danes, who granted him this support, perhaps believing that Æthelwold would become another puppet king if he emerged successful. In the first years of the tenth century, Æthelwold incited the uprising of a large Viking force from East Anglia against Edward, who rushed there with an army to put an end to the challenger's prospects. Though the Danes under Æthelwold emerged victorious from the bloody Battle of the Holme in December of 902, Æthelwold died in battle, and his uprising subsequently ended.

It is also difficult to determine the extent of King Edward's power in the first years of his tenure. In the royal charters issued in his name, he is mentioned as the "King of the Anglo-Saxons," but it is unlikely that he exercised as much influence over English Mercia as his father had. The charters of King Æthelred of Mercia, who had recognized Alfred as overking since the 880s, do not mention Edward in the same manner. In fact, Mercian sources emphasize Æthelred's sovereignty as king and especially Æthelflæd—Alfred's daughter—as queen. In fact, sources such as the *Annals of Æthelflæd* and *Mercian Register* depict the queen as a very strong ruler herself, especially after the death of her husband in 911, acting independently and pursuing policies that would benefit Mercia.

Mercian coinage, on the other hand, tells a different story. It is issued in Edward's name, suggesting that Mercia was, at least nominally, under his control. It seems that though Edward exercised some form of power over Mercia, even taking command of Mercian forces in a campaign in 909, Mercian kings were relatively free to operate in their domains in the first few years of the tenth century.

After Æthelred's death in 911, Edward's rule over Mercia became firmer. He inherited some of the most important Mercian centers, such as London and Oxford, which greatly strengthened his position. From this point on, Edward also developed a better relationship with his sister Æthelflæd of Mercia, and it is plausible that the two coordinated their most important political decisions in the following years. The fruits of this relationship were manifested in the joint policies against the Vikings throughout the Danelaw. These policies included not only offensive military campaigns in East Anglia and eastern parts of Mercia but also the continued construction of key defensive burhs in territories still controlled by the Anglo-Saxons to keep the borders safe. The royal charters from this time refer to the Vikings of East Anglia and Northumbria as two separate armies and political entities, suggesting that the leadership of the Danelaw was decentralized.

The construction of burhs made it difficult for Vikings to cross into the West Saxon or Mercian countryside and pillage the lands. Over time, they were constructed closer to the border between the dominions of the Anglo-Saxons and the Danelaw, such as at Hertford and Witham in Essex. These defenses were set up to check potential Viking offensives from East Anglia into the lands north of the Thames River, those that led directly to London, which was a crucial center of power. The burh network spread out like a spiderweb, each supporting the next and enabling the whole system to be sustainable.

It appears that this policy was soon relatively successful. Burhs constructed in the English heartlands eventually caused some Viking centers to submit to the Anglo-Saxon rulers of Mercia and Wessex.

By 918, most of the large cities south of the Humber thus appear to have submitted to the Anglo-Saxons, with individual Viking leaders striking agreements and offering to pledge their allegiance. Because of the lack of West Saxon charters in this period, it is difficult to determine what exactly caused such a shift in political organization. However, evidence suggests that the most elite Vikings likely kept their estates after pleading with Edward. It is thus likely that gradual West Saxon and Mercian military domination forced the Viking leaders to submit one by one, though this was done carefully to keep the peace instead of exploiting Viking trust. The Danes, who saw benefits in aligning with the kingdoms of Mercia and Wessex, thus negotiated on behalf of their subjects. We know that this large-scale transfer of the Danelaw lands south of the Humber into Edward's control was a profound process because of the coins minted in the West Saxon king's name.

With the death of Æthelflæd in 918, Edward was essentially the most powerful Anglo-Saxon king, and he proceeded to quickly assert his power over Mercia. The *Anglo-Saxon Chronicle* mentions him pushing to the site of the queen's death at Tamworth in Staffordshire, where the Mercian people decided to submit to him, along with three Welsh rulers, who had probably been under Æthelflæd's influence. Edward then took Ælfwynn, the daughter of the late Mercian queen, to Wessex, perhaps to deal with the potential threat of a succession challenger sooner rather than later. This incident essentially gave Edward a level of control over Mercia similar to his father Alfred's, once again uniting two of the strongest Anglo-Saxon kingdoms.

Moreover, in the next two to three years, Edward continued his policy of "defensive expansion" by constructing burhs all around his realm. In this way, he made his control of the vast Mercian territories firmer, even making advances in the Northumbrian Danelaw territories. The *Chronicle* remarks that Edward was chosen as the "father and lord" not only by the English and the Danes south of the Humber but also by Ragnald of York, the prominent Viking leader of the northern Danelaw. The exact circumstances surrounding Edward being chosen as overlord are unclear, but it suggests that Ragnald struck a mutual recognition treaty with Edward in which he retained control of York and surrounding territories north of the Humber.

On the other hand, Edward was recognized as the sole leader of the Anglo-Saxons, who were starting to be called the "English." The reigns of Alfred and Edward had done a lot for this important identity transformation, which would be finalized during the reign of Edward's successor.

The King of the English

Historians disagree on the nature of Anglo-Saxon nation-building or unification, and the prominent stance is that it was never consciously initiated. Anglo-Saxon rulers, ever since they could be called kings and their realms in Britain called kingdoms, were motivated by personal gain. Anglo-Saxon kings were aware of their tough political environment, and increasing political power at the expense of others was always the chief motivation behind the reigns of kings such as Offa of Mercia or Alfred of Wessex. These rulers were great because they could adapt to changing circumstances and emerge from extremely challenging times as dominant figures. This is true even though these rulers were often referred to as "over-kings" or "kings of the Anglo-Saxons" or "kings of Britain."

There are also complications in defining "unity" among the Anglo-Saxons. What exactly does this word entail when we consider the complex ethnic, linguistic, and cultural makeup of the British Isles during the Middle Ages? Where exactly did the Anglo-Saxon realms end? How could a ruler be objectively considered the king of the Anglo-Saxons? Better yet, how could a ruler be considered the king of the English?

Thus, when we speak of King Æthelstan of Wessex as the first king of the English after 927, we must clear up all this confusion, especially because Æthelstan did not directly inherit all the territories previously controlled by his father Edward. The events immediately following Edward's death in 924 remain unclear, but it seems that Æthelstan initially only succeeded him in Mercia, whereas his brother Ælfweard inherited the throne of Wessex. We don't know whether Edward had divided the lands between his sons before his death. This explanation is valid, as Frankish kings in Europe had practiced this way of succession for quite a while.

Ælfweard may also have been proclaimed king in Wessex because Edward had died in Mercian territories, where he had been accompanied by Æthelstan, who had a history of being involved in Mercian affairs. For example, Æthelstan had participated in the campaigns with his aunt and uncle, Æthelflæd and Æthelred, and was more known to the Mercian court. However, Ælfweard died less than three weeks after Edward. Æthelstan thus became the king of both Mercia and Wessex, though he initially faced minor resistance in Wessex when he tried to impose his power. Importantly, he was proclaimed king in September of 925 at Kingston-upon-Thames—a place chosen specifically because of its location on the border between Wessex and Mercia.

Frontispiece of Bede's Life of St Cuthbert, showing King Æthelstan presenting a copy of the book to the saint himself.

Æthelstan ruled for about fifteen years until his death in 939, which makes his great achievement of English unification that much more impressive. By the time of his accession to the throne, the only major Anglo-Saxon realm not under his rulership was Danish Northumbria, centered around the city of York. (Previous West Saxon and Mercian kings had already regained control of East Anglia and eastern Mercian territories.) Æthelstan became the first southern Anglo-Saxon ruler of Northumbria, as well. He managed this through a marriage alliance between his sister and Sihtric, the Viking ruler of York, in 926.

Sihtric, who had previously also ruled the Viking-controlled Kingdom of Dublin, had become the King of York in 921 after the death of Ragnald of York. The Danish ruler's position may have been weakened due to his prior wars with the Brittonic kingdoms of the north, forcing him to negotiate with Æthelstan.

Importantly, Sihtric died only about a year after marrying Æthelstan's sister, and the *Chronicle* mentions that it was the West Saxon king who "succeeded the kingdom of the Northumbrians." It is difficult to grasp the extent to which Æthelstan was initially accepted by the Northumbrian people as their king, but he may have been first challenged by Guthfrith, a cousin of Sihtric who led a small force from Dublin. This resistance was unprepared and fell short of preventing Æthelstan from imposing his power in York, however.

Crucially, other northern kings also submitted to Æthelstan at Eamont in July 927. Among them were King Constantine of Alba (Scotland) and King Owain of the Brittonic Kingdom of Strathclyde. Additionally, the Welsh also accepted Æthelstan's overlordship. The Welsh kingdoms of Gwent, Deheubarth, and Gwynedd had proclaimed their allegiance to the Mercian and West Saxon kings at the beginning of the tenth century and extended it to Æthelstan, as well. All these rulers appeared as witnesses in Æthelstan's royal charters for the next several years and regularly attended the West Saxon court, residing there as the most respected figures. This confirms the extent of the overlordship and influence Æthelstan had achieved in the first three to four years of his reign.

Æthelstan's control of Northumbria was by no means firm, however. The Northumbrians had always considered themselves separate from other Anglo-Saxon kingdoms and had a special identity. This had been the first time a ruler from south of the Humber had successfully imposed his rule on Northumbria, and Æthelstan was rightfully faced with dissent.

To improve his standing in Northumbria, Æthelstan made generous land grants to different nobles and members of the clergy.

But the question of the territories at the border between Northumbria and the Scottish domains in the north complicated the matters. These lands, formerly part of the old Kingdom of Bernicia, had been under the control of Ealdred of Bamburgh until his death in 934. That year, Æthelstan launched a northern invasion, going farther than any other Anglo-Saxon king had previously campaigned. The reason for the invasion is unclear, but a conflict between King Constantine of Alba and Æthelstan after the death of Ealdred is a possibility. Together with Æthelstan were the Welsh rulers who had pledged their allegiance to Æthelstan, suggesting that his influence was tangible at this time.

According to the *Chronicle,* Scotland was attacked both on land and by sea, though the exact details of the campaign—and, more importantly, its outcome—are also shrouded in mystery. We know that Æthelstan was back in Buckingham in central England later that year, issuing a charter in which Constantine was referred to as a sub-king. In later charters, however, beginning from 935, Constantine no longer appears as a witness, while all the other kings who had pledged loyalty to Æthelstan were still mentioned.

The strained relationship between Æthelstan and Constantine escalated into a full-scale conflict a few years later. The *Chronicle* records that a decisive battle took place in 937 at Brunanburh (whose exact location has not been determined) between West Saxons under King Æthelstan and a combined force of Scots under King Constantine, Britons of Strathclyde under King Owain, and Vikings from Dublin under King Olaf Guthfrithson.

Olaf had succeeded his father three years earlier as King of Dublin and had allied with the Scots after marrying Constantine's daughter. Possibly, his campaign from Ireland into northern England was his bid for the throne of York, which he believed had been unjustly lost to Æthelstan.

The allied forces launched an invasion in late 937 but were eventually defeated at Brunanburh by Æthelstan in a bloody battle. There were many casualties on both sides, including important family members of the kings involved in the battle. Æthelstan's victory was seen as decisive, and a poem was dedicated to him in the *Chronicle* to celebrate his achievement. As we will see, however, the question of the dominance of English kings in Northumbria would remain largely unresolved until years after the death of Æthelstan.

Æthelstan was thus the first King of the English, ruling over the lands that had been taken over by the Anglo-Saxon migrants after the end of Roman rule in Britain. But he was also more than that. He was the strongest political leader in the British Isles. He exacted tribute from the Welsh and received their military assistance; he had successfully subdued the Brittonic kingdoms of the north and the Vikings from Dublin. In some of his charters, Æthelstan is referred to as "emperor," and this notion is not far from reality. The House of Wessex was the most powerful royal house in Britain at the time.

Æthelstan's reign was the period in the Anglo-Saxon history of England when the royal court was most involved with European affairs. Through royal marriages and frequent involvement with European leaders, Æthelstan provided a great example for other tenth-century Anglo-Saxon rulers. For example, to bolster his international reputation and legitimacy, Æthelstan pursued a friendly foreign policy with the Franks. After the dissolution of the Carolingian Empire, the rival royal families descended from Charlemagne also sought legitimacy and influence. It is in this light that the marriage between Eadgyth, the half-sister of Æthelstan, and the soon-to-be Emperor Otto of the Holy Roman Empire should be viewed.

Æthelstan is not just remembered for his conquest of Northumbria and his privileged position as the most powerful ruler in Britain. He was also a great reformer and strengthened the domestic legal and administrative framework of his kingdom. Æthelstan was faced with new challenges as the first Anglo-Saxon king to rule such a vast piece of territory, close to the modern borders of England. He decided to centralize his rule to govern more effectively. He produced the most legal texts and royal charters of any ruler to make the practice an inherent part of kingship and thus legitimize his rule in all Anglo-Saxon lands. He also held frequent councils and moved from one city to another. These councils, known as witans, were a crucial part of Æthelstan's administration. Officials of different ranks, members of the clergy, nobles, ealdormen, and many other figures usually attended and discussed relevant affairs. It can be argued that this practice played a big role in the parliamentarian tradition modern England is known for today.

Æthelstan also understood that he was a Christian king. He knew that he had to carefully choose his actions and cultivate good relations with the Church. During his reign, the clergy played an important role in creating and spreading new laws, most of which were based on other great Anglo-Saxon codes, such as Alfred's. Æthelstan consulted regularly with Archbishop Wulfhelm of Canterbury, who drew up many of the laws concerning royal relations with the Church.

Overall, Christianity became more prominent in the English laws during Æthelstan's reign, and the fusion of the two aspects of life became a staple of Medieval European kingdoms. His four codes issued at Grately, Exeter, Faversham, and Thunderfield address a wide range of social and economic hardships that might have been prominent at the time. They are concerned with matters such as the failure to pay tithes to the Church, thievery, the possession and exchange of property, and the procession of justice affairs. Æthelstan's laws were extensive and ambitious, demonstrating his commitment to impose and maintain order in challenging circumstances.

Æthelstan was also one of the most pious and educated Anglo-Saxon kings. Again, in this respect, he built on the foundations laid by his grandfather, Alfred the Great. For example, the fact that Æthelstan continued to issue laws in the vernacular Old English shows Alfred's influence, and so does his patronage of culture.

Importantly, the archbishopric of Canterbury had come under direct West Saxon control by the time Æthelstan became king, and he used this position to increase his leverage over the Church. Throughout West Saxon lands, for example, the king exerted the most influence in religious matters, even promoting and appointing loyal bishops to different dioceses.

Æthelstan also did a great deal to better integrate the Church of Northumbria into his realm, as it had developed separately since the invasion of the Vikings. Many monasteries and churches were founded in the lands formerly controlled by the Danes to combat the possible backsliding of Christian values in these areas. He was especially involved with the cult of Saint Cuthbert, the patron saint of Northumbria, located in Durham, to which he graciously donated many times during his reign, including during his northern campaign. Among his donations was a copy of Bede's *Life of Saint Cuthbert*, written entirely in Old English and featuring an illustration of Æthelstan presenting the book to the saint.

In general, Æthelstan donated extensively to different religious institutions all around his kingdom and beyond it, forging relations with foreign bishops throughout Europe. He also avidly collected ancient relics and old manuscripts, many of which he gifted to various monastic establishments. His commitment to these matters was mimicked by his successors, and ecclesiastic revival can be considered a characteristic of tenth-century England. No doubt, political motivations lay behind Æthelstan's actions, but they nevertheless resulted in a rich and rare cultural legacy in a time of great turmoil.

The House of Wessex

Æthelstan, the first King of the English, united all the lands of the Anglo-Saxons, ending years of Viking dominance in Northumbria and making all the rival kings of Britain submit to him. However, though his reign was overwhelmingly positive for the kingdom, problems started to appear after Æthelstan's death at the young age of about 45 in 939. The most obvious problem Æthelstan's successors faced was keeping the north in check. The Northumbrians' historical reluctance to accept southerners as kings, paired with a renewed Viking interest in controlling York and its surrounding territories, complicated matters for kings Edmund and Eadred.

Edmund, brother of Æthelstan, ascended the throne with no difficulties in 939, but his authority in Northumbria was very quickly challenged by a familiar figure—Olaf Guthfrithson, who returned with a small force from Dublin in 940. The people of York proclaimed Olaf as king, and he proceeded to turn his attention to the English heartlands. He directed his efforts to taking the "Five Boroughs"—the important centers of Nottingham, Lincoln, Derby, Leicester, and Stamford—all located in eastern Mercia. He was endorsed in this endeavor by Archbishop Wulfstan of York, whose motivations for supporting Olaf remain unclear.

King Edmund finally confronted the Danish leader at Leicester, but he was unsuccessful in his siege and was forced to recognize Olaf as the ruler of the area. Only after the death of Olaf two years later did Edmund successfully reconquer the "Five Boroughs" and drive out the Norsemen who had returned to eastern Mercia with Olaf's offensive. In 944, the reconquest of Northumbria was completed when Edmund took back York from Olaf's brother Ragnald and another Viking leader, Olaf Sihtricson. After Edmund's death in May 946 and the succession of his brother Eadred as the new king, Northumbria was again lost, this time to the legendary Viking Eric Bloodaxe, who would not be driven out until 954.

Despite these hardships throughout the 940s and the 950s, with Northumbria and eastern Mercia repeatedly targeted by the Vikings, the development of social, economic, administrative, and cultural processes in England never ceased. The progress in these fields showed during the reign of King Edgar, nicknamed "the Peaceful" because of the relative lack of military activities during his almost sixteen-year tenure as king, starting in 959. Edgar had ruled Mercia since the death of his father in 955 and inherited the southern part of the kingdom from his brother, Eadwig, after his death.

King Edgar largely followed policies like those of his predecessors, continuing to assert firm rule over Northumbria and expanding on the legal framework. By the time he became king, the West Saxon model of governance had already become very mature, with a clearly defined administrative body that delegated the legal authority of some of the most powerful noble families and ealdormen.

The laws issued during the era of the House of Wessex had already introduced changes to taxation based on the "system of hundreds"—a new unit of land division. By the end of his reign, Edgar had also transformed the monetary system of his kingdom, centralizing the production and distribution of coins and introducing a new dimension of unity that is a testament to his rule in all the Anglo-Saxon realms.

More importantly, however, the ecclesiastical society of England underwent a profound transformation during the tenth century, with the leading figures of the Church making important changes that were endorsed by the king. Three religious figures were at the head of these changes—Archbishop Dunstan of Canterbury, Bishop Æthelwold of Winchester, and Archbishop Oswald of York. Our knowledge of these reforms comes almost entirely from biased sources, mostly biographies produced after Edgar's reign. Nevertheless, texts from the latter half of the tenth century are dominated by religious accounts, where the main motivations for the reforms are spelled out. It appears that the reformers sought to reverse the alleged decline of monastic life in England that had taken place after the Viking invasions.

The reformers were also heavily influenced by Bede's *Ecclesiastical History*, which criticized the Anglo-Saxon religious practices, and the ongoing continental monastic reform movement. They argued, much like their European contemporaries during the tenth century, that the English Church had fallen into disarray, with monasteries populated by clergy who had families and owned extensive property. Instead, the reformers believed that the clergy should live their lives according to the Rule of St. Benedict—in celibacy and with full focus on religious activities.

The contacts the English kings had forged with Christian kingdoms (and, therefore, with Christian clergy in Europe) certainly amplified these sentiments. The reforms were mostly pushed in the monasteries of Wessex and Mercia, where, by the year 975, many Benedictine-style monasteries and nunneries had been established. The religious officials, with support from the Crown, often confiscated the possessions of clergy who lived in the old monasteries, driving them out and installing monks and nuns in their place to keep the institutions running. Edgar expressed his support by granting numerous donations to new monasteries, further boosting interest and activity.

In 970, the reformers introduced laws that imposed uniform rules on all Benedictine monasteries in the kingdom to avoid diverging from the original rule book, which was translated into Old English and widely distributed to boost its appeal and reach. The enforcement of uniformity can be seen as a major political move to assert the unity of a kingdom ruled by one king. Still, the reformers encountered many difficulties in enforcing the reforms, especially in Northumbria, where monastic life did not change as significantly.

The leaders of the reforms had also been Edgar's close political allies since the king's youth, supporting his claim to the throne after the death of his brother, Eadwig. If looked at in this sense, the Benedictine reforms in England in the tenth century were also directed toward increasing the influence of these religious officials in the royal court. By the late tenth century, the Benedictine reform movement in England had not only greatly affected the ecclesiastical affairs in religious institutions throughout the kingdom but also strengthened the position of the Crown. As we will come to see, despite these changes, the authority of later West Saxon kings would be put to the test in the final decades of the millennium.

Chapter 7: From Æthelred the Unready to William the Conqueror

In the final chapter of the book, we will look at the later history of the Anglo-Saxons, starting with the reign of Æthelred, who has been given the title "the Unready" because of the troubled nature of his rule. As we will come to see, Æthelred would be unable to maintain stability in the kingdom because of many different domestic and external factors that plagued his reign. The late tenth century would also bring a renewed wave of large-scale Viking invasions, which eventually crippled the power of the West Saxon kings and forced them to adapt to changing political circumstances. New Viking activity would even result in the expulsion of the House of Wessex and the emergence of Scandinavian rulers on the English throne for several decades. This chaotic part of Anglo-Saxon history ended with a succession struggle in the mid-eleventh century, when a seemingly unlikely bid succeeded the throne of England, marking a new era in the history of the Anglo-Saxons. We will dive deep and analyze the complex procession of events from Æthelred's accession to William of Normandy's conquest of England in 1066. Finally, we will assess the era of Anglo-Saxon dominance in Britain and the material and cultural legacy with which the Anglo-Saxons are remembered in history.

Æthelred the Unready

The reign of King Æthelred the Unready, from 978 until 1016, including a brief interregnum caused by his overthrow and return in 1013-1014. It is generally considered one of the low points of Anglo-Saxon kingship, and not just because it led to the collapse of the House of Wessex's power. Contemporary and later chroniclers note a complete degradation of England's socio-political and economic spheres at the time, no doubt accelerated by a renewed wave of Viking invasions from Scandinavia. These invasions, which increased in severity throughout the 990s and reached their peak in the first decade of the eleventh century, took a great toll on the English king, who failed to maintain the unity of his kingdom and was forced to abandon his subjects.

In short, King Æthelred was given the nickname "the Unready" for many reasons. Certainly, his inability and weakness of character contributed to the decline of his kingdom's power. Upon closer observation, however, Æthelred's reign appears to have been troubled with problems from the outset—problems rooted deep in the nature of the Anglo-Saxon society of the late tenth century.

To understand the troubles that plagued Æthelred's reign, it is important to look at the events of the second half of the 970s that led to him becoming king. Æthelred's father, King Edgar the Peaceful, died in July 975, and the *Chronicle* describes his death as a great tragedy —a sentiment that undoubtedly stems from the king's religious inclinations and his patronage of the monastic reforms during his reign. The people mourned the death of a beloved leader who had guaranteed them peace and security for the fifteen years he had been king.

However, powerful individuals, such as Ealdorman Ælfhere of Mercia, used the chaos provided by Edgar's death to reclaim lands the Church had gained during his reign by forcefully expelling monks and nuns from religious institutions. In the *Life of St. Oswald*, the biographer notes a widespread crackdown on monks and monasteries previously under Edgar's patronage in an event that historians have deemed the "anti-monastic reaction."

This reaction was not necessarily against the new form of monasticism and Christian practice since those who seized the moment were benefactors of the Church. Instead, it appears to have been a move to reclaim some of the political power that had been undermined by the prominent leaders of the Church during Edgar's reign. Some nobles, for instance, justified their actions by claiming that they had been coerced into giving up their lands to the Church to comply with the king's new regulations.

It was in this chaos that Edward, son of Edgar and his first wife, Æthelflæd (who was thirteen years old at the time), ascended the throne. This was largely made possible thanks to the influence of friends in his father's court, such as Archbishop Dunstan of Canterbury. Unexpectedly, however, the young king was mysteriously murdered in March 978—less than three years after he ascended to the throne—during a visit to his half-brother, Æthelred, the son of King Edgar from his second wife, Ælfthryth. Edward, tragically murdered in unclear circumstances, was venerated as a martyr. It was another tragedy, one that called into question the integrity of the reign of Æthelred, crowned king less than two weeks later. Æthelred, himself four years younger than Edward, may have been an ignorant victim of the intrigues of the royal court.

Æthelred's rule was unique. As king, he was characterized by his contemporaries and later writers as weak, passive, and largely unsuccessful, influenced by various interest groups and never quite able to assert authority over his most powerful subjects. The *Chronicle* tells of his inability to control the Anglo-Saxon nobility, his tendency to make impulsive and violent decisions, and his naivety when dealing with the Vikings.

As we mentioned, it was the combination of all these factors that gave him the title "the Unready." However, the sources that provide the most detailed accounts of Æthelred's reign, like the C, D, and E versions of the *Anglo-Saxon Chronicle*, were compiled after it had ended, in the court of a rival king—Cnut the Great. Because these accounts are not contemporary, they are inherently biased due to their knowledge of the disastrous nature of Æthelred's tenure as king. Thus, when speaking of Æthelred, it is important to counterbalance these sources with primary accounts produced by the king's contemporaries, such as the A version of the *Chronicle,* though such sources contain much fewer details.

A depiction of Æthelred the Unready.

In the second half of the 980s Æthelred appears to have gained more influence in the kingdom's political affairs. Early in his reign, he was the victim of court rivalries between different interest groups, including ones stemming from the monastic reform and its reaction after Edgar's death. The names of some of the most powerful figures that had dominated the witness lists of the royal charters for the first few years of Æthelred's disappeared in the 980s. Some, like Bishop Æthelwold of Winchester, died (in his case, 984). The disappearance of other names from the royal charters, like Queen Mother Ælfthryth, suggests their influence or power had declined.

By 985, King Æthelred appears to have also issued his first law code and regained control of centralized coin minting. Charters from this time show a shift in policy and preferences for choosing allies. Æthelred granted a lot of land back to the Church as a conscious effort to recoup its losses during the anti-monastic reaction. Thus, in about ten years, Æthelred partially overcame the influential figures of the old system and undermined their interests in favor of new groups with whom he began to build personal relationships. However, by this time, King Æthelred was faced with a threat that significantly affected his decisions and forced him to appropriate many resources to keeping his kingdom secure.

Though the Danish influence had been significantly reduced in England since the reign of Æthelstan, not all the Danes had been forced to leave England with the conquest of Northumbria. As we remarked earlier, most Danes, now Christians, were well-integrated into the kingdom. It certainly seemed that the Vikings had been largely dealt with. The raids that took place in the early 980s were very localized and small in scale. In fact, there is no reason to suspect that Viking activity of this scale had completely ceased during the tenth century, as Viking realms had persevered in parts of Britain and Ireland. Despite catching the English by surprise at places like Southampton, Devon, Portland, or Cornwall during this period, the Vikings were quickly driven back.

This pattern of small-scale Viking raids on the English coastal areas changed in 991 when a large raiding party of ninety ships sailed to England from Norway, led by Olaf Tryggvason—the future Norwegian king. This force targeted important areas in Essex, pillaging towns such as Ipswich before confronting an English army at the Battle of Maldon in August. We don't have many details about how the battle played out, but we know that it ended in a Viking victory, with the English ealdorman and leader of the army—Byrhtnoth—slain in the field. King Æthelred was forced to negotiate and supposedly paid off the Vikings with a huge sum of 10,000 pounds to stop their attacks before proceeding to build up his fleet to catch the treacherous Vikings. However, he was betrayed by one of his ealdormen, who let the invaders escape.

The raid of 991 was the first of many destructive large-scale Viking attacks that were to come for the next two decades. Olaf Tryggvason returned in 994 with a similar-sized force, accompanied by Sweyn "Forkbeard" of Denmark, first attacking London and then targeting the coasts of Essex and Sussex. The Vikings were paid off once again, this time with gold and silver worth 16,000 pounds. As a guarantee that they would stop the attack, Olaf Tryggvason converted to Christianity and sailed back to Scandinavia. The amounts paid to the Vikings in exchange for peace were huge sums, and the *Chronicle* mentions that these kinds of payments continued well into the first decade of the eleventh century. The accounts are likely exaggerated, especially as it would have been virtually impossible to collect coins worth this much. The amount paid to the Viking armies probably included a large portion of valuables, such as relics from churches or other forms of booty.

Tribute was not just paid to the Vikings in exchange for peace. Sometimes, the English hired soldiers from the Viking army as mercenaries, with the agreement that they would defend the English shores from other Viking attacks. All in all, it was a widespread solution, practiced well before Æthelred became king. It was often pursued separately by local officials to keep their lands safe. Still, despite the best efforts of the English, these measures would not be enough to dissuade further Viking raids, which intensified in the late 990s and caused great destruction and turmoil.

The House of Denmark

Viking attacks continued with more ferocity in 997, three years after Æthelred had struck a peace deal with the previous army. The invaders first pillaged the shores of southwestern England, moving around for the following two years before raiding Normandy in the year 1000. Another force also attacked Sussex and later Devon the following year.

All these attacks had forced King Æthelred to adapt his policies, but it was becoming clear that resisting such fast-paced invasions would be a challenging task—one that required cooperation from local leaders. The *Chronicle* mentions that some ealdormen, such as Ulfcetel of East Anglia, were defeated in 1004 when they tried to confront the raiding Vikings. Others were reluctant to commit their forces to the costly struggle against the Scandinavians. Duke Richard of Normandy was ready to cooperate with the English, having agreed to mutual peace and a defensive alliance against the Vikings in 991. This alliance was reconfirmed when Æthelred married Richard's daughter, Emma, in 1002. The need to search for new allies confirms that the Viking raids were a significant threat at this time.

While Æthelred's decision to ally with the Normans can be justified, the same cannot be said of his policies for dealing with the Vikings in his realm. The "Saint Brice's Day Massacre"—arguably the most infamous event of Æthelred's reign—took place in November 1002. The king, in a decision that appears to be that of a paranoid ruler, ordered all Danish men in England to be killed, believing they had been conspiring with the invading Vikings to overthrow him. This decree was likely directed toward Danes who had recently settled in England as opposed to those who had lived in the kingdom for generations, by now well assimilated with the Anglo-Saxons. Perhaps, Æthelred wanted to eliminate the Scandinavian mercenaries who had agreed to fight with the English, as there were instances when they had been disloyal. Archeological evidence of mass graves containing the skulls of tens of males with Scandinavian genes, unearthed at Dorset and Oxford in the 2000s, has been identified as proof that the massacre did indeed take place.

A large army returned from Scandinavia in the year 1009, led by a Danish commander named Thorkell, who had accompanied Sweyn Forkbeard in his previous raids. This invasion proved to be too much for Æthelred, who had been struggling with endless court intrigue. We know that the king had lost the support of some of his most powerful allies, including the nobility and ealdormen of various provinces, because they no longer appeared in his charters as witnesses at the beginning of the eleventh century. Æthelred had tried to prepare for an impending Viking attack by commissioning the construction of a large English naval force, but this project had faced many setbacks, prone to corruption and betrayal.

Thorkell's army, when it landed in Kent in 1009, was paid off by the local ruler and made its way into Sussex, where it mercilessly ravaged the English countryside for the next few months. The English were unable to strike back, leading the Vikings to sack Canterbury in 1011 and take Archbishop Ælfheah (who was later murdered) prisoner. Æthelred was then forced to pay a ridiculous sum of money as a tribute—the *Chronicle* says 48,000 pounds of gold and silver—as part of the peace agreement with Thorkell. The Viking leader not only agreed to send his soldiers home and cease attacks on England but also joined Æthelred with a force of forty-five ships.

A year later, Sweyn Forkbeard, now king of both Denmark and Norway, returned with a large force and launched a full-scale invasion of England, making his way from Kent to the East Midlands. What happened next was an almost instant collapse of whatever power Æthelred had maintained. English ealdormen refused to fight the Vikings under Thorkell. One by one, the lands of England fell to the invaders, like dominoes. The "Five Boroughs" submitted to Sweyn with little resistance—a thorn in the side of Æthelred, who tried to resist the invaders. With the help of Thorkell, Æthelred put up a fight at London but could not chase the Vikings to inflict decisive casualties. Sweyn moved west, pillaging the countryside until Æthelmær's surrender, which eventually forced the king to surrender London as well. In late 1013, Æthelred was forced into exile in Normandy.

The Scandinavian king only lasted as the king of England for a few months before suffering an unexpected death in February 1014. Naturally, his army declared his son, Cnut, as the new king. The Anglo-Saxon nobility, however, who had submitted to Sweyn during his conquests, were reluctant to accept his son as their new overlord. Instead, they "invited" Æthelred back to be king again. This invitation was likely based on certain demands from the nobles, who had reasons to feel mistreated or undermined. The *Chronicle* mentions that they made Æthelred promise to solve his previous mistakes and grant amnesty to those who had betrayed him the previous year. Thus, in hindsight, Æthelred's return to the throne was doomed from the beginning. Nevertheless, he accepted.

Hearing this, Cnut was forced to flee back to Scandinavia. Æthelred, however, could not hold on to the power or authority that would guarantee the loyalty of his subjects. He proceeded to campaign in Lincolnshire, punishing the nobles who had supported Sweyn. This resulted in yet another rebellion, this time led by his own son, Edmund "Ironside."

Edmund established himself in the north, where anti-Æthelred sentiments had been the strongest, and quickly gained local support. Edmund was likely motivated by his desire to gain the throne for himself because he had been disregarded as a potential successor by Æthelred in favor of Edmund's half-brother, Edward. Edward, the son of Æthelred by his second wife Emma of Normandy and a teenager at this time, was already starting to be involved in political affairs beside his father.

Edmund's bid for power, however, was also short-lived. Cnut returned to England after having replenished his forces in Denmark and took the fight directly to the territories of Wessex. Æthelred was not ready to confront the returning Vikings as he had fallen ill, and Edmund led the resistance this time. Just like his father, however, his allies, including Thorkell, defected to the enemy.

Æthelred died in April 1016 as Cnut was pillaging the lands of England and negotiating terms of peace with local nobles. At the Battle of

Assandun, fought in October 1016 (the exact location of which has not been determined), Cnut decisively defeated Edmund's forces and forced him to surrender. The two leaders agreed to divide the Kingdom of England, with Edmund only retaining control of the lands of Wessex. This division did not last long, however. Edmund died a month later, and Cnut assumed control of England. He was now the king of Denmark, Norway, and England, a political entity referred to as the North Sea Empire. The House of Wessex, which had united and ruled England for over a century, had fallen.

Perhaps because he was a foreign king or the lack of royal charters produced during his nineteen years as king of England, we are left with the sense that the reigns of Cnut and his two successors from the House of Denmark were a transitory period. This is partially due to the events of 1066, which ended the dominance of this dynasty that ruled the North Sea Empire.

By all means, Cnut was one of the most powerful rulers England had ever seen—and certainly the most competent and experienced since at least Edgar the Peaceful. England had been at its lowest as he ascended the throne of England in 1016 and, as a foreigner with a history of hostility with the English, he had to do a lot of work to reverse the decline of English power. The policies adopted during his reign, as well as the fact that it marked a brief period of relative peace in England, testify that he achieved stability in a complex environment. The fact that he is one of those rulers with the title "the Great" also supports this.

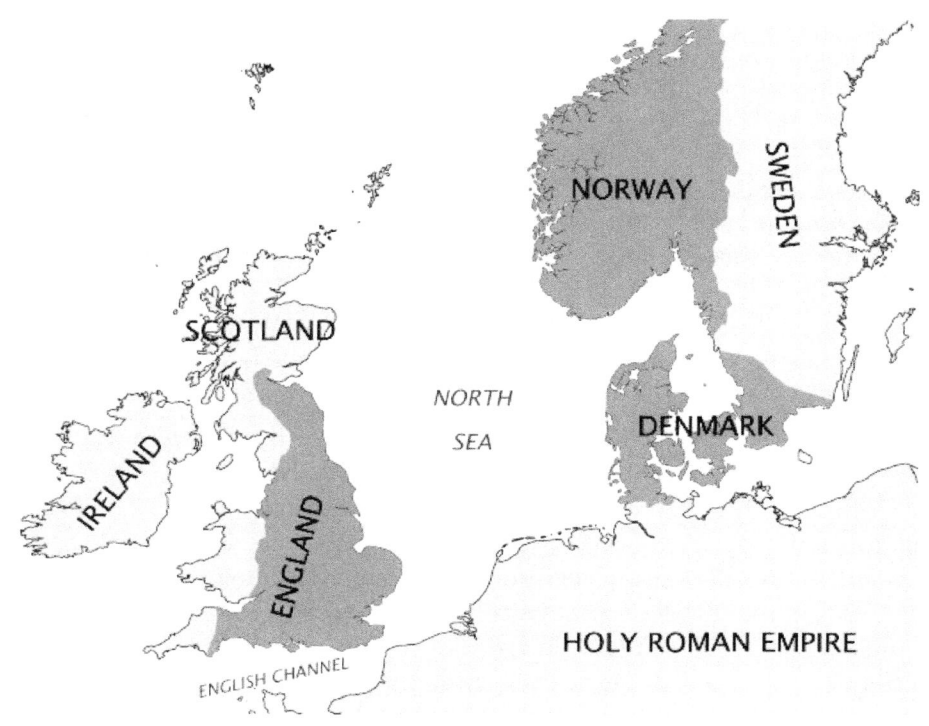

A map of Cnut's North Seas empire.

As King of England, Denmark, and Norway during an age when it took information weeks to be delivered from one place to another, Cnut found himself in a rather unique position in 1016. He realized the need to adopt several measures that would ensure the safety of his position in England, especially as he was often absent, busy attending to matters in Scandinavia, such as domestic rebellions. To strengthen his control over England, Cnut divided the lands he had conquered into four parts, assigning each to one of his supporters in 1017. He kept control of Wessex, delegating East Anglia to Thorkell, Northumbria to Erik of Hlathir, and Mercia to Eadric Streona.

In addition, Cnut eliminated resistance from the House of Wessex, forcing Æthelred's sons, who might have had claims to the throne, into exile to the court of their mother's family in Normandy. The same year, Cnut married Æthelred's widow, Emma, in a bid to further strengthen his image as a legitimate king. The marriage was likely negotiated by Emma in exchange for her sons' safety and an important position for her in Cnut's court, something to which the king appears to have agreed.

A year later, in 1018, Cnut passed his own law code, endorsed by Archbishop Wulfstan of York and drawing heavily from Anglo-Saxon legal tradition. Overall, it appears that it was Cnut's intention to be seen as the continuation of Anglo-Saxon kingship—as another in the line of succession and not a usurper of the throne. Cultivating a good relationship with the archbishop affirms this, as does Cnut's conscious attempt to reconnect with the peaceful and stable times of the past—especially those under King Edgar. For a foreign ruler who had conquered the English throne and forced members of the royal family into exile, Cnut was nevertheless quite tolerant of local customs, traditions, and religious practices. He was an active benefactor of the Church, especially in the south, donating lavish gifts to Canterbury and Winchester.

Although he put many Scandinavians into positions of power as ealdormen and in lower administrative roles, the makeup of English administration had again become Anglo-Saxon-dominated by the end of his reign in the 1030s. The relatively short-lived Viking nobles installed by Cnut were initially granted many lands throughout England, but their influence was kept in check by a similarly powerful Anglo-Saxon class of elites, led by Earl (a title increasingly used at this time) Godwin of Wessex. Earl Godwin and other influential nobles, though a new class compared to the old aristocracy, gradually accrued more power in England. This was made possible by Cnut's frequent absences, which created a small power vacuum in the kingdom, even though he would often delegate regents to rule in his name. Throughout the 1020s, Cnut campaigned extensively in Norway and defeated rebellions that challenged his rule in Denmark, for example.

All in all, Cnut the Great was a compelling ruler of the North Sea Empire and one of the most successful kings of England from the House of Denmark. The kingdom would be plunged once again into a succession struggle upon his death in 1035. His son, Harold Harefoot, acted as king for the following five years, although he was not crowned until 1037 due to the nobility's hesitation to declare their support for him. His half-brother, Harthacnut, was supposed to inherit the throne but was absent, trying to consolidate his position in Denmark, much like his father. Only after the death of Harold Harefoot in 1040 did Harthacnut return to England to claim the throne peacefully.

Restoration of the House of Wessex

Harthacnut was the last member of the House of Denmark to rule England in the eleventh century, and his reign was very short-lived—the king suffered a stroke in early 1042 and died in June of that year. The question of succession was again up in the air, but the transition of power was smooth and unchallenged this time. Sometime before his death, Harthacnut, perhaps realizing his ailing age, had invited Edward, son of Æthelred the Unready and Emma of Normandy, back to England. It is likely that since Harthacnut was unmarried with no children, he saw Edward as a natural successor—a sentiment that was shared among the English public, including the elites. This is alluded to in the *Chronicle*, which mentions that the people of England had chosen Edward as the next king. However, he was also the only logical candidate to take over the throne after Harthacnut. So, the elites' support for him does not necessarily mean Edward was their preferred choice as king.

Edward's reign as King of England would last for about twenty-three years until January 1066, making him the longest-reigning monarch in England since his father, Æthelred. The early years of Edward as king were naturally marked by political intrigue. Despite his royal lineage, he was virtually unknown since he had spent most of his early years in exile in Normandy with his mother's family. In fact, Edward, already about forty years old when he ascended the throne, was a much more foreign ruler than Cnut, Harold Harefoot, or Harthacnut had been. Life in exile had made him a Norman French who spoke French in private. His royal court was also comprised of figures who had been close allies of Cnut, such as Earl Godwin of Wessex and Siward of Northumbria. Naturally, these actors had accrued much more influence in England than the new king, so the first few years of Edward's reign were spent in endless political maneuvering.

Edward was forced to accept the fact that he did not have the leverage to exercise authority over his more powerful subjects. He must cater to their needs and demands to gain favor among the English and Danish aristocracy of his kingdom. It was only after making concessions to these interest groups that Edward was finally crowned as king on Easter Day in 1043, about two years since his arrival in England when Harthacnut had still been alive.

Godwin of Wessex was the earl whose support Edward most desperately needed. An experienced earl of English origins, Godwin had been part of the royal court for many years and held considerable sway in the kingdom. To expand his power, Edward realized he had to give something to the earl of Wessex in return—and he did.

At first, he granted Godwin's sons, Sweyn and Harold, earldoms in the West Midlands and East Anglia, and then married Godwin's daughter Edith in January of 1045. This significantly increased the influence of Godwin and his family, but it was not long before the earl and King Edward became rivals, especially over foreign policy matters. Most importantly, Edward decided not to campaign in Denmark to help Danish King Sweyn Estridsson against the Norwegian King Magnus' invasion even though King Sweyn, supported by Godwin, had personally asked for Edward's help. Godwin wanted to help King Sweyn because King Magnus aspired to invade England and claim the throne for himself, something that never transpired because of Magnus' death in 1047.

Tensions between King Edward and Earl Godwin further escalated in 1051-1052 when Edward appointed his Norman friend Robert of Jumièges as the new Archbishop of Canterbury despite the English clergy and Godwin favoring another candidate. Robert had come to England with Edward in 1041 and had been the bishop of London since 1043. He was one of Edward's closest allies since the beginning, and his appointment as the new archbishop further reduced Godwin's influence in the kingdom. Edward also appointed Norman clergy and nobles to positions of power within his kingdom, a naturally unpopular move for the English aristocracy. To gain some favor with the public, Edward then proceeded to disband the royal fleet, viewing it as an unnecessary tax burden.

By then, however, the relationship between Edward and Godwin had been strained, and an incident involving Edward's brother-in-law Count Eustace of Boulogne put the kingdom on the brink of civil war. Eustace and his Norman men got into a fight with locals in Dover, and Edward demanded that Godwin, as the earl who presided over Kent, punish the townspeople. Godwin refused. Archbishop Robert, a close friend and ally of Edward, then accused Godwin of plotting a conspiracy against the king, prompting earls loyal to Edward—Siward and Leofric—to muster their men and prepare for a fight with Godwin. Godwin, on the other hand, was supported by his sons Harold and Sweyn, who also prepared to go to battle. Tensions were as high as ever, but in the end, neither side was ready to fight. As a result, Godwin and his sons fled. Harold went to Ireland, while Godwin and Sweyn went to Flanders. Having successfully expelled his opponents, Edward, endorsed by Archbishop Robert, divorced his wife and sent her to a nunnery.

Sweyn Godwinson died in exile, but his father and brother recouped their losses and returned to England in 1052 with a large army to confront Edward. This time, support for the king was not as firm. Edward negotiated a settlement with Godwin and Harold, reinstating them to their old positions and agreeing to get rid of the Normans in his court. In fact, the domains of Godwin and Harold were expanded at the expense of those held by the king and his Norman allies, which was supported by earls Siward and Leofric, who kept their lands as part of the agreement. Edward also took Edith back as his wife. He had to accept that, after a crisis that spanned two years, the power of the Godwin family had only increased.

Throughout the 1050s, as all the old prominent members of the court, including Godwin, died, Edward decided to grant even more lands to members of his family. Harold Godwinson was appointed as the new Earl of Wessex, while his younger brothers Tostig, Gyrth, and Leofwine were promoted to dominant positions in Northumbria, East Anglia, and the southwestern Midlands. This placed considerable influence in the hands of the Godwinson family, who were now just as powerful as the king himself.

Though most of the Godwinsons' power was concentrated in southern England, control of these earldoms gave them the ability to collect taxes, raise armies, and preside over local political and judicial affairs. Contemporary sources give us limited insights into Edward's intentions. It is unknown whether he believed he had been forced to give up such control and influence. This is a logical explanation if we consider that Edward gradually withdrew from active political affairs in the second half of the 1050s, increasingly spending his time away hunting, for example. He devoted less attention to both domestic and foreign policy affairs. Harold and Tostig Godwinson campaigned against the Welsh and the Scots in this period, not the king. Thus, the House of Wessex under King Edward had once again declined about fifteen years after its restoration as the ruling family of England in 1042.

As Edward's power and influence gradually declined well into his reign, the obvious question of succession to the throne became more prominent. Edward had no children, and it was not exactly clear who he favored as the next king. The fact that Edward never named a successor caused the whole crisis in 1066 after his death.

William of Normandy was perhaps the most unlikely claimant to the throne. An illegitimate son of Duke Robert I of Normandy, he would take quite a while to consolidate his power in the duchy before he was in a position to throw in his bid for the throne of England. William was related to Edward—he was the king's cousin once removed—but this relationship was by no means enough to make him a logical candidate in the eyes of his rivals, especially Harold Godwinson.

Importantly, William claimed Edward had promised him the throne of England in secret during the crisis of 1051-1052. Few contemporary sources mention that such a meeting took place between Edward and William. For example, only in the D version of the *Anglo-Saxon Chronicle* is the event even mentioned. It states that William visited Edward in 1051, perhaps to support the English king in a time of crisis against Godwin and his family. At the time, however, William was involved in a war in the County of Anjou, so his visit with Edward is unlikely.

Even if William did visit Edward, it is unclear whether the king entrusted him with succession. Norman sources mention another meeting taking place between William and Archbishop Robert, who had supposedly traveled as a dignitary on Edward's behalf to bring the Norman duke the news that he had been chosen as successor. However, the sources do not provide many details about the nature of this visit.

Alongside William of Normandy, whose potential candidacy as the next king remained relatively unknown to the English until 1006, there was also a bid for King Edward's exiled nephew—Edward the Exile. He was the son of Edmund Ironside, who had been forced to flee England in 1016 after the conquest of Cnut. Edmund had returned to England in 1057 with his family but died soon afterward and was buried in London. Instead, it was his five-year-old son Edward Ætheling who was next in line in the House of Wessex. All other male members of the House of Wessex had died by then. However, Edward was too young, and his mother held too little influence to properly press his claim during King Edward's lifetime, let alone after his death. By the time of Edward Ætheling's arrival in court, King Edward had already become passive at attending to state affairs, having delegated most of the work to the Godwinsons. Young Edward was thus never involved in royal matters, and the fact that he had no army, unlike William, made his candidacy as the next king even weaker.

The Norman Conquest

The events of 1066—one of the most important dates in English history—are very complicated because of the intricate relationships between the different actors during the crisis that followed Edward's death. Edward died in early January and probably entrusted the kingdom to Harold Godwinson, the most obvious candidate for becoming the next king.

Harold was Edward's brother-in-law, the most powerful earl in the kingdom with vast domains. He came from a respected and well-established family, had experience in governance and warfare, and was largely supported by other earls. Importantly, Harold was also of Anglo-Saxon origin from a local family, giving him an advantage over William. And while Edgar Ætheling was from the royal House of Wessex, the elites could not have pledged their support solely based on this factor. Finally, as if all these factors had not been enough, Harold claimed that King Edward had made him the successor on his deathbed.

Still, Harold's hasty coronation on the same day Edward was buried shows his adamance to become king and his potential awareness that others were just as capable of asserting their power in England.

One such contender was King Harald Hardrada of Norway. Hardrada's involvement in the power struggle had partially been a matter of chance. An experienced warrior who had spent his youth as a military commander in the Kievan Rus and the Byzantine Empire, Hardrada had become the king of Norway in 1046. An ambitious individual, he wished to also claim the throne of Denmark but failed to achieve this despite launching many raids into the Danish territories. Though the throne of England had never been among King Harald's objectives, he was invited as a claimant in late 1065 by Tostig Godwinson, who had by then strained his relationship with his brother Harold.

To better understand the struggles of 1066, it is thus important to examine the events of 1065 that turned Tostig against Harold—more specifically, the rebellion in Northumbria against Tostig.

Tostig had served as Northumbria's earl for about a decade, but the locals were unhappy with his rule. While Tostig was in the south visiting King Edward, the Northumbrians revolted, taking control of York and sacking Tostig's estate there. Their main demand was the expulsion of Earl Tostig and the installation of Morcar, the younger brother of Earl

Edwin of Mercia, as the new earl. The rebels pushed as far south as the East Midlands, pillaging Tostig's lands and pressing their demands before a peace was negotiated by Harold Godwinson. Tostig was stripped of his earldom and forced into exile. He was furious, believing that Harold had incited the rebellion and used it to expand his own influence in the north at the expense of his brother.

Around the same time, Harold had also married the sister of Earl Eadwig and the newly appointed Earl Morcar, securing an alliance with this powerful English family. Harold likely intended to build as many good relationships with the locals as possible so they would support his candidacy as king after Edward's death.

Tostig, feeling betrayed by his brother and the future king, fled to Flanders, where he assembled a small force and tried to return to England, possibly intending to become king. His attempt was unsuccessful, however, as Harold's forces easily repelled Tostig's fleet, forcing him to flee to the court of King Malcolm of Scotland.

In Scotland, Tostig Godwinson joined King Harald Hardrada of Norway, who had already launched his invasion to take the English throne. It is possible that Tostig invited Harald to throw in his bid for the throne, hoping to regain his earldom as a reward. For Hardrada, who envisioned himself as the next king of England and the reviver of Cnut the Great's North Sea Empire, Tostig could have proven a valuable ally in cementing his position as king.

Hardrada, who had assembled a sizeable army in the spring, landed in the Orkney Islands in early September, which were controlled by Norway. Then, he moved on to the town of Dunfermline on the southeastern coast of Scotland, where he met Tostig and King Malcolm of Scotland. Tostig, with his small force that paled in comparison to Hardrada's, joined the Norwegians and set sail for Northumbria.

While the Norwegians under Harald Hardrada were pillaging the Northumbrian countryside throughout September of 1066, the news of King Edward's death had already reached William of Normandy. The duke had already prepared a large fleet to cross the English Channel in late summer, but he was delayed by unfavorable weather. The exact size of William's army is unknown, and many sources greatly exaggerate the number of men at his disposal in 1066. It can be assumed that William had assembled a force of about 10,000 men, having mustered up his army from not only Normandy but also Brittany, where he had campaigned in previous years.

Luckily for William, King Harold Godwinson of England had already moved north to meet Harald Hardrada when he decided to cross the channel in late September. Throughout the summer, the English king had maintained a fleet that patrolled the southern shores of England, anticipating a potential invasion from William. Seeing that there was a more immediate threat in the northern part of his kingdom, Harold Godwinson marched to Northumbria to confront the Norwegians.

Covering a distance of about twenty-five miles per day, Harold and his army's march from London to York took only nine days—an exceptionally small amount of time. Still, when they arrived on September 25, they found the city decimated by Harald Hardrada. The Norwegian force had moved east and encamped at the village of Stamford Bridge. The English quickly proceeded to the village, trying to catch the Norwegians off-guard.

The ensuing battle resulted in heavy casualties on both sides. Chroniclers describe a vicious battle for the narrow crossing on the river, which was only defended by a single Norwegian. He stopped the initial English advance, killing tens of English soldiers before falling himself, having allowed the Norwegian forces to mobilize and form a defensive. Nevertheless, the English were victorious, and both Harald Hardrada and Tostig Godwinson were killed in battle. The survivors negotiated a truce with King Harold and agreed to sail back to Norway.

Stamford Bridge had been an amazing victory for the English. It was one of the most decisive victories over the Vikings in history, comparable to Æthelstan's triumph at Brunaburh more than a hundred years earlier. Certainly, it would have been instrumental in further legitimizing Harold's kingship, as he had successfully defended his kingdom from a large foreign invasion. Unfortunately for the English, however, William of Normandy's forces of landed at Pevensey just three days after the Battle of Stamford Bridge. The Normans proceeded to build a small fortification at Hastings, which they used as their headquarters while raiding the surrounding areas.

This called for a prompt response from Harold Godwinson, who was most likely already on his way back to London when he learned about William's invasion. He had left a part of his force in the north and decided to replenish his troops once he reached London, resting for a week. Then, he headed south to Hastings, where he met the Normans in battle. On October 14, at the Battle of Hastings, the English were defeated by the Normans. Harold Godwinson, the last crowned Anglo-Saxon king, was killed in battle, possibly after being struck by an arrow in his eye. His army was routed after the death of its leader.

The English fled to London, trying to organize further resistance and giving their support to Edgar Ætheling as the next king. Joined by earls Morcar and Edwin, they believed William would strike there next. However, William instead continued to ravage the southern countryside, moving east and eventually taking Canterbury. He successfully eluded the English forces that chased him down.

Eventually, the English leaders submitted to William one by one, and he was ultimately crowned King of England on Christmas Day, 1066, in the newly constructed Westminster Abbey. In exchange for submission, William spared the lives of the English nobles, including Edward. The era of Anglo-Saxon dominance in England was over.

Conclusion

It took William a lot of work to consolidate his power over England after the conquest of 1066. Many Anglo-Saxon nobles either tried to organize rebellions in the first few years of his reign or fled the kingdom. William, on the other hand, began replacing the English elite with Normans, though he kept the existing governmental and administrative systems in place. The Anglo-Saxon system was very sophisticated for its time, with England already divided into units that determined important matters, such as taxation. Instead of trying to shake up the system, William put some of the most prominent Normans in positions of power to better control the affairs of his kingdom.

He also promised amnesty to many of the old nobility, though he expected them to provide military support and raise armies from their domains in times of need. Many were stripped of their lands, which were redistributed to William's loyal followers, most of whom were either distinguished Norman commanders or noblemen themselves. Others chose to emigrate. The result of breaking up old estates and their redistribution is mentioned in the Domesday Book, a manuscript that recorded the results of the kingdom-wide survey of 1086.

In the Church, Anglo-Saxons were also increasingly replaced in favor of Norman clergymen. This ensured that the English Church would no longer persist as a potential rival of the Norman king.

In addition, William constructed several important fortifications throughout the kingdom, which he garrisoned with loyal troops to dissuade new rebellions from the English resistance. King William, nicknamed "the Conqueror," had to ensure that the situation in England was constantly under control as he was often absent, attending to matters in his home duchy on the other side of the channel.

All in all, after the initial changes implemented by William took root, a radically new England emerged. It had a new elite and was ruled by a new dynasty that had originated in northern France. The Norman Conquest also resulted in widespread social and cultural changes, such as the displacement of many Old English words and the increase of French influence. Latin was again used for official documents instead of Old English, a major change that affected the higher echelons of the new society.

It is estimated that fewer than 10,000 Normans settled in England during the post-conquest period by the beginning of the twelfth century, and they were well integrated into English society. In time, new distinctions emerged based on origins and dwelling place. Norman Englishmen, for example, were those born in England but of Norman origin. But these distinctions also faded with time.

In hindsight, William had achieved in England what no other conqueror could. He fundamentally transformed the nature of English society and never faced a real threat that could undo these changes. Similar processes had been attempted during the initial Viking conquest, but the scope of that invasion in the ninth century never reached as far as the Norman Conquest of the eleventh century. The Scandinavian invaders' motivations were very distinct from those of the Normans (who were themselves descendants of Vikings). William was accepted as the English king without much difficulty, and his descendants would continue to rule England.

Where does the Norman Conquest stand in the broader history of the Anglo-Saxons? It stands as the event that marked the end of Anglo-Saxon dominance in England, an era that had begun sometime during the fifth century. In fact, the consequences of William's conquest can arguably be best compared to the Anglo-Saxon settlement of Britain after the fall of Rome in the Early Middle Ages. The effects of both processes were widespread and long-lasting.

Still, the legacy of the Anglo-Saxons lived on in England to this day. The socio-cultural changes brought by the Normans eventually resulted in the development of Middle English by the fourteenth century as the mother tongue of most of England's population. It combined elements of

Old English with new words brought by the Normans. What also survived was the political order established during the Anglo-Saxons' dominance. The post-conquest borders of England, as well as the country's modern borders, were largely forged in the Middle Ages by the Anglo-Saxons, as were many of the most important cities. The history of the Anglo-Saxons is compelling to examine, full of fascinating stories and memories that are still deeply rooted in popular culture.

Part 2: Medieval England

An Enthralling Overview of the English Middle Ages

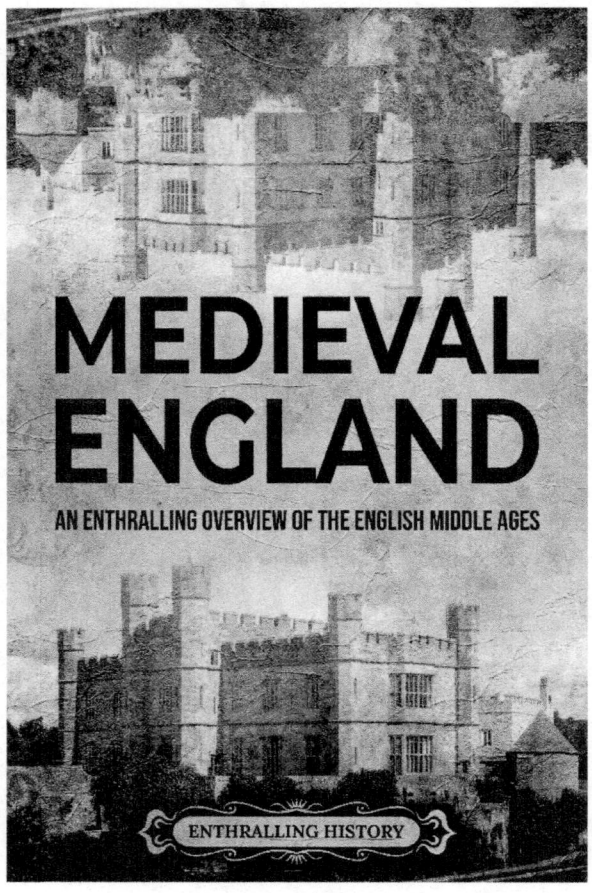

Introduction

When you hear the phrase medieval England, what do you think about? Knights in armor charging into battle on horseback? Kings with golden crowns sitting in castles? Maybe you even picture small towns with thatched roofs, a muddy road, and a pig ambling through the streets?

The time period known as the medieval period, also called the Middle Ages, has been incredibly romanticized in books, movies, and ultimately in our memories since it ended some six hundred years ago. Some people picture it as a grand time full of noble deeds, exciting battles, and simple living. Others refer to this period as the Dark Ages, indicating a time of filth, poverty, and general ignorance. The truth, as it often is, lies somewhere in the middle of these two extremes. Medieval England was neither as glamorous nor as horrendous as we often paint it; it was a lot more varied than those simple images we usually picture.

The medieval period in England covers roughly six hundred to eight hundred years. That's a whole lot of time for things to happen. To put it in perspective, six hundred years ago from today would be in the early 15th century. Shakespeare wasn't alive yet. Columbus hadn't yet sailed the ocean blue. The United States of America wouldn't become a country until over three hundred years later. In six hundred years, humans have gone from walking and riding as the main means of transportation to airplanes and cars. Six hundred years ago, most people still believed that the earth was at the center of the universe, and now, we have sent men to the moon.

The point is that a lot can happen in six hundred years. Medieval England in the year 600 looked quite different from medieval England in 1485. During this time, England saw the rise and fall of several royal dynasties. It saw barons repeatedly rebel against the king's authority and even England's first popular uprising. There were both foreign wars and civil wars. It was a period that saw the conversion to Christianity and the church becoming the most powerful institution in the Western world. The law system contained both the infamous and cruel trials by ordeal and the origins of the trial by jury. It was a time of knights and monks and peasants and lords. Over these six hundred years, England and its people went through a lot of changes, ordeals, and developments. There was a lot more to these six hundred years than castles and knights.

This book hopes to cut through those stereotypes to take a realistic look at the Middle Ages. We will talk about the armored knights charging into battle, but we look at why the use of armored knights in military strategy declined throughout the period. We will learn about some of the cruel and gruesome punishments used in the justice system, but we will also examine why the system was designed that way. We will talk about the corruption and immense power of the medieval church, but we will also see the role the church played in local life.

This book is about the real medieval England. Some of it may be similar to what you have always thought about the Middle Ages, but a lot of it may surprise you. For example, did you know that the famous Christian martyr Thomas Becket began as a politician, not a priest? Did you know that the infantry was strategically better than the cavalry? Did you know that women in the Middle Ages could work the same jobs as men? Did you know that King Arthur isn't English, that the Vikings are kind of responsible for the start of England, and that the Black Death might be the result of one of the first acts of biological warfare?

There are a lot of fascinating things to learn about the medieval era, and this book will walk you through them while also giving you a comprehensive understanding of the entire period. Whether you already know the basics or have no idea what years medieval England even covers, you'll be able to follow along and learn something new as this book takes you on a tour of one of the most interesting periods in English history.

Chapter 1: Early Middle Ages (600–1066)

In the year 600, England didn't exist, but by 1066, the English people had been united under a single king for close to a century.

The story of the Early Middle Ages in England is thus the story of how a nation came to be. Over these five hundred years, the disparate groups that inhabited the area joined into a nation with a single king and a distinct culture. There was a lot going on in England during this time. From the development of towns to Viking raids, this is how the nation we call England got its start.

Setting the Scene: England before 600

If we want to understand England in the medieval period, it helps to know a little bit about what was going on before that. The English were not actually the original inhabitants of Britain, so how did they get there, and who was living there first?

Prior to the Middle Ages, England, or rather Britain, was part of the Roman Empire as the province of Britannia. Emperor Claudius had his generals conquer the island in 43 CE, although it took much longer than this for the Romans to actually subdue all of the southern tribes living on the island at the time. These original tribes were the Celtic Britons (they weren't the native inhabitants of the island either; like the Romans and the Anglo-Saxons, they came over from the continent). Rome was never able to fully conquer and hold the northern part of the island (Scotland), but the south (England and Wales) was under firm Roman control, despite numerous rebellions, for around four hundred years.

During this time, the Celtic Britons inevitably became Romanized. They lived in Roman-style houses, wore Roman-style clothing, and even spoke a type of British Latin. Britain was covered in Roman roads and Roman settlements. By the 4th century, the people living there were fully Romano-Britons.

A map of the five provinces of Roman Britain
https://commons.wikimedia.org/wiki/File:Roman_britain_400.jpg

You might be surprised to learn that Britain was a Roman province for so long. We typically don't think of Britain as being Roman. Today, there are very few traces remaining of Roman Britannia, and while other previous Roman provinces speak Romance languages (like French and

Spanish), which have their roots in Latin, the British speak English, which is a Germanic language. If the British people were fully Romanized by the 4th century, what happened?

In short, Rome fell. It was sacked by the Visigoths in 410, but by that time, things had been going downhill for a while anyway. We often think of the sack of Rome as the beginning of the end for the Roman Empire, but by this time, things were pretty much already over for the province of Britannia. The empire was already collapsing due to a combination of external threats and infighting. One of the various emperors vying for control during the period removed the Roman legions from Britain to fight elsewhere, and they simply never returned to the remote island province. Britannia was left high and dry without a Roman military presence.

While that might sound great, what it meant was that the inhabitants no longer had imperial protection. No Roman legions were protecting them, and unfortunately, there were a lot of groups who were happy to take advantage of that.

So, life suddenly got very hard for the Romano-Britons. They found themselves attacked by numerous barbarian groups: the Picts of Scotland, the Scotti of Ireland, the Angles and Saxons (both Germanic tribes), and the Jutes, who were a Norse tribe. The Angles, Saxons, and Jutes eventually moved past raiding Britain to settling there, and for the sake of convenience, we typically refer to them collectively as the Anglo-Saxons.

By the time we pick up with England two hundred years later, in 600 CE, at the start of the Middle Ages, the land was divided into several competing Anglo-Saxon kingdoms. The English nation eventually formed out of these nations.

But what happened to the Celtic Britons? Not only did they no longer have Roman military protection, but without Rome, the economic system that had been sustaining the province also collapsed, along with functions and services related to the imperial government. Roman towns with their now useless public buildings and marketplaces were abandoned, and then the Anglo-Saxons arrived.

We will talk more about this in Chapter 4, but tradition tells us that the Celtic Britons were pushed out of the area that would become England by Anglo-Saxon conquerors. Some chose to migrate to Brittany, an area in what is now northwestern France, and they did not completely disappear from the isle of Britain. Wales is a Celtic nation, as is Cornwall.

While the Britons maintained the area that became Wales, within a generation or two after the Romans departed, Roman Britannia had been fully replaced by *Angleland*, the land of the Angles.

Anglo-Saxon England

Thus, at the beginning of the Middle Ages, the area that would become England was effectively Anglo-Saxon, but it was not yet England. At the beginning of the 7th century, this area was divided into the Anglo-Saxon Heptarchy, which consisted of seven competing kingdoms: Northumbria, Mercia, Wessex, East Anglia, Sussex, Essex, and Kent.

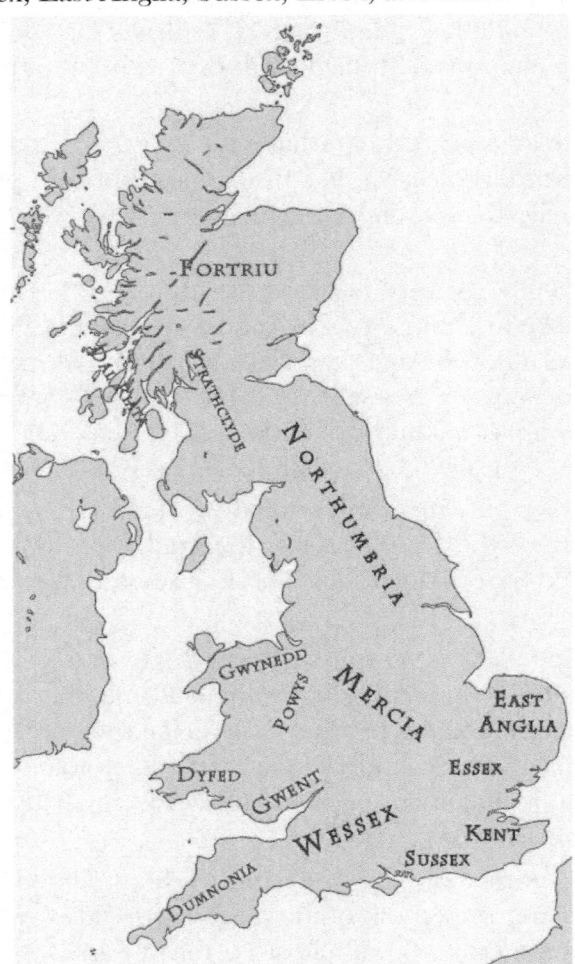

The kingdoms of the Anglo-Saxon Heptarchy, along with the Welsh and Pict kingdoms
https://commons.wikimedia.org/wiki/File:British_kingdoms_c_800.svg

We'll get into greater detail about who exactly the Anglo-Saxons were and what they were like in Chapter 4, but for now, let's talk about how England, or rather the area that would become England, developed during the period when the Anglo-Saxons were in charge.

As we already discussed, when the Romans left, the towns they had built were completely abandoned. So, in the 5th and 6th centuries, there were no towns in England. The Anglo-Saxons at this time lived in a tribal and rural society. There was pretty much only one way to get rich in this world, and that was to take things from your neighbors. Warfare was a profitable business, and the elites of this society gained power and wealth by making war on and conquering their neighbors. There were many more than seven Anglo-Saxon kingdoms, but the seven of the Heptarchy were the ones that came to dominate as the different groups vied for power during the 5th, 6th, and 7th centuries.

While warfare can be highly profitable in the short term, it is also not the most viable long-term economic plan. The more territory you conquer, the more funds you need to rule that area. If your funds are coming solely from campaigns, that means you now have to conquer even more territory. Eventually, a kingdom simply gets too big to run off the spoils of war alone.

Now, warfare also provides one with a surplus of various goods (the things you take from the people you conquer). These surpluses can be used to develop a much less risky and more tenable economic plan: trade.

In 7th-century England, towns again began to appear. Trade flourished, and permanent settlements again became viable. As the economy continued to develop, communities developed around the production of certain key goods. There were settlements that focused on producing salt, mining iron, and harvesting timber.

So, over the first two centuries of the Middle Ages, Anglo-Saxon society grew and prospered. It remained a time full of war and other hardships that one would expect to find in the 6th and 7th centuries, but it was not the dark ages some have made it out to be.

The Viking Age

By the late 8th century, the Anglo-Saxon kingdoms were flourishing, but they were still very much competing kingdoms. It would take a significant outside threat to unite these kingdoms, and that threat was the Vikings.

The first Viking raids on England began in the 790s. These raids, though relatively small in scale, were devastating for the coastal settlements. The Vikings were Norse raiders who came from several different areas, such as Denmark, Sweden, and Norway. Although they had many differences, the Vikings all shared at least one crucial skill. They were excellent shipbuilders.

Vikings made many different kinds of ships, but the ones typically used in raids were called longboats. As the name suggests, these ships were long and narrow and, importantly, had shallow draughts. This meant that they could travel easily in shallow water. In these ships, the Vikings were able to land right on the beaches of settlements near the water and then swiftly push their boats out to sea again. They were also able to navigate rivers, extending the reach of their raids.

These fast and deadly raids were bad enough for the Anglo-Saxons, but things got much worse in the 9th century. The Vikings began to make more substantial attacks on the Anglo-Saxon kingdoms. They did not stop at burning and looting but began to conquer territory. Some even chose to settle on the island. In 865, the Viking threat became an all-out invasion with the arrival of the *mycel hæþen here*, or Great Heathen Army.

The Great Army was a Norse or Viking force that quickly set out to conquer the Anglo-Saxon kingdoms. In truth, the army was a more disparate group than the name suggests. It was not one large unified force but was rather made up of many distinct groups. Remember that although the Vikings were all Norse, they came from many different areas. The Great Heathen Army reflected this.

Of course, this variance among its members did not make the Great Heathen Army any less devastating for the Anglo-Saxons. The Great Army conquered Northumbria and installed a puppet king. East Anglia soon followed. Mercia held out longer, but it, too, fell to the Norse. Wessex was the last to submit, but eventually, the king of Wessex, King Alfred, was driven from his kingdom by the Vikings in 878.

At this point, it certainly looked like Angleland had become the land of the Norse instead, but if that had stayed true, England would probably look very different today. What happened?

King Alfred of Wessex had been driven from his kingdom, but he was not dead. In the same year, 878, King Alfred fought a battle against the Norse, and he won a decisive victory. From the brink of defeat, Alfred managed to push the Norse out and reclaim Wessex. This incredible victory and his subsequent reign earned Alfred a name that few monarchs managed to pull off: Alfred the Great.

The Rise of the Wessex Dynasty

Alfred's victory in 878 was crucial, but it was not the end of things. In 878, Alfred made a deal with the Norse Guthrum that required Guthrum to convert to Christianity and leave Wessex. Guthrum then established a kingdom in East Anglia, so while Wessex was recovering, the Norse still held sway over a large part of England. The boundaries negotiated by Alfred and Guthrum were made official around 886. The area controlled by the Norse would later come to be called the Danelaw, and it included the Anglo-Saxon kingdoms of Northumbria, East Anglia, Essex, and parts of the original Mercia.

The kingdoms of England in 886
https://commons.wikimedia.org/wiki/File:Britain_886.jpg

When Alfred died in 899, his children continued the fight against the Danes. Alfred's son, Edward the Elder, became the king of the Anglo-Saxons, a title his father had created. This means the House of Wessex continued to be in charge. Alfred's daughter, Æthelflæd, had married the king of the Mercians and was known as the "Lady of the Mercians."

With Alfred's death, the Danes again tried to conquer Mercia and Wessex, but both Edward and Æthelflæd built a ring of forts to protect their kingdoms. In 910, Edward won a decisive victory against the Danes at Tettenhall, ending their plans of reconquering Wessex.

Starting in 912, Edward was able to go on the offensive. Step by step, he regained the Anglo-Saxon kingdoms of Essex and East Anglia. His sister Æthelflæd again mirrored Edward's moves and also went on the offensive. She began to retake the Danish Five Boroughs, which were part of the area that had originally been part of Mercia. Æthelflæd had made enough progress with her campaign to receive a promise of submission from the Danes in Northumbria when she died in 918.

Upon hearing of his sister's death, Edward halted his campaign against the Danes to go to Tamworth, where he was able to get the Mercians to accept him as king, making an even larger Anglo-Saxon kingdom. Edward then succeeded in gaining back the rest of Mercia from the Danes. When Edward died in 924, the House of Wessex now had control of most of England, with the expectation of Northumbria, where a Norse king sat at York.

Edward was succeeded by his son, Æthelstan. Æthelstan was able to finish what his father started but with surprisingly less violent means. Æthelstan had his sister marry the Norse king in York, a man by the name of Sihtric. When Sihtric died in 927, Æthelstan gained control of Northumbria and became the first king to rule all of the English people. The year 927 is thus the start of England as a nation, and Æthelstan is widely considered to be the first king of England.

Taking a step back from the details that led to Æthelstan becoming the first king of England, there are two ways you can read the events that led to the domination of Wessex in the Anglo-Saxon kingdoms. You could argue that the Wessex dynasty, beginning with Alfred the Great, was the savior of the Anglo-Saxons. They drove the Danish invaders back and united the Angles into a more powerful kingdom that would be better equipped to defend itself.

However, you could also argue that the rise of the Wessex dynasty and the unification of the Anglo-Saxons under them was the simple product of opportunism. Alfred the Great and his descendants took advantage of the Danes weakening their Anglo-Saxon rivals. As they worked to push the Danes out, Wessex was able to easily consolidate the conquered Anglo-Saxon nations under their control. In a way, the Wessex kings were simply a different conqueror.

There is likely some truth to both interpretations. There can be no doubt that without Alfred the Great, the Danes would have most likely conquered the Anglo-Saxons, and England might have never come to exist. However, it is equally true that Wessex was not the only Anglo-Saxon kingdom and that the ultimate dominance of its rulers was largely due to their ability to take advantage of the opportunity created by the Norse takeover. So, ultimately, the Vikings are kind of responsible for the unification of England.

England under the Wessex Dynasty

We will talk more about this era in our discussion of the Anglo-Saxons, but for the sake of chronology, there are a few things you need to know about England under the Wessex dynasty. England was now under the rule of a single king, but it was not united in the way we think of nations today.

When Æthelstan became the king of the English in 927, he was ruling over several rather disparate areas. Things that are vital to government, such as currency, measuring systems for land ownership, and laws, differed greatly across England. Depending on where you were, you could be under a Mercian, West Saxon, or Danish style law system.

This might sound like an absolute logistical nightmare today, but in the 10th century, English kings were far less concerned with having everything in their administration the same. For the most part, local areas continued using their own systems, especially those that were using the Danish law, although a few changes were instituted. The kingdom began to use the same type of currency, and the Wessex system of dividing the kingdom into shires and those into even smaller units called "hundreds" was expanded. Eventually, there were national rules about how often the courts that presided over these localities had to meet.

Although these changes may seem insignificant, they were the beginning of the creation of an English nation that was unified in practice as well as in name. Living under the same king was one thing, but using the same coins and the same systems created much more commonality between the Anglo-Saxons in Wessex, Mercia, and elsewhere in England.

This process of practical unification would continue into the 11th century, only not under the Anglo-Saxon kings. In 1013, the Danes returned.

The Return of the Danes

To understand how the Danes managed to invade England again, we first need to talk about the Anglo-Saxon king at the time: King Æthelred. When Æthelred's father, King Edgar, died in 975, there was a dispute about whether the throne should pass to Æthelred or his older stepbrother, Edward. Both brothers had supporters, and although Edward initially seized the throne, he held it for less than three years. Edward was murdered, and Æthelred took the throne in 978 at the age of twelve.

Taking the throne after the assassination of the previous king and doing so as a child set the mood for most of Æthelred's reign. In short, he was not a good king. In fact, history has dubbed him Æthelred the Unready, and it was during the reign of Æthelred the Unready that the Vikings again began to raid England.

Æthelred was unable to deal with the Viking problem. He only succeeded in making it much worse by massacring Danes on St. Brice's Day in 1002. Æthelred was unable to fend the Danes off, so he paid them continuously higher tributes to buy peace. However, the raids only continued to get worse. In 1013, the English people had had enough. They accepted Sweyn, King of Denmark, as their king. Æthelred was forced to flee the country, seeking asylum with his family.

King Sweyn did not rule England long, however. He died in 1014, and the English invited Æthelred to return on the condition that he would be a better king, which he happily agreed to, again becoming the king of the English in 1014.

Sweyn's son, Cnut, however, was not happy with this arrangement. In 1016, Cnut led another Danish invasion of England. Æthelred died during the conflict, and his son Edmund Ironside was eventually defeated by Cnut. Cnut allowed Edmund to maintain control over Wessex, which proved to be an inconsequential arrangement because Edmund died within a few months, leaving Cnut ruler of all of England. For the next twenty-five years, England had a Danish king.

For nineteen of those years, Cnut ruled England, doing so from 1016 to 1035. There can be no argument that Cnut was an effective king. During his reign, he managed to conquer Norway, so he was the king of England, Denmark, and Norway. Cnut gained great popularity with the English people through his conversion to Christianity and dedication to maintaining the law. Under Cnut, England saw almost two decades of security and relative peace.

Despite his successes, Cnut's death again left England with a problem of succession. Cnut had two wives, one of whom was Æthelred's widow, Emma, and he had sons by both her and his other wife. Both his sons naturally felt that they had a claim to the throne. Harold, Cnut's son with his first wife, seized the throne of England first, holding it for five years before he suddenly died in 1040. Harold's early death gave his brother, Harthacnut, the son of Cnut and Emma, the chance to seize the English throne. Harthacnut ruled for only two years before he died suddenly. Neither of Cnut's sons was well-liked by the English people.

It was surprisingly one of Æthelred's sons who next took the throne after the death of both of Cnut's sons. Edward the Confessor was the last of the Wessex dynasty to rule England. He reigned from 1042 to 1066. Although Edward had a fairly successful reign, he and his wife Queen Edith failed to have any children. When he died childless in 1066, England was again thrown into confusion over the succession. This time, an outside threat decided to take advantage of that confusion. It would soon be the end of Anglo-Saxon England.

England from 600 to 1066 was an emerging nation. Although there was much progress in terms of economic growth and political unity, there was also an almost constant state of warfare due to both foreign invaders and infighting over succession issues. The monarchy had proved to be both a powerful consolidating force and the source of many issues. Starting with Æthelstan in 927, the kings and queens of England would continue to have an enormous impact on the country for the next eight hundred years, through the Middle Ages and beyond.

Chapter 2: High Middle Ages (1066–1272)

David Carpenter's book on this period of English history bears the title *The Struggle for Mastery*, and it certainly is an apt description. Beginning with the Norman Conquest in 1066, moving through the eighteen-year civil war known as the Anarchy, and ending in the 13th century with the conflicts between the barons and kings, the High Middle Ages in England was dominated by struggles for power. While the Early Middle Ages saw the establishment of the king and his government, the High Middle Ages would test that government and the extent of the king's power.

The Norman Conquest

In 1066, Edward the Confessor died childless, and, as usually happens with monarchies, the lack of a direct heir led to problems. Immediately after Edward's death, Harold Godwinson, an earl, was named the king. The quick appointment of Harold suggests that the powerful men of England were at least in partial agreement about Harold's appointment, and their quick action may also have been an attempt to preempt the rival claimants to the throne. However, Harold's appointment did not stop his rivals. If Harold wanted to keep the throne, he would have to fight for it.

The first trouble was not William of Normandy (later known as William the Conqueror) but someone far closer to home. Harold's brother, Tostig, joined forces with the king of Norway, Harald Hardrada, and attacked York. King Harold rode north with his army and engaged the forces of Tostig and Harald at Stamford Bridge on September 25th, 1066.

The Battle of Stamford Bridge was a decisive and total victory for King Harold. Both Tostig and Harald were killed in the battle, and the remains of their forces fled in ships. Harold had successfully defended his right to be the king of England, but unfortunately, there was still another rival. Three days after Harold's victory at Stamford Bridge, William, Duke of Normandy, landed in the south of England with an invading force.

Why did the duke of Normandy feel he had a right to the English throne in the first place? King Edward's childlessness was not just a subject of discussion on his deathbed. William of Normandy claimed that Edward had named him as his heir. It is possible that Edward might have made such a promise to William sometime around 1051 in an effort to maintain peaceful relations with Normandy, but it would not have been a serious promise since King Edward was still healthy and might even have had children at that time.

Norman narratives would later state that in 1064/1065, while acting as Edward's ambassador to Normandy, Harold Godwinson had confirmed William's appointment as heir and even swore an oath to William. It seems highly unlikely that this story is entirely true considering its source, but in 1066, Harold was condemned for breaking his oath. Since he never got the chance to defend himself, we will never know what exactly happened. What we do know is that William used this story to justify his invasion.

King Harold's army met William's at the Battle of Hastings on October 14th. Some consider Harold's move to confront William so soon after the Battle of Stamford Bridge as reckless, but it is always difficult to judge with the gaze of hindsight. The Battle of Hastings did not go well for King Harold, so it is easy to say that his decision to confront William at that time was unwise.

We'll get more into the details of the battle in our later chapter on battles, but needless to say, the Normans won the Battle of Hastings. The English force was almost entirely annihilated, including King Harold and his brothers. William was the only rival to the throne left standing, and it did not take him long to claim his place. William was crowned king of England in London on December 25th, 1066.

Just as Anglo-Saxon and then Danish rule had brought changes to England, the rule of the Normans would have a great impact on the

English nation. The first change was in the ruling elite. After putting down several rebellions in the first five years of his reign (1066-1070), William I had had enough of the remaining English aristocracy. They were removed from power and replaced with William's Norman appointees.

William didn't just stop at changing the faces in power, though. He also made some changes to the system. Although we often think of the feudal system as being a staple of the entire medieval period, it was only under Norman rule that England adopted a true feudal system, although the system that was in place before the conquest was feudal-like. We will discuss this system in greater detail in Chapter 5.

The Anarchy

As with both the Anglo-Saxon dynasty and the Danes, the Norman rule of England was also destined not to last, and it, too, ended due to problems with succession.

After William I, his son, William II, ruled England. When William II died without children, his brother Henry I took the throne. Things seemed set since Henry I had a son, William, who would become king after him. However, in 1120, William died when the *White Ship* sank in the English Channel. His death led to a period of English history that would become known as the Anarchy.

After William's death, King Henry I named Matilda, his daughter, as heir to the throne. However, when Henry died, the barons did not support Matilda's claim. She was married to Geoffrey Plantagenet, Count of Anjou, whom the Anglo-Norman barons disliked. Henry's nephew, Stephen of Blois, seized the throne.

Because Matilda was in Normandy at the time of Henry I's death, Stephen arrived in England first and was able to seize the throne with relatively little difficulty. However, his reign did not follow the pattern of this promising start.

The majority of Stephen's reign, in fact, all but one year of it, took place during the Anarchy, an English civil war that lasted from 1135 to 1153. This eighteen-year war was essentially a fight between Stephen and Empress Matilda (empress because her first husband was Holy Roman Emperor Henry V) for the English throne.

We do not have the space here to dive into a detailed account of the Anarchy. As the name suggests, it was a complex and chaotic time in English history. Stephen's problems extended beyond Empress Matilda's claim to the throne. In the west, the Welsh managed to raid and eventually seize control of some areas, and in the north, King David of Scotland invaded and conquered substantial areas of English land.

During this period, both Stephen and Empress Matilda granted lands and favors to try to win support. Various people switched sides throughout the war, and many took advantage of the chaos to try to gain more power. Earls waged war on other counties, and castellans and the garrisons stationed at the various castles across England terrorized the local populations. The national currency, which had been established by the Anglo-Saxon kings, fractured, with Stephen, Empress Matilda, and even some barons all issuing coins in their own name.

This did not mean that all of England was burning constantly, as the name "Anarchy" might suggest, but the constant warfare meant that at times in certain places, anarchy became very real. This was especially true in the border areas between the area controlled by Stephen and that controlled by Empress Matilda. Even as England was broken into multiple pieces, law and order still reigned within these smaller pieces controlled by people like King David, King Stephen, and Earl Robert (Empress Matilda's brother and supporter in the conflict).

So, what brought an end to the chaos? The war had proven to be a firm stalemate. While Matilda had returned to Normandy in 1148, her son Henry continued the fight in England in 1153. The powerful men of England were reluctant to enter into a final decisive battle since they did not want to give up their local power again to a powerful king. The church also refused to take sides, refusing to recognize Stephen's son Eustace as heir. Everyone appeared to be waiting for something to break the stalemate so that they could side with the victor.

The thing that broke the stalemate was ironically the same thing that had caused the civil war in the first place: the death of the male heir to the throne. In 1153, Eustace died, and Stephen was left without an heir. His other son, William, showed no desire to ascend the throne, so, in 1153, Stephen made Henry, Empress Matilda's son, his heir, effectively ending the Anarchy.

As it turned out, Henry did not have to wait long for his throne. Stephen died a little less than a year later in 1154, and Henry became Henry II.

The Angevin

Henry II marked the beginning of a new ruling dynasty in England, one which was to last for the remainder of the medieval period: the Plantagenets.

Henry II was the son of Empress Matilda and Geoffrey Plantagenet, making him the first English king in the Plantagenet line. However, historians often refer to Henry II and the two kings following him (Richard the Lionheart and King John) as the Angevins.

The Angevins were English kings with an empire. In fact, as a whole, they spent more time on the continent than they did in England. The Angevin Empire stretched from northern England to the Pyrenees Mountains, including part of Ireland and large areas of France (Anjou, Normandy, Aquitaine, Maine, and Brittany).

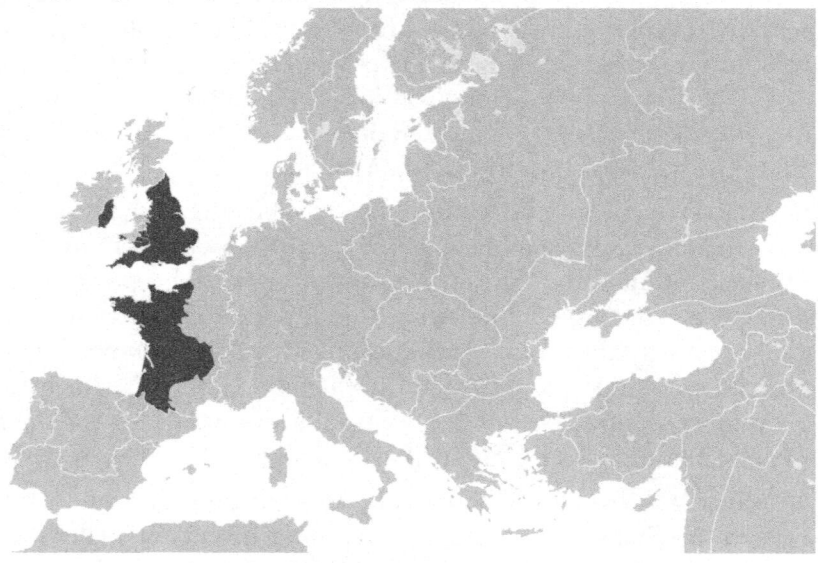

The Angevin Empire
https://commons.wikimedia.org/wiki/File:Angevin_Empire_1190.svg

This large empire was not the result of conquest but rather of Henry II's position when he became the king of England. He inherited the title of count of Anjou and Maine from his father and was made duke of Normandy by the king of France in 1150. Perhaps his most successful maneuver was marrying Eleanor of Aquitaine in 1152. This marriage made him duke of Aquitaine. So, by the time Henry II became the king of England in 1154, he already held vast areas of land in western France.

Unfortunately, besides lots of land, Henry II also had lots of sons—five to be exact. He soon ran into problems with trying to find places for all of them to rule. His sons rebelled against him several times. Eventually, his son Richard allied with King Philip II of France and forced his father into a settlement. King Henry II died shortly after.

Despite his family issues, Henry II had an enormous lasting impact on England, and his reign was indeed a critical one in English history, largely because of the changes he made to the judicial system.

In brief, Henry II wanted greater control over local matters, and after the Anarchy, there was a greater push to develop a system that could more effectively keep the peace. Henry II's changes were complex, but they created a system with distinct procedures. Decisions were now made by juries and heard by the king's judges rather than local courts.

The new system was voluntary, so the amount of people who took their cases to it indicates that it had appeal. This was the start of a system that would last until the 1970s in England. We'll discuss law and order in the medieval period in greater detail in a later chapter, but this was one of the lasting impacts that Henry II had on England. His empire would not be as lucky.

Henry's youngest son John became the king in 1199 following the death of his brother, Richard the Lionheart. Although Richard spent only around six months of his reign in England, his military and diplomatic skills had kept the Angevin Empire together throughout his ten-year reign. King John was less skilled in these arts.

King Philip II of France took advantage of the opportunity and began seeking to drive King John out of France. Through both ill luck and bad decisions, John lost the Angevin Empire's continental holdings little by little. By 1204, he was effectively only the king of England, but King John's troubles did not stop with his continental failures. The rest of his reign would cement his place as one of England's worst kings.

The Magna Carta and the Barons' Wars

Fighting wars takes money, so to continue his military expeditions in France and win back Normandy, King John needed funds. He thus spent a good deal of time after 1204 finding ways to gain wealth, a task that was only heightened by the inflation during this period.

Squeezing every coin you can get from your subjects does not make for a popular king, and John did not stop there. The popular new judicial system developed by his father, Henry II, might have been a way for John to gain some popularity, but he failed to use it. Justice became a farce under King John, further antagonizing his subjects.

The barons became increasingly hostile to King John, and in 1212, the king discovered a plot to kill him. While he managed to gain control of the situation that time, three years later, tensions exploded again. This time, instead of trying to kill him, the barons sought to make John agree to a list of demands. These demands were the Magna Carta (the Great Charter), and it was one of the most significant moments in English history.

The Magna Carta was a document of sixty-two chapters that put a limit on the king's power. Specifically, it sought to do things like restrict the king's ability to raise funds and stop him from treating individuals however he pleased. The Magna Carta was the first time that restrictions were placed on an English king. It was a landmark moment in that it subjected the king to the law. Before this, the king had always been above the law since he was the one who made the laws. Now, there was something higher than the king.

The Magna Carta was a document prepared by the barons, so its concerns were mostly baronial. It did little to protect the common people, but the general idea and parts of the Magna Carta would become precedents for later democratic hallmarks like the American Bill of Rights. Some chapters of the Magna Carta, such as "To no one will we sell, to no one will we deny or delay right or justice," are still in force today.

Of course, King John did not want to agree to these demands, but the barons went to arms, and he was forced to seal the charter at Runnymede, a meadow near the Thames.

Unfortunately, the peace the Magna Carta seemed to ensure did not last long. King John asked the pope to condemn the Magna Carta, which he did, meaning that King John did not have to follow it. The barons instead went to war, rebelling against King John and offering the throne to Louis, the son of the king of France. Thus began the First Barons' War in 1215.

Louis might have succeeded in becoming the king of England were it not for King John's death. With King John dead, most of the barons switched their support from Louis to John's son, Henry, who was nine years old at the time. Without the support of the rebellious barons, Louis was defeated in 1217.

Although Henry III ruled for far longer, he ended up facing similar problems as his father. Henry III's expensive foreign campaigns were unpopular for the same reason King John's had been, and the local officials he appointed were detested. His half-brothers, the Lusignans, were also unpopular and helped fuel a growing English dislike of foreigners. Again, there was trouble with the barons, and in 1258, Henry III agreed to reforms. But like with his father, the paper reforms proved ineffective. In 1263, the Second Barons' War broke out, with the rebelling barons being led by Simon de Montfort.

During the conflict, both Henry III and his son and heir, Edward, were captured. It seemed as if Simon de Montfort and the barons would win, but Edward escaped capture and defeated Montfort at the Battle of Evesham. The war continued for two years after this. It finally ended in 1267, and Henry III was restored to the throne.

Henry III's victory did not come with the total restoration of royal power. During the later years of his reign, after the war, he was forced to agree to some of the barons' requests, such as restricting the king's local officials to prevent abuses and confirming the Magna Carta. He negotiated with Parliament to secure funds for his son's crusade, marking an important transition in English history. The king was now looking to Parliament for the approval of taxation, something that would become a staple of the English system. King Henry III died in 1272, and the reign of his son Edward would mark the beginning of the last medieval period: the Late Middle Ages.

The years 1066 to 1272 saw massive changes in the monarchy and powers that governed the English nation. In 1066, William I established himself as a strong conquering king. He was able to introduce a feudal system that theoretically placed a lot of power in the hands of the monarchy. However, by 1272, Henry III had accepted the fact that if he wanted to remain the king of England, he would need to please the barons.

While we often think of the medieval period as a time in which monarchs ruled with absolute sovereignty, this period in English history shows us that that was not always the case. Limits could be placed on a king's power. However, those limits often had to be confirmed with the sword rather than the pen.

Chapter 3: Late Middle Ages (1272–1485)

You might think that this last period of the Middle Ages would be a time of prosperity that ushered England into the Renaissance age. However, for the most part, the opposite is true of the Late Middle Ages. This was a time of great hardship and ruin for England. From the devastation of natural events like the Great Famine and the Black Death to the strain brought about by conflicts like the Hundred Years' War, the Peasants' Revolt, and that famous civil war now known as the Wars of the Roses, England from 1272 to 1485 was anything but boring, no matter one's station.

So, how did England make it through these two hundred years and into the Renaissance age? The many hardships would ultimately force a change in the attitude of England's rulers and people. The end of the Middle Ages would be brought about less by the events themselves and more by the changes in people's mindsets that these events produced.

Unity through War

Edward I took the throne in 1272 after over fifty years of fighting between the barons and the king. Edward himself had even participated in these conflicts, as he had beaten Simon de Montfort's forces at the Battle of Evesham and restored his father, Henry III, to the throne during the Second Barons' War.

It thus might have initially seemed that Edward I would experience similar infighting with the barons that had plagued both his father (King Henry III) and grandfather (King John). However, by the end of his reign, Edward I would be one of the most successful kings in English history. How did he transform his predecessors' legacy?

Both King John and Henry III had struggled with internal conflicts, and Edward I, whether he meant to or not, essentially put an end to this by introducing a different kind of conflict. During his reign, Edward I would conquer Wales and nearly conquer Scotland as well. His military prowess saw England's focus shift from infighting to external wars.

Edward I's conquest of Wales was both brutal and effective. He fielded an enormous force in 1277 for his first invasion and then further subdued the Welsh by crushing their revolt in 1282, during which the members of the Welsh ruling family were killed. By 1283, Wales was effectively under English control. Edward I's conquest and subsequent control over Wales was so successful because of the massive amounts of capital Edward poured into the campaign. Not only was Edward I's invading army big enough that the Welsh had virtually little hope of resistance, but he also built a series of castles in the conquered territory to cement his control over the area. It was expensive but highly effective.

Wales was not the only place to keenly feel the strong military aptitude of Edward I. Edward I was also known as the Hammer of the Scots. The exact reason for Edward I's invasion of Scotland is tied to a succession dispute that we will not get into here, but suffice it to say, in 1296, Edward I invaded Scotland.

Edward Longshanks—Hammer of the Scots

Edward I's Scottish campaign was not nearly as successful as his conquest of Wales, largely because of the problem administrators to this day struggle with—lack of funds. The expense of Edward's Welsh conquest had not left him with enough money to repeat the same strategy in Scotland. Edward I also faced stern resistance in Scotland from figures such as William Wallace and Robert the Bruce.

While Edward I defeated Wallace in 1298, he marched again on Scotland in 1306 when Robert the Bruce was declared the king of Scotland. Edward I was able to best Robert the Bruce at the Battle of Methven in 1306, but he died in 1307 before he could finish his Scottish conquest. The campaign was left to his son, Edward II.

Edward II did not have the same military ability that his father possessed. In 1314, Robert the Bruce's forces defeated those of Edward II at the Battle of Bannockburn, effectively ending the English hopes of conquering Scotland, though a treaty was not signed until 1329.

Edward II's defeat at Bannockburn marked the sharp difference between him and his father. While Edward I had been able to effectively rule England, bringing national unity through foreign campaigns, Edward II was not a great military mind. He would soon find himself suffering from the same problem that his grandfather (Henry III) and great-grandfather (King John) had faced: discontent barons.

Edward II's reign can be described as little more than a disaster. The brazen promotion of his personal favorites, such as Piers Gaveston and the Despensers, led to poor governmental choices. It also greatly angered the ruling elites, who were being overlooked. The barons put pressure on Edward II to make changes in the Parliament in both 1311 and 1327, but they failed to make substantial and lasting reforms.

In the end, Edward II was deposed by his own family. His wife, Queen Isabella, and her lover, Roger Mortimer, invaded England in 1326. Edward II was captured shortly after, and his son Edward III was made king in his place in 1327.

Edward I's campaigns against Wales and Scotland had briefly united the king and barons under a common goal, but Edward II's military failures and poor kingship had again introduced the problem of baronial discontent. It was becoming more and more clear that England could only be governed effectively when the king had the support of his barons.

The Great Famine

Let's take a break from kings and barons to discuss what life was like for the everyday person in the Late Middle Ages. At the beginning of the 14th century, England, like the rest of Europe, was doing rather well economically. Agricultural productivity was at a high with more land in use than ever before, and the population had grown over the last two centuries as a result. This was not simply an era of subsistence farming. Surpluses allowed for trade to flourish, and towns offered places for peasants to both sell and buy various goods.

However, the society was still based on agriculture, and this left it vulnerable to agricultural disasters. The Great Famine, which began in 1315, was devastating to such a society. Although famines are often caused by drought, the Great Famine was the result of a very different weather problem: heavy rainfall. The Great Famine was caused by a period of heavy rainfall and cool temperatures. Not only did this lead to crop failures, but the wet conditions also meant that hay could not be made to feed the livestock.

The recent population growth made the famine all the more devastating. Before the famine, many peasants had finally been able to acquire their own land, and there were many farming communities developing in fringe locations with land that was harder to cultivate. These settlements were in their earlier precarious stages when the famine struck. The people sold land in droves and moved toward larger population centers in the hopes of being able to buy food. However, food prices quickly skyrocketed. People began to eat their livestock, and cooperation in small farming communities collapsed. By 1322, between 10 and 15 percent of the English population had died of starvation. Despite this devastation, the populace recovered relatively quickly once the weather began cooperating in 1322. By 1330, both the population and commerce had recovered.

Even though it had relatively few long-term effects on English history, the Great Famine shows us just how uncertain life in the Middle Ages could be, especially for the lower classes. Not just England but all of Europe faced huge losses of life because of the weather. While it was in some ways unavoidable, it also demonstrates the inability of medieval governments to deal with such crises effectively. This was a time of instability, where people were moved and torn by the whims of nature as well as the whims of kings.

The Hundred Years' War

In 1340, King Edward III made a decision that would greatly affect all of the English people for a long time to come. He declared himself the king of France. Edward III was not the first English king to make this claim, but he was the first one prepared to push his point. France and England had begun a period of conflict that would last for over one hundred years.

It can be easy to assume that the Hundred Years' War was the result of nothing more than Edward III's vaulted ambitions, but that far oversimplifies the matter. The French monarchy was also showing signs of great ambition, and Edward III needed to protect English trade in Flanders. Furthermore, Edward III seemed to have understood what made his grandfather Edward I so successful. Edward III's fight against France gave unity to his reign. Instead of arguing with their king, the

French wars gave the English elite a place to cooperate and attain their own ambitions. After all, warfare is a very profitable business. Much like his grandfather, Edward III quelled infighting with an external conflict.

The actual fighting of the Hundred Years' War was not one hundred years of constant fighting but rather one hundred years of various campaigns in France (it also lasted longer than a hundred years, with most historians saying it began in 1337 and ended in 1453). There is not enough room to even begin to discuss the progress of the war here, but some notable battles include Crécy (1346), Poitiers (1356), Agincourt (1415), the Siege of Orléans (1429), and Castillon (1453).

The war was started by Edward III, and it would not end until the reign of Henry VI. Five English kings would continue this conflict with France, with some being more successful than others. Henry V became a national hero thanks to his victories, such as the one at Agincourt, and the military failures during Richard II's reign led to the first popular uprising in English history.

The Peasants' Revolt

To understand what led to the Peasants' Revolt in 1381, we must first understand how closely war and taxes were tied together in the medieval period. In the Middle Ages, taxes were the direct result of war. A king could only directly tax his subjects when there was an express need, i.e., the defense of the realm. This principle had also been used to justify taxation for aggressive wars, such as the French campaigns.

By this point in English history, taxation was also no longer solely in control of the king. Parliament had to approve taxes. Therefore, if kings wanted to continue their wars, they often had to agree to certain demands to get Parliament to approve their taxation plans. This check on a king's power was the result of over a century of baronial discontent and pressure on various kings.

What all this means is that in the eyes of the majority of the English population, defeat in warfare was the direct result of poorly managed funds from taxation and that taxation was the result of both Parliament and the king. To pay taxes for successful military campaigns was one thing, but to be forced to pay for losses was grating.

Unfortunately, the logic of war only exacerbates this issue. Whether you are winning or losing, wars are expensive. However, when you are winning, you can at least partially offset that expense with the spoils you gain. Thus, a war that is going poorly inevitably ends up costing more than a war that is going well.

In the late 1370s, the war was not going well for the English, and the English were being taxed heavily. From 1357 to 1371, there had been no direct taxation of the English people at all, but with Richard II's ascension to the throne in 1377, there was direct taxation every single year for four years. Despite this, there were still no great military triumphs. In 1381, when a third poll tax was issued, a popular revolt erupted.

This time of heavy taxation might not have resulted in an uprising were it not for the fact that the people were already resentful. The Black Death (which we will discuss in detail in a later chapter) had reached England around 1348, killing enough of the population to cause a labor shortage. The labor shortage meant that workers suddenly had the leverage to demand better wages and working conditions. However, the government, which was comprised of people who had to pay these workers, passed a maximum wage law, limiting the amount workers could demand. Such treatment naturally bred resentment, which boiled over under the heavy taxation from 1377 to 1381.

The revolt was concentrated in southeast England, and it was initially quite successful. Led by Wat Tyler, the rebels successfully marched into London. Tyler was even able to gain a meeting with the king and the mayor of London.

However, at the meeting, things quickly went south for the rebels. The mayor of London killed Tyler, and the king somehow managed to convince the rebels to go home by making promises of reform, promises that were not carried out. After dispersing, the rebels found themselves on the wrong end of the law, and many were punished. The revolt had come to nothing.

The death of Wat Tyler (the image shows King Richard twice, both talking to the peasants and watching Tyler's murder)

Despite its failure, the Peasants' Revolt of 1381 is a crucial event in English history. While the barons had issued the Magna Carta over a century earlier, this was the first time that the masses had defied the king's government. It was a landmark moment for this alone, but it also showed signs of something that would become a national sentiment by the end of the Middle Ages: weariness of war.

In the medieval period, war was the thing that made and broke kingdoms. As we have seen thus far in this chapter, war was often the sustaining factor that kept kings in power and governments stabilized, but it could also turn and become the thing that brought those very governments down. War was a unifying factor, but it was a volatile one. It would take one more brutal internal conflict before England would begin seeking a different path.

The Wars of the Roses

The Wars of the Roses is one of the most famous conflicts in English history. Even the incredibly popular *Game of Thrones* series is based on this particular event. Its lasting impact on the popular imagination is due in no small part to Shakespeare, who wrote a multi-play series about the event. Many of the things that come to mind when you hear the Wars of the Roses is likely because of Shakespeare. The idea that supporters of the different factions picked either a white or a red rose to show their support? Shakespeare. Richard III was an evil, ugly hunchback who murdered his nephews? Shakespeare. While the Bard didn't get everything wrong about the Wars of the Roses, we must remember that Shakespeare wrote his plays over a century after the events and that he was writing to entertain, not for accuracy.

So, what really happened during this conflict that would only later come to be called the Wars of the Roses? It was a chaotic time that saw two noble houses completely annihilated in their contest for the throne. We cannot hope to cover all the messy details here, but we will explore a basic overview of this war that brought an end to the Middle Ages in England.

Although the bloodshed officially began in 1455 at the First Battle of St. Albans, the problems that led to the war started long before then. Henry VI, who ascended to the throne as an infant after the untimely death of Henry V in 1422, was a weak king. Even when he had reached the age to govern in his own right, Henry VI was not a capable ruler. As this fact became more and more obvious, other men were eager to step into the role of being England's practical ruler while Henry VI continued to wear the crown.

One man who sought this role was Richard, Duke of York. By 1450, Richard saw himself as the best man to become the right hand of the king (which, in the case of Henry VI, meant ruling England). However, Richard did not anticipate that Henry VI would view Richard's offer of assistance as a threat. Matters were only made worse by the fact that Richard strongly disliked the man Henry VI had picked instead: Edmund Beaufort, Duke of Somerset.

Richard of York vied for power for five years without bloodshed before things reached a boiling point in 1455 at St. Albans. There, the Yorkist faction defeated the Lancastrian force (Henry VI was of the House of

Lancaster) and captured Henry VI, marching him back to London. Henry VI remained the king, with York as his chief counselor and the de facto ruler of England.

Unfortunately, this would turn out to be only the beginning of a series of battles and conflicts between the Houses of Lancaster and York that would last for a little over thirty years, with the final claimant to the throne defeated in 1487. The advantage swung between either side like a pendulum. Below is a short list of how the battles went:

- 1455: First Battle of St. Albans – Yorkists win
- 1459: Battle of Ludford Bridge – Lancastrian win; Richard of York flees the country
- 1460: Battle of Wakefield – Lancastrian win; Richard of York killed.
- February 1461: Battle of Mortimer's Cross – Yorkist win led by Edward, Richard's son
- February 1461: Second Battle of St. Albans – Lancastrian win
- March 1461: Edward of York declared King Edward IV
- 1470: Henry VI restored to the throne
- 1471: Battle of Tewkesbury – Yorkist victory; Henry VI is killed in the Tower of London; Edward IV is the undisputed king

These dates give some idea of the absolute chaos of the time, but they only scratch the surface. Law and order suffered, as men seized power and then were ousted by rival forces. The fighting was brutal and left many people on both sides of the conflict seeking revenge for lost loved ones. It seemed like Edward IV was sitting victorious on the throne in 1471, but that was not the end to this drama.

When Edward IV died in 1483, his son became Edward V. However, only a few months later, both of Edward IV's sons were declared illegitimate. Edward IV's brother Richard was declared king. He became Richard III. It is widely believed that Richard III then had his nephews killed to secure his claim.

History does not remember Richard III fondly, but it might have seen his actions differently were it not for what would happen two years later. The final bloodshed of the main claimants to the throne in the Wars of the Roses was the Battle of Bosworth in 1485. Richard III was killed, and Henry Tudor took the throne. Losing the Battle of Bosworth was seen as divine judgment for Richard's wrongs, and he has been seen in infamy ever since. We might think of Richard III very differently had he won that battle.

But who was Henry Tudor anyway? Henry V's widow, Catherine de Valois, married a Welshman, Owen Tudor. Catherine's sons with Owen Tudor were thus half-brothers to Henry VI. One of their sons, Edmund Tudor, then married a woman named Margaret Beaufort, who could trace her lineage in a direct line back to John of Gaunt, Duke of Lancaster, who was the third son of Edward III. Henry Tudor was the son of Edmund and Margaret Beaufort, and he claimed a right to the throne through both lines.

If Henry Tudor's claim sounds dubious, that's because it was. No contemporaries would have picked Henry Tudor as a strong claimant to the throne, but, thanks to the Wars of the Roses, by 1485, Henry Tudor and Richard III were the only real claimants left standing. (A pretender would be presented after Richard's death, with his defeat officially ending the wars.) With the defeat of Richard III at the Battle of Bosworth, Henry Tudor was effectively the only option. He became Henry VII. To further solidify his claim and put a final end to the bloodshed, Henry VII married Elizabeth of York, Edward IV's daughter. The Houses of Lancaster and York were united, and the war was finally over. England had entered a new era. The Middle Ages was over.

The End of the Middle Ages

Why exactly does this moment mark the end of the Middle Ages? After all, we have seen several dynasties come and go throughout the medieval period, and the Wars of the Roses was not the only civil war that plagued England during this time.

England in the Middle Ages had been formed and defined by warfare. The war with the Viking invaders had originally united the country under the Wessex dynasty, and throughout the next five centuries, warfare served as both the bane and boon of many English kings. Success in war solidified one's rule, but a lack of military prowess often led to rebellion. War was the sole force behind taxation rates, and law and order collapsed several times under the pressure of internal warfare. Although we often romanticize and exaggerate it, there can be no doubt that the medieval period was a violent time.

The end of the Wars of the Roses marked the beginning of a transition away from war being the government's primary purpose. Although Henry

VII did deal with rebellions and could be quite ruthless to his political opponents, he strived to maintain the peace during his reign, passing the throne to his son, Henry VIII. This was the most stable the English throne had been in a long time. It was a throne based on the hereditary and sovereign right of the king to rule rather than on the right to rule through conquest. The personal authority of kings was a far more stable thing to rely on than their military authority (although the personal authority of kings would eventually come to be challenged in England during the English Civil War of the 17th century).

This does not mean that war had no place in England after the Middle Ages. Henry VIII would renew the conflict with France, and the defeat of the Spanish Armada by the English in 1588 would prove to have enormous effects on England's future. Over a century after the Wars of the Roses, another civil war would again strike England. Thus, wars would continue to be a shaping factor in English history, but it was no longer the axis around which the entire nation, particularly the government, turned. Industry and trade had been making steady progress, and as England moved into the Renaissance period, things like religion and art would become increasingly important definers of the English nation. England had begun as a nation bound together by conquest and the need for defense. It grew into a nation with a unique culture, systems, and people. We will examine these aspects more closely as we continue to look at medieval England in closer detail.

Chapter 4: The Anglo-Who?

As we already discussed in Chapter 1, the Anglo-Saxons were not the original inhabitants of Britain, but they were the ones who gave England (Angleland) its name. The first king of England was Anglo-Saxon, and the language of England (English) is derived from the Anglo-Saxon language. Clearly, the Anglo-Saxons are important to English history. They are the start of English history, but who exactly were the Anglo-Saxons, and what were they like?

The Dark Ages?

For a long time, the period between the Roman departure from Britain and the Norman Conquest, which was when the Anglo-Saxons held sway over England, had been known as the Dark Ages. This name comes from the idea that this period saw very little forward progress in anything like knowledge or culture. History from this perspective viewed the Anglo-Saxons as poor barbarians who were barely able to scrape up enough to get by.

Of course, this view of the Anglo-Saxon period has been proven wildly inaccurate. The belief that the period from around 400 to 1100 was a dark age bereft of culture and progress comes from an overly sentimental attachment to Rome and its culture. Rome referred to these people as barbarians, and historians for a long time followed the Roman perspective.

Still, it wouldn't be fair to act as though that's the only reason the Anglo-Saxon period has been dubbed the Dark Ages for so long. In some ways, it was the Dark Ages, at least in hindsight, because we know relatively little about this period. There are a handful of written sources such as St. Gildas's *The Ruin of Britain* (likely written sometime in the 6th century), the Venerable Bede's *Ecclesiastical History of the English People* (written in the 8th century), and the *Anglo-Saxon Chronicle* (first compiled during the reign of Alfred the Great in the 9th century). These few sources, which cover over five hundred years of history, are not much, especially when compared to the wealth of sources we have on ancient Rome.

Then there is also the fact that we must question the reliability of the sources. For example, both St. Gildas and Bede have clear biases and probable inaccuracies in their accounts. They display a devotion to the narrative, which, while it makes their accounts more interesting, also makes their accuracy questionable. For instance, Bede says that the Anglo-Saxon settlers (or invaders, depending on how you look at it) had two leaders, Hengist and Horsa, who were descended from the god Woden. Not only is the divine ancestor part highly questionable, but Hengist and Horsa also mean stallion and horse. These two were likely nothing more than mythical figures like Romulus and Remus from Roman mythology.

What all this means is that historians were likely making some assumptions about the Anglo-Saxons because they didn't have a lot of evidence to go on. So, how do we know that many of those assumptions were inaccurate? While the written sources may be few, we do have another way to gain insights about Anglo-Saxon England. There is a wealth of archaeological evidence, which has only been discovered in the past century, that has caused us to rethink the way we view the Anglo-Saxons.

Take, for example, the famous site of Sutton Hoo. Sutton Hoo was a burial site that was first excavated in the late 1930s. In it was found a variety of treasures: burial masks, buckles, weapons, jewelry, and more. These grave goods—items buried with the dead—showed us several things about the Anglo-Saxons. They did have wealth—enough even to bury quite a bit with their dead—and their society had structure and culture. The grave goods were an indication of status, showing the existence of a hierarchy, and the practice of burying the dead with such elaborate goods shows a belief system and rituals. The Anglo-Saxons were more than poor barbarians practicing only subsistence farming.

A replica of the Anglo-Saxon Helmet found at Sutton Hoo

British Museum, CC BY-SA 2.5 <https://creativecommons.org/licenses/by-sa/2.5>, via Wikimedia Commons

https://en.wikipedia.org/wiki/Sutton_Hoo#/media/File:Sutton_Hoo_helmet_reconstructed.jpg

Since the discovery of Sutton Hoo, there have been even more archaeological finds from the Anglo-Saxon period. Thus, our knowledge of this "Dark Age" is continuing to grow. However, the simple fact remains that we will never have as many exact facts about this period as we would like, but much the same could be said for many eras of history. Now, let's look at some specifics about the Anglo-Saxons.

Where Did They Come From?

The Anglo-Saxons were Germanic settlers that came to Britain after the Romans left. Specifically, according to the Venerable Bede, there were three main groups: the Angles, the Saxons, and the Jutes. Their movement to Britain has come to be known as the English settlement.

The written histories then go on to tell us that the Anglo-Saxons conquered the south and southeast of Britain in a reign of terror, annihilating the native Britons and pushing them into the west, which later became Wales. This version suggests that the English people are almost entirely descended from Scandinavian and Germanic peoples.

As we have already discussed, we have learned to be wary of taking everything these written histories say for granted. Archaeological and scientific evidence (such as from the field of paleobotany) suggest that the reality of the English settlement is more complicated than one group simply replacing another. It seems more likely that the native Britons assimilated into the Anglo-Saxon culture, much as they had become Romanized while they were a Roman province. The Anglo-Saxons may not have settled Britain in the enormous numbers that we once thought, but they did manage to form a society where they formed a higher level of the social hierarchy than the Britons. The Britons may then have gradually adopted the Anglo-Saxon language and culture to gain more social status in this new society. The Britons disappeared because they became Anglo-Saxon, not because they were massacred, so the Anglo-Saxons that lived in England may have included far more Britons than we originally thought. They were a combination of peoples that developed over time into a distinct English people.

Conversion to Christianity

When the Anglo-Saxons first came to England, they were undoubtedly pagan. Remember, Bede claims that their leaders were descended from Woden. However, by the time of Alfred the Great, many of the Anglo-Saxon kings were Christian. Alfred even required the Viking king Guthrum to convert to Christianity in 878. How did this religious change occur, and what did it mean for the Anglo-Saxons?

The story of how Christianity came to England is quite dramatic. Apparently, Pope Gregory I, before he was the pope, saw some beautiful slave boys in the market at Rome. When he asked who they were, he was told that they were the Anglii. He thought the name fitting since they looked like angels, and Gregory believed that they should be heirs of the angels in heaven. He made up his mind then and there to convert the English people to Christianity, but then he became pope and was no longer free to travel as a missionary. He thus sent Augustine in his stead in 597, and that was how Christianity came to England. Augustine would even become known as the "apostle to the English."

Whether this story is true or not, there are some problems with it. Firstly, Christianity had already reached Britain long before this while it was still a Roman province, and even the Anglo-Saxon kings of the time were aware of Christianity. King Æthelberht of Kent had a Christian wife before Augustine ever arrived. We should also be wary of the way this narrative suggests that Augustine's arrival simply brought Christianity to the Anglo-Saxons. For one, Augustine and the missionaries who came with him were not the only ones responsible for converting the Anglo-Saxons. Missionaries from Ireland may have had greater overall success. Also, the process was much more gradual than the story suggests. It took many decades, and it was made easier by the fact that the people were allowed to keep many of their practices and even temples. Pagan temples had their idols removed and were changed into churches. Pagan holidays became Christian feast days for saints. The Anglo-Saxons as a whole did not so much flip a switch to Christianity as much as they slowly slid into it.

Why is the conversion to Christianity an important thing to know about the Anglo-Saxons? While traditional historians, specifically Bede, may have placed too great an emphasis on how much this conversion affected Anglo-Saxon society, it did have a huge impact on the Anglo-Saxons, especially on their kings.

To put it simply, converting to Christianity proved to be a smart power move for Anglo-Saxon rulers for several reasons. The Roman Catholic Church was by now an established power to which many European kingdoms were connected. Converting to Christianity thus gave Anglo-Saxon kings connections and status they had not had previously. There were also the members of the clergy. Their presence gave the courts of Anglo-Saxon kings distinction, and they were useful because of their knowledge of writing. With writing, kings could issue demands that affected a much larger radius, which means they could expand the areas they controlled. The rituals of Christianity were also beneficial to Anglo-Saxon kings. Kings could place themselves in superior positions by acting as the godfather at baptisms. There was also the uniformity of Christian worship. All across their kingdom, churches could meet and pray for their king. Finally, the structure of the church proved useful. With the establishment of churches and monasteries, kings had the opportunity to see people loyal to them in institutions that would become the center of local life.

Thus, in many ways, Christianity truly did transform Anglo-Saxon England. Over the course of the 7th century, as Christianity spread, kings were able to use it to widen their control and increase their power. It was at this point that the many Anglo-Saxon tribes across England were consolidated into the seven kingdoms of the Heptarchy.

What Were They Like?

So far, we have talked about what the Anglo-Saxons were not, where they came from, and how Christianity changed them, but what were they really like? Although we are still limited by what information we have on this period, here are some things we know about Anglo-Saxon culture.

Let's start with the language, which is a key component of any culture. The Anglo-Saxons spoke Old English, which is not nearly as similar to modern English as the name suggests. Old English and modern English are two different languages, though modern English is certainly derived from Old English. For instance, contrary to what you might have heard, Shakespeare did not write in Old English. He used Early Modern English. Old English is a different beast altogether. For instance, Old English has gendered nouns and uses cases, and if you don't know what either of those are, that just shows you how different Old English really is.

The first page of Beowulf in Old English
https://commons.wikimedia.org/wiki/File:Beowulf.firstpage.jpeg

As we mentioned in the first chapter, Britain is one of the only former Roman provinces whose modern language is not a Romance language (deriving from Latin). One reason for that may have been because of the importance the Anglo-Saxons placed on their language. Being able to speak Old English well, that is, without sounding like a Briton, was important for social status. The Anglo-Saxons were convinced that they were better than the native Britons, and speaking Old English was thus a mark of "superior" ethnicity. This hierarchy then encouraged native Britons to learn how to speak Old English just as the Anglo-Saxons did as a way to increase their social status, which helped to ensure the spread and dominance of the language.

Old English is also something that differentiated the Anglo-Saxons from the Germanic tribes on the continent. Although Old English is in the West Germanic group of languages, it emerged sometime around the 5th century on the isle of Britain, indicating that rather than simply being immigrants, the Anglo-Saxons were their own group of people fairly early on in the Middle Ages.

There was more than just their language that made the Anglo-Saxon culture unique. The Anglo-Saxons valued kin and family highly, and it had a great impact on their customs. For example, your family was responsible for avenging your death rather than the law. This practice got so out of hand that a system called the *wergild* had to be established. The *wergild* set a price on a person's life, which would then be the fine the guilty party had to pay if they killed or injured that person.

This system of using blood money to halt a constant cycle of revenge killings shows us a lot about the Anglo-Saxons. While they were a people who valued warfare and honor, the realities of how this played out were often complex. Anglo-Saxon values might make it important that you avenge your kin, but such practices were too chaotic to endure for long, so the *wergild* was established. Another example of the strain in Anglo-Saxon values and life can be found in their conversion to Christianity. The Anglo-Saxons clearly believed in the idea of revenge, but Christianity has a clear "turn the other cheek" doctrine. To get around this, some Anglo-Saxons would delay their conversion to Christianity until after they had dealt with a past grievance. After most of their society had converted, the Anglo-Saxons maintained a strange union between a society that valued kin and honor and a religion that valued humility. They were a society that produced poems about both religious piety and battles.

Although we may find it hard to understand, Anglo-Saxon society flourished despite these apparent contradictions. It simply shows that whatever we may know about the Anglo-Saxons on paper, the realities of their culture were far more nuanced and complex than we often give them credit for.

What Happened to the Anglo-Saxons?

The Anglo-Saxons were doing fairly well in England, but, as we already know, that didn't last. In 1066, the Normans conquered England. So, why is it that it's still England (the land of the Angles) today? What exactly happened to the Anglo-Saxons after the Norman Conquest?

The Norman Conquest did bring about large changes in Anglo-Saxon society. It was at this point that the language mutated into what we call Middle English, and even then, it did not have the same status as it once did, with French and Latin being the languages that signaled elite status. Speaking of the elite, the Anglo-Saxon nobles were almost entirely replaced by Normans, and the government systems and structures were also altered under Norman influence. England would never be the same after the conquest.

However, that is not to say that the Anglo-Saxon influence was completely wiped out. Although the elites may have turned to other languages, most people still spoke English, and that language has persisted in England and indeed has gained traction in many parts of the world thanks to British colonialism. Also, many of the modern towns and ports in England have their origin in the Anglo-Saxon period. There can be no doubt that the Anglo-Saxons are the people who first formed England, and in that respect, their influence continues to be felt to this day.

Chapter 5: Societal Structure

When you think about society in medieval England, you likely picture something resembling feudalism. A lord owned the land and had peasants that worked it and paid homage to him in exchange for small plots of their own where they could grow food for subsistence. This lord who ruled over the peasants was, in turn, under the king and had to supply knights and other things to the king when required. It was a basic social pyramid, with the king on top and the majority of the population sitting on the bottom.

While that is a fairly accurate picture of how feudalism worked in medieval England, the societal structure in this period was a bit more complicated than that. For around the first five hundred years of this time period (from 600 to 1066), England technically wasn't a feudal society, and even when they did become one, England did have some free peasants, which means not everyone fit as cleanly into that social pyramid as we might think. Also, as we have seen from the numerous revolts and internal fighting throughout this period, feudalism caused problems and needed to be reformed.

So, there is a bit more going on in medieval English society than just the King → Lord → Peasant structure. The eight-hundred-year period did not have a single stagnant society but a developing and changing one.

Before Feudalism

We often think of feudalism as a primitive form of society, and while that may be true in some ways, it also gives us the wrong idea about where feudalism comes from. Feudalism is not the default setting of society. Other social structures existed before it. In England specifically, it was not until the Norman Conquest that England adopted a fully feudal system, so what was society like under the Anglo-Saxons in the Early Middle Ages?

The Anglo-Saxons started as a tribal society. Instead of large kingdoms, they were divided into many smaller tribes that were constantly fighting since warfare was quite profitable. Conquering your neighbors gave you not only access to all their stuff but also to slaves, who could then be sold or used for free labor. Through this system, larger and more powerful tribes began to emerge. And the bigger a tribe got, the more defined the social hierarchy became.

How does that work? Imagine a king in charge of a group of one hundred people. He only gets tribute from those one hundred people, and he doesn't have a large enough force to win many battles. His wealth, therefore, probably does not differ too much from the people he rules over. Sure, he is still in charge, but his house, clothing, and other stuff look about the same as everyone else's. In other words, the gap between the top and bottom of society is very narrow. Now, picture a king ruling over five thousand people. Not only is he getting more tribute, but he also has a much bigger force to win battles with and acquire even more wealth. This king's clothing, living quarters, etc., will probably start to reflect the wealth he has gathered. The gap between the top rung and bottom rung of the social ladder is widening.

This change does not just affect the king. The wealth reaches other people too, and we begin to see the emergence of the elites. However, we are still a long way off from the feudal system. As social hierarchies became more defined in Anglo-Saxon society, the practice of paying tribute became much more organized. Manors, which were the estates of these elite, collected tribute from the peasants in the surrounding area. As kings and *thegns* (nobles) alike realized that staying put and collecting tribute might be more stable and profitable than constant warfare, the kingdoms of the Anglo-Saxon Heptarchy emerged. The development of these kingdoms with manors and nobles had already begun on the continent, so it did not take long for them to become established in England.

At this point, you might be thinking that this sounds an awful lot like feudalism. Why isn't this considered feudalism? The Kingdom of Mercia provides a good illustration of why this system of the Anglo-Saxons, though feudal-like, was not quite feudalism yet. Until the rise of Wessex, which came with the Viking raids, Mercia was the most dominant of the

Anglo-Saxon kingdoms. In the 8th century, the Mercian kings controlled large swaths of territory, but their control was not of the sort that the Wessex dynasty established over England in the 10th century. Mercian kings conquered areas and turned them into client kingdoms. These kingdoms had to pay homage to Mercia in the form of tribute, but that was pretty much where the control stopped. The kingdoms kept their kings, laws, and customs. The Mercian kings were collecting tribute, but they were not "ruling" these territories. The feudal structure of the Normans would bring a lot more direct control.

Feudalism in Medieval England

It was the Norman Conquest in 1066 that fully introduced feudalism to England, but English feudalism was not exactly like that on the continent. As a conquering king, William I was in a position with a lot of power, and he used that power to strengthen the position of the king.

William created a chain through which the king owned all the land. The king gave the land to the lords, who then divided and subdivided it until it reached the bottom rung of the ladder with villeins, who were people that held small areas of land in exchange for their labor. The goal of this system was to ensure that everyone was ultimately loyal to the king.

This feudal chain was unique to England. In other feudal systems of the time, vassals only owed allegiance to their direct lord and not the king. William I's incredibly strong position after conquering England allowed him to partially invent this new system, which had the potential to give the monarchy substantially more power. The key word here is "potential" because this system essentially ensured loyalty to the king on paper. It would take a strong king to make that loyalty a reality.

These changes worked their way down to the peasantry as the new Norman barons reorganized their fiefs. Interestingly, this period saw a decrease in slavery in England, which, although it may have been in part due to efforts of the church, had a far less altruistic reason. The Norman barons were often absentee landlords. Many of them owned land on both sides of the Channel, and they preferred to receive their profits from the English holdings in the form of cash. It was, therefore, more beneficial for them to split their land among peasants who would work it and then pay them a tribute than to own slaves.

While slavery decreased, that did not mean that the lower classes were getting freer. The number of free peasants also decreased during this time, as land reorganization and the new feudal system increased the number of villeins. Villeins were not slaves, but they were classified as unfree. They rented land from a lord and, in exchange, worked part of the lord's land as well as their own. They also often had to pay their lord fees for various things, such as marrying one of their daughters off.

Men harvesting wheat
https://commons.wikimedia.org/wiki/File:Reeve_and_Serfs.jpg

Villeins had very few legal rights. They were unable to leave the land and unable to take legal action against their lord concerning the land. However, at this time, being a villein also brought with it a certain level of stability. Lords rarely kicked villeins off their land since they needed them for work, which offered some protection from the instability of farming. Also in this agricultural society, having access to land meant having access to food you could grow. If you didn't want to starve to death, it was better to be a villein than a free peasant with no land.

The People of Medieval England

Feudalism was the basic social structure of medieval England, but there was more to overall society than just the lords who owned the land and the peasants who worked it. There were, at its most basic, four types of people: peasants (the laborers), knights (the fighters), nobles (the administrators), and clergy (the prayers).

The peasants by far comprised the majority of the population. Although many of them worked as villeins or tenants on a lord's estate, there were also, though very few, peasants rich enough to own their own land. Many of them had holdings that were too small to feed their families and also offered their labor to nearby lords or better-off neighbors to earn the necessary income. Even if you did own your own land, if you were a peasant, there was a high chance that you spent some of your time working someone else's land. Still, farming was not the only occupation. Even though this was a primarily agricultural society, not everyone was a farmer. There were towns, which meant that there were craftsmen and traders. These skilled workers were a bit higher up the social chain than the peasants who worked the land, but they were still part of the working majority. Their labor just happened to not be farming.

As you can probably guess, these were the people that kept England running. The peasants were the ones growing the food and producing various goods, and their lives were centered around whatever job they performed. Villeins and rural peasants farmed their whole lives, and craftsmen became fully devoted to their trade from an early age. As this was the overwhelming majority of the population, your lot in life could vary wildly as a peasant. You might own enough land to feed your family comfortably. You might be barely scraping by and die of starvation during a bad year. You might be a blacksmith with a small shop in a town. You might find yourself under a lord who treated you horribly. You might work the land of a lord you would never see. There were a lot of possibilities, but wherever you were, you spent your whole life working, and most likely, you were working for someone else.

Besides a need for lots of labor, England in the Middle Ages also needed fighters. Enter the symbol of the medieval period: the knight. But were knights really what we picture them to be now? Heroes riding around in plate armor, defending damsels, fighting in crusades, and talking about chivalry? For the most part, no. In terms of social standing, knights were lesser nobles who held land under the more powerful magnates like barons. In exchange for the land, they provided military services for their lord and the king.

Thus, most knights were the medieval period's small-time landlords. Don't be too disappointed, though! They did do a lot of fighting. There was the Hundred Years' War with France and multiple crusades, which gave knights plenty of opportunities to make a name for themselves. But as for simply riding around the country doing chivalrous deeds? Knights didn't do that, and during the numerous internal conflicts that England suffered during this period, knights often ended up being the ones terrorizing rather than protecting the local population.

Now we have reached the top of the social hierarchy: the nobles. Technically, knights were nobles as well because they held a title, but we are focusing on the bigger nobles: the barons, earls, and even the king—the men who controlled England. These magnates controlled huge swaths of land. They divided this land among lesser nobles like the knights, who they could then command. They ran the judicial system and oversaw the protection of the realm. They granted positions and gave land to people under them. In other words, these were the administrators who ran England.

Based on the simple pyramid structure, you would think that the king would be the most powerful of these men. Although William the Conqueror designed the system so the king would wield the most power, this was not always the case. The First and Second Barons' Wars were clear proof that the magnates felt that they should and could keep the king in line. By the end of the Middle Ages, Parliament could refuse to grant the king funds for war, which was a major check on royal power. Even though nominally the king was at the very top of the hierarchy in medieval society, his ability to act as the top was often challenged by those immediately under him. The feudal system that William the Conqueror had created frequently did not work in practice as it did on paper.

The final class of people in England was the clergy. The clergy was definitely toward the top of the social hierarchy, but just how high depended on what position they held. The archbishops of Canterbury and York, as well as the bishop of London, were often amongst the most powerful men in the nation. Besides these individuals, the church as a whole played a significant role in English society. Monasteries and bishops often controlled land and employed peasants to work it just as nobles did. The bishops in any town were a huge part of the normal processes of life, playing a role in births, deaths, baptisms, and marriages. We will discuss the role of the clergy more extensively in the chapters on faith and the church, but at this point, suffice it to say that the clergy was a vital and powerful group in the social make-up of England.

Changing Structure

The feudal system was a hallmark of the medieval period, but by 1485, things were evolving. The Black Death had killed so many people that it caused massive labor shortages, and for the first time, peasants could demand more for their labor. The Peasants' Revolt of 1381 is clear evidence of a world that was beginning to change, with the bottom of the social hierarchy pushing the top for the first time. The Renaissance era would see more and more growth in the urban population, and the social structure that relied so heavily on the peasants farming the lord's land would slowly disappear with the rise of industries and the middle class.

These changes took a long time, and some of England's early social structure survived. The monarchy would continue to be the effective head of the government until the very end of the 18th century. The nobility is still around in England today, though they do not hold the power they once did. England has undergone many eras of reform, but its social hierarchy still exists. Some things from the medieval era have proved to be longer lasting than others.

Chapter 6: Status of Women

You can probably already guess that women in the Middle Ages had fewer rights than their male counterparts. After all, women didn't even get equal voting rights in England until 1928, so it shouldn't come as a surprise that around a thousand years before that, there was some sexism present in the English system.

The better question then is what form did this take? Did women have absolutely no rights in the Middle Ages? What was their status under the law? What options did women have in the course of their life, if any? While it's accurate to say that women had fewer rights in the Middle Ages, there is a little more going on for the female half of the population than that for these eight hundred years of English history. Here's what it was like to be a woman in medieval England.

Eve vs. Mary

Perhaps the best way to capture the somewhat paradoxical view of women in this period is to look at two religious figures: Eve and Mary. Both of these women from the Bible had a large place in the religious understanding of the day, and that translated into how this society viewed women in general.

In the Christian account of the original sin, the serpent tempts Eve to eat the fruit from the forbidden tree. Eve eats it and convinces Adam to do likewise, causing the couple to be expelled from paradise and the overall fall of man. The medieval church saw Eve as the primary guilty party in this narrative. She was the one who had fallen first, and she dragged Adam down with her. Thus, women were not only more prone to sin, but they were also temptresses who would pull men into sin with them.

Whatever your personal religious views, you must remember that in the medieval period, the church was a powerful social institution. This view of Eve had a major impact on the way society viewed women. Because women were more likely to sin, they were regulated to an inferior position in society. Men needed to have authority over women because women could not be trusted.

This understanding of Eve goes a long way in explaining how the inferior status of women was justified in the Middle Ages. However, there was a bit more complexity to medieval attitudes toward women. Besides Eve, there was another female figure that was important to the medieval church, and this one had a much more positive reputation.

As the Middle Ages progressed, Mary, the mother of Christ, became increasingly important to the church. She was venerated as one of the most important saints. Eve had been the source of original sin, but Mary was the source of salvation since she gave birth to Jesus Christ. Women were paradoxically both responsible for the fall and the redemption of mankind.

The two contrasting characters of Eve and Mary pushed women into two extremes. Women were either temptresses or saints. Unfortunately, the result of these two opposing roles was that women couldn't win either way. They were condemned, either for being morally weak like Eve or when they failed to live up to the virginal perfection that Mary represented. Both the extremely high and extremely low standards placed women in a tough position, and it meant that throughout the Middle Ages, women were consistently seen as inferior.

The Role of Women in Society

Although women were viewed as inferior, this underlying assumption did not play out in medieval society the way we might expect. Due to the more recent practices of the 19th and 20th centuries, we tend to think of sexism as restricting women to the role of homemakers. Progress was when women were finally allowed to join the workforce and leave the home.

The idea that women should not work was not that prevalent in the Middle Ages. As we discussed in the last chapter, the majority of the English population at this time were laborers, and the women worked just as hard as the men. Wives and daughters worked alongside their husbands and fathers in the fields. Even as towns grew and more people turned to trades rather than farming, women continued to hold a fairly equal position in the type of work that they did. Women did the same jobs as men. The workforce did not have the gender segregation that we now see as a mark of sexual inequality.

That is not to say that there were not tasks that were more often given to women. Women at all levels of society were responsible for tending their households, and images of this time commonly depict a peasant woman with a distaff, which was a tool used for spinning wool. However, while there were duties that tended to fall to the women, there was not a strict restriction on what work women could do. Making a living and feeding your family was hard, and women were expected to contribute wherever they could.

Noblewomen also played a greater role in medieval society than you might initially think. They were responsible for their households just as peasant women were, and the larger size and political aspect of a noble household often meant that these duties were quite extensive. Noblewomen could be witnesses for legal documents, oversaw estates in their husband's absence, acted as patrons, and could even become involved in warfare, particularly during England's internal conflicts. While they legally had few rights and were officially labeled as lesser, women still did quite a bit in medieval society.

Marriage vs. Nunnery

While they might have been working alongside the men, women were still extremely limited in what they could do, and one way we see this is in the number of options a girl in medieval society had. There were basically two. If you were born a girl in the Middle Ages, you could either get married and work for your husband and family or become a nun.

Let's start with the second. What would being a nun mean for a woman in the Middle Ages? First of all, there were technically two religious paths a woman could take: nun or anchoress. Nuns lived in monasteries, while anchoresses lived on their own (kind of like female hermits) or in small groups. Both involved a life devoted to religious purposes and a vow of chastity.

Contrary to popular belief, being a nun did not necessarily mean being around only women for the rest of your life. There were double monasteries that housed both men and women. These double monasteries were run by an abbess and were thus one of the only places in medieval society where a woman could hold a position over a man. These double monasteries often played a significant role in culture and politics, so abbesses could wield a good deal of influence both within and outside their monasteries, especially in the Early Middle Ages. As the medieval period progressed, double monasteries became less common, and the church increasingly sought to isolate religious women for the sake of purity. Even so, completely separating nuns from men was never really possible. Priests had to tend to the nun's spiritual needs, nuns had to conduct business with their local communities, and workmen and servants had to occasionally enter the nunneries.

The life of a nun also wasn't truly open to everyone. Nuns typically came from families with at least a certain amount of wealth since girls had to pay dowries and often bring a few necessary items, such as bedding, when entering a nunnery. Although this was naturally exclusive, these payments and other gifts were what allowed nunneries to function. So, if your family had enough money, a life of religious devotion was the only alternative to marriage that women had at this time, and many chose this life out of a desire to avoid marriage.

The vast majority of women, however, went with the first option: marriage. As you might have guessed, marriage in this period was not based on love matches. Women rarely got to pick their partners (to be fair, men also didn't get much of a say). Marriages were arranged by parents, other kin, or even lords, and they were a business transaction as much as a personal agreement. Women in this period could own land, which meant that marriage was often deeply steeped in concerns about property. When a woman married, her legal identity became part of her husband's, so whatever land she had would belong to her husband. Even those in the lower classes, where there was little concern about property, could not marry freely. Tenants needed approval from their lord to marry. Almost any marriage in the medieval period had to be approved by those other than the couple involved. It wasn't until the 12th century and reforms were headed by the church that emphasis began to be placed on the consent of the couple.

What did marriage mean for a woman? Women were to obey their husbands. The work they did and the role they played were determined by their husbands. This subservient role and the fact that marriages were arranged often cause us to assume that many marriages were unhappy at best and abusive at worst, but that was often not the case. If for nothing more than practical reasons, a husband and wife greatly benefited from forming a working partnership. Trying to survive on your own was very difficult in this period, so a relationship of mutual trust and reliance was preferable. That's not to say that abuses of this system didn't happen because the system itself did little to protect women, but it would also be a mistake to think that every married woman was miserable. Marriage was a fact of life for virtually everyone, and most people likely chose to make the most of it.

Till Death Do Us Part

With marriage or religious devotion being the only option for women, there was a group that naturally did not fit well into this system: widows. Widows occupied a peculiar position in medieval society. Before marriage, a woman was under the control of her father. After getting married, she was under her husband, but as a widow, she was in her own power. Widows had the legal status of *femme sole*. Rather than being folded into a man's legal identity, a *femme sole* was a woman with her own legal identity. She could own land, run a business, and make her own decisions.

That did not mean that being a widow was the secret desire of every woman, for the position had a lot of complications. Upon the death of her husband, a new widow would need to secure her dower—her share of her husband's estate typically arranged at the time of marriage—and also make arrangements for the guardianship of her children. If there were any complications, the cases to sort these aspects out could become long and complicated. For much of the medieval period, though, a widow would often maintain control of a significant part of her husband's lands or business.

Even after settling these things, widows faced the looming prospect of remarriage. As a *femme sole*, a widow had the right to choose her next husband, but there was certainly pressure from family and, in some cases, the king himself depending on the property and titles that a widow held. It did happen that widows were sometimes forced to remarry. Kings used marriages to widows as a way to bestow lands and titles on their favorites. Ironically, if a woman was rich and did not need to remarry to secure herself financially, she would likely face pressure to remarry. If a woman was poor with many children and needed to remarry for security, it would often be more difficult to find a match. If a woman chose not to remarry, she was able to run her own property and finances. It was perhaps for this reason that many women remained widows for the majority of their lives.

The rights of widows decreased over time, as new laws and customs saw inheritance settled more and more often on solely the male heirs. By the Victorian period, widows held a lesser social position than they had in the Middle Ages.

Powerful Women of the Middle Ages

Because women were viewed as inferior, they rarely held real political power, but even so, history also tends to overlook the role that some women played in shaping the Middle Ages. Here are some of the women that left a mark on medieval England:

- **St. Hild of Whitby** - St. Hild, also called Hilda, was the founder and abbess of Whitby, a double monastery with both men and women. Hild was famous for the ordered way she ran the monastery. Under her leadership, Whitby produced several bishops and even a famous poet. She was well-respected and had considerable influence, as seen by Whitby hosting the Synod of Whitby, an important early church conference, in 664.

- **Æthelflæd** - Æthelflæd was the daughter of Alfred the Great, King of Wessex and later King of the Anglo-Saxons. She married the king of Mercia when she was sixteen, and while her husband was struggling with poor health, she led the Mercians in their efforts to drive back the Vikings. When her husband died in 911, Æthelflæd became the Lady of the Mercians. She ruled Mercia alone for seven years, during which time she allied with her brother, the king of the Anglo-Saxons, in continuing to push the Vikings out of England until she died in 918.

- **Empress Matilda** - The daughter of Henry I, Matilda fought her cousin Stephen of Blois for the English throne for eighteen years, causing the English civil war known as the Anarchy. Although she never successfully ousted her cousin, Matilda controlled large areas of England during the Anarchy, and she eventually left more because of a stalemate rather than defeat.

- **Eleanor of Aquitaine** - Eleanor was not only a powerful woman in England; she was perhaps the most powerful woman in 12th-century Europe. She was married to the king of France for fifteen years, and after that marriage was annulled, she married Henry Plantagenet, who became Henry II of England. As the queen of

England, Eleanor played a large role in politics. She aided her sons in their rebellions against their father, and when her son Richard became king, she was one of the main people running England while the king was gone on his crusade. After Richard's death, she continued to aid her next son, John, as king, playing a role in several English military victories on the continent. Eleanor of Aquitaine was the wife of two kings, mother to two more, and she wielded significant influence and power with all of them.

- **Isabella of France -** Queen Isabella was married to King Edward II and earned the nickname the She-Wolf of France for her treatment of her husband. In 1326, she joined forces with her lover, Roger Mortimer, against her husband and helped to overthrow Edward II in 1327. Isabella and Roger Mortimer effectively ruled England for the next three years until her son Edward III had Mortimer killed. Isabella eventually retired to a nunnery.

- **Margaret of Anjou -** Margaret of Anjou was married to Henry VI and was one of the leaders of the Lancastrian forces in the Wars of the Roses. With Henry VI being a rather weak king at the best of times, Margaret was the main driver of royal interests during the conflict. She relentlessly tried to secure the kingship for her son but was ultimately defeated by Edward IV at the Battle of Tewkesbury.

These women are clear examples that men were not the only ones involved in the bloody power struggles of the Middle Ages. Queens did not always follow their kings. Still, although these women held great influence, they were connected to this influence through the men in their lives. Women in the Middle Ages worked alongside men, but they remained inferior in the eyes of both society and the law.

Chapter 7: Food, Clothes, Work, and Entertainment

Learning about the medieval period through major events like wars is fascinating, but it does leave us rather unclear on what daily life in the Middle Ages was actually like. What did they eat? What did they wear? What holidays did they celebrate? What was there to do in medieval England?

With around eight hundred years of history to cover, we cannot hope to tackle everything about daily life in the Middle Ages. That would take a whole book on its own! However, we will look at some of the more interesting tidbits about food, clothing, work, and entertainment in medieval England.

Food

Food is both something that we all need and something that can mark our differences. Not only is food an indicator of our culture, but it can also be an indicator of our social class, and in medieval England, this was especially true. The table of a lord and the table of a peasant looked very different.

Perhaps the most notable difference was meat. While lords would eat meat with almost every meal, meat was a luxury for peasants. Even though there were forests with deer, rabbits, and other animals for hunting, as well as rivers and other bodies of water with fish, peasants were not allowed to access this food source. Hunting was for the nobles. If a peasant was caught hunting in the lord's forest or fishing in the lord's pond, they would likely lose a hand. That was too high a price for a side of meat to go with your dinner.

Livestock was also not the abundant source of meat that you might think. Maintaining animals was expensive, and a cow was worth far more as a producer of milk than as a side of beef. Also, cheese and other dairy products made up a large portion of the peasant diet, so cows were more valued as dairy animals rather than sources of meat. The only animal that peasants regularly raised for meat were pigs. Pigs had little trouble taking care of themselves. They could find enough food to keep themselves alive with their foraging, so they were a food source that did not drain more resources than they were worth. Pork was thus the meat of choice for many peasants, but they were not able to enjoy it often. Those who lived close enough to the sea were also able to add more fish to their diet.

The freshness of meat was another marker of social class. Because the lords had regular access to it, they frequently enjoyed fresh game and fish. On the other hand, almost everything peasants ate was preserved. The meat they ate was typically salted or pickled.

There were other differences in what the poor and rich ate. While bread was a staple for everyone, the type of bread you ate depended on your wealth. White bread was made from wheat, which was much more difficult to grow and was thus typically only enjoyed by the upper classes. The majority of people ate darker bread made from rye and barley. When harvests were bad, peasants might also have to add other ingredients to make their bread, such as acorns.

Besides bread, another food that almost everyone in medieval England ate was pottage. Pottage is a thick stew that can contain a wide variety of different ingredients ranging from meat to vegetables and cereals. Like bread, the quality of the ingredients in a pottage varied between classes.

You might be thinking that with all of this bread and pottage, people were typically drinking water, but that was not the case. While sources of fresh water were fairly abundant, that water was also very dirty. Drinking water from your local river could easily make you sick. Although there was milk to drink if you had a cow, the drink of choice for most people was ale. Lords would have had access to wine as well.

So, if you were a peasant in the Middle Ages, you probably ate bread, cheese, and whatever vegetables you could manage to grow. If you did get to eat meat, it was probably pork or maybe mutton, and you likely drank ale that you made yourself. Lords had access to fresh meat and fish and higher quality bread, ale, and even wine. The wealthy also enjoyed access to various imported spices and dried fruits. However, it was at a banquet that the upper classes really showed off what their wealth meant in terms of food. A medieval banquet included normal dishes like stews and pies alongside exotic dishes like peacock and porpoise. There were also massive sculptures made out of sugar. These banquets were extravagant and showed just what the upper classes had access to in the Middle Ages, but even when they weren't hosting a banquet, the meals of the rich could still have ten courses. If you were poor or even just average, you had to rely mostly on the food you grew and preserved yourself, but if you were rich, your food would be fresh, covered in imported spices, and sometimes even sculpted.

Clothing

The differences in what people ate were a clear marker of social class, but what about what they wore? Even today, clothing choices can tell us a lot about someone's personality and place in society.

Surprisingly, the clothing style of nobles and peasants in medieval England did not differ drastically. Everyone wore the same basic styles and designs. What differentiated noble clothing was not the type of clothes but the materials used and the cut. While peasants' clothing was typically made out of wool, of which England had an abundance, nobles might also have had silk outfits. Nobles' clothing could also have furs and expensive decorative items like pearls and gems. In terms of cut, noble clothing tended to be overall better made with a finer and more fitting cut. In medieval times, it was likely that people were easily able to distinguish between the clothing of a noble and a peasant in the same way that we can tell the difference between a man's and a woman's running shoe today, even though their basic designs are the same. Clothing was still a sign of social class, but fashion did not differ as much across society as you might think.

Even more surprising than the similarities in clothing between peasants and nobles was the similarities between men and women. Although there were differences in style between the sexes, men and women wore the same basic garments. You could still tell the difference, but we are a long way off from the men wearing pants and women wearing dresses dynamic that came to dominate fashion for so long.

So, just what was everyone wearing? The main medieval garment was the tunic. Tunics were basically long shirts, often gathered at the waist with a belt. They tended to be a single color and had long sleeves. Men's tunics typically went to the knee, so they would wear hose or leggings underneath them. Women's tunics went all the way to the ankle. The exact style of tunics evolved over the medieval period. Tunics began as loose-fitting garments, but over time, they became much more close-fitting. The style of sleeves varied during the period as well, from close-fitting sleeves to sleeves with long cuffs, sleeves that were loose around the upper arm and then tightened, and more. Men's tunics also got progressively shorter over the Middle Ages.

Medieval clothing was all about layers, though. People typically wore a linen shirt under their tunics, or they might wear two tunics at once, with one acting like an undergarment. When they were outside, which was a good bit of the time for most people, a cloak or coat was added to the outfit. Cloaks were simply shaped pieces of cloth fastened at the shoulder with a brooch or chain. They could even be knotted. Like cloaks, coats were long, reaching well past a person's knees.

Besides tunics, another piece of medieval garb that everyone wore was hats. You did not walk around with a bare head in medieval England. Even indoors, both men and women wore hats. The basic headgear for women was called a wimple. It was a large piece of, usually white, cloth that wrapped over the head and under the chin, covering the hair and neck. A veil or hat might also be added to the wimple, especially when going out. Men wore close-fitting linen caps called coifs as their indoor head coverings. Like women, they would wear additional hats on top of this piece when going out or dressing up.

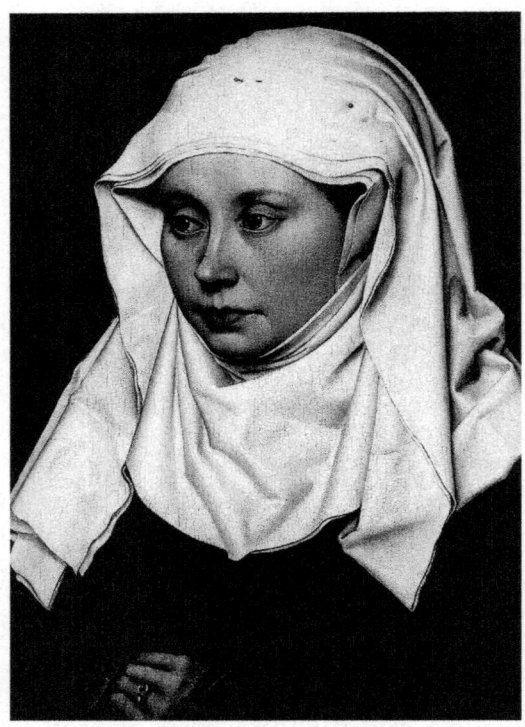

Portrait of a Woman by Robert Campin (shows a medieval woman in a wimple)
https://commons.wikimedia.org/wiki/File:RCampin.jpg

Speaking of dressing up, how fancy did medieval clothing get? Did they add decorations and embellishments to their outfits? Like us today, medieval people found ways to make their basic clothes more exciting, but overall, they kept things pretty simple. Embroidery might be used to decorate a tunic, but it was typically restricted to just around the cuffs, neckline, and maybe the hem. It would have been very rare to see a tunic covered from neck to hem in embroidery. Fur might also be used as a trimming for both warmth and decoration. That didn't mean that their tunics were boring, though! Bright colors, such as blue, red, green, and yellow, were standard, and there were elements like fringes, tassels, and even feathers added to give decoration. Belts, brooches, chains, and hats were also places where a person could add precious stones or metals to their outfit, adding style and, more importantly, displaying their wealth.

Although clothing did not differ greatly between the social classes, it was still seen as a very important way to demonstrate rank. There were laws that restricted who could wear what type of materials, and there were even limitations on the imports of fine materials like silk to limit the number of people who had access. The upper classes took steps to ensure that a peasant could not rise above his station with his clothing. The social classes were strictly divided, and there was no way for someone to pretend to be higher on the ladder than they really were.

Work

Now that we have a better idea of what people ate and what they wore, what did they do? In medieval England, the majority of people spent most of their time working.

There were two general types of jobs that a peasant could have: farmer or craftsman. Most people were farmers, and most of these farmers lived as tenants on lands owned by a lord. They were responsible not only for growing their own food but also for growing the lord's food as well. Some of the more well-off farmers owned their own land, and you could rent yourself out as a laborer to earn extra when times were hard.

Being a craftsman was the other option for a peasant, although they were a bit higher up the social ladder than the farmers. Craftsmen lived in towns or cities and produced particular goods. Examples of craftsmen would be a stonemason, blacksmith, baker, carpenter, miller, and goldsmith. Craftsmen relied on the upper classes of society since they were the ones who could buy what the craftsmen made. Craftsmen also often banded together in guilds. The guilds controlled entrance into the craft, which allowed them to control the labor supply and prices. It took a long period of study under a master before someone could hope to earn the approval of the guild and enter the craft in their own right.

When it came to exactly what type of job you ended up with in medieval England, there wasn't much choice. If you were a man, you likely ended up with whatever job you were born into (if your father was a farmer, you were probably going to be a farmer), and if you were a woman, you helped your husband. There was not an intense gender division of labor in the peasant classes, so women would work in the fields alongside their husbands and even help run their husbands' businesses in a town.

So, what if you weren't a peasant? Didn't nobles just sit around all day? While nobles certainly did not work nearly as hard as peasants, they did have a role to play in society. Lords were the organizational sector. Their estates produced surplus goods, their courts handled legal business, and their men defended the realm when it was needed. The lord himself likely did not do all of this, but his steward and other staff oversaw the bureaucratic and administrative tasks that were necessary for keeping England running as a whole.

So, when it came to work in medieval England, the bottom line is that everyone had a job to do. In fact, it was illegal to be jobless! In a society where most things, from growing food to making tables to keeping accounts and more, were done by hand, everyone had to work to ensure that society could maintain the necessities of life. This was a world where not having a job and a role would mean starving to death.

Entertainment

All of that talk about the necessity of work is making medieval life seem quite grim and hard. Did they ever have fun? Obviously, the noble classes had plenty of free time to amuse themselves, but let's start with the peasants. If you were a peasant in medieval England, would you ever get a day off or have time for entertainment?

In the Middle Ages, you didn't get vacations, and most people never traveled at all. However, they did celebrate frequent holidays, which they would have called feast days. The feast days in medieval England frequently had pagan origins, but they were tied to the Catholic Church. Besides the ones most of us still celebrate, like Easter, Christmas, and Valentine's Day, there were quite a few more, such as St. Crispin's Day, Michaelmas, All Saints' Day, Candlemas, St. John's Day, and around forty to sixty more. Yes, you read that right. There were as many as sixty holy days (that's where we get the word holiday) in a year.

While many of these feast days were more significant than others, the church insisted that people refrain from working on these holy days. Each day had its own traditions, such as exchanging gifts, and there might be plays and games to celebrate as well. Besides the numerous feast days, people also got Sundays off for the same reason. So, even though work was crucial, peasants in medieval England did not work 365 days a year.

Peasants found ways of entertaining themselves that were not tied to feast days as well. Traveling performers, called troubadours, were popular, especially for the music they provided. Telling stories, singing, and dancing were all ways to spend time. We might often picture the Middle Ages as grim, but the people, like all people, knew how to have a good time.

Of course, if you happened to be wealthy, you did have more opportunities to have a good time. What did the nobles do for entertainment? There was a large variety of options. Like the peasants, nobles celebrated the feast days and also enjoyed a performance by a good entertainer, though those who entertained nobles often held permanent positions at a castle. Minstrels provided music, and jesters were early comedians. These people would usually perform during or after meals, which for nobles could be a form of entertainment themselves with their extensive number of courses and extravagant dishes. Dancing might also follow meals.

When they weren't eating, nobles liked to get in a good bit of exercise. There were many popular outdoor activities, such as hunting, falconry, and tournaments. Hunting at this time was quite the affair. Forests were fiercely protected, and if a noble lacked one of his own, he could pay to hunt on someone else's estates. As we already mentioned, the price was high for peasants who hunted in a nobleman's forest. Falconry was immensely popular in this period, with even women participating in the sport. Tournaments were chances for knights to prove their valor and included jousting and the melee (a mock cavalry battle).

What did nobles do if it was raining then? Rain is not uncommon in England, but there were several ways to pass the time. Games from the East had made their way to England by this time. Chess was perhaps the most popular, but backgammon and dice were also well-loved. Gambling was frequent, but it did not have the negative reputation that it does today.

Knights Templar playing chess
https://commons.wikimedia.org/wiki/File:KnightsTemplarPlayingChess1283.jpg

Overall, there was more to do in the Middle Ages than you might think. They may not have had our modern entertainment options like TV, but they found plenty of ways to entertain themselves with sports, games, music, and more.

In medieval life, the split between the nobles and peasants showed itself in almost every aspect of daily life, from food to clothing and from work to entertainment. While this divide was sharp, we can still see a unified culture in the many shared aspects of daily life like similar clothing styles, feast days, bread, and more.

Chapter 8: Art and Architecture

When it comes to the medieval period, most of our attention is spent dwelling on the knights on horseback, castles, and kings, but medieval society, just like modern society, had many aspects. It may have been a more violent time in general, but the Middle Ages did find time to make a pretty hefty contribution to the world of English art.

It's pretty hard to make a living today as an artist, so how would it have been possible in the Middle Ages? Not only can you not sell records of your latest ballad or copies of your newest book to make ends meet, but it was also incredibly difficult to make art a serious side gig. Peasants were far too busy with the amount of work necessary to simply survive to be composing great epics in their spare time, yet somehow art still existed in the Middle Ages. How?

There are a few things you need to know about art in the medieval period to understand how this was possible. Perhaps most important was that art tended to have a practical purpose. The Anglo-Saxons made many beautiful things, but those things were also usually functional. Instead of using their sculpting skills to carve a statue, an Anglo-Saxon would probably use them to decorate a buckle, shield, or brooch. Even their function as status symbols was practical since it helped families to position themselves within the social hierarchy. As we progress through the Middle Ages, artistic objects get less obviously functional, but they often still have a practical purpose. For instance, much artistic skill was devoted to making religious items. The grandest architecture of the day is displayed in churches, which were buildings that served as both centers of local life and whose purpose made more elaborate designs appropriate. Even an item like the Bayeux Tapestry was politically functional, as it allowed the Normans to immortalize their version of the events surrounding the Norman Conquest. In all, art in this period rarely existed for art's sake. Whether religious or political or purely practical, art was mixed into many other aspects of medieval life. It was because of these other functions that art was able to flourish as much as it did during the Middle Ages.

Two other things in medieval life made art possible: monasteries and patrons. Monasteries were one of the only places a person could devote themselves to something other than manual labor. This did not mean that every monk or nun was a poet, but it did mean that the poets and historians that did exist, especially in early medieval England, often owed their careers to the support of a monastery. As the Middle Ages progressed and monasteries became less common and played less of a vital role in medieval life, patronage became another avenue through which an artist might find support. Patrons were wealthy benefactors, often aristocrats or clergy, who gave monetary and other support to an artist. Such support was the only way an artist could pursue their work and also not starve to death. The patronage system of supporting the arts gained increasing importance through the Renaissance and Victorian periods, but it had its start in the medieval era.

So, artists in the Middle Ages were not lone creators trying to convince the world of their genius. They had to have outside support, and their work often served several different roles in society. Let's look closer at various kinds of art in the Middle Ages.

Literature

In a time with high illiteracy and little leisure time, the written word did not have the same centrality that it does now, and what did exist differed greatly from what we now think of when we hear the word literature.

Perhaps the biggest difference between literature in medieval times and today was the lack of the novel. The first English novels did not appear until the 18th century. In the Middle Ages, poetry was far more popular than prose. Although prose was beginning to make headway by the end of the Middle Ages, it would be another few hundred years before the novel first appeared.

Why was poetry so much more popular? Remember that most of the population was illiterate. Books and stories were not written to be privately read but to be performed and read publicly. The earliest form of English literature was oral stories, like *Beowulf*, which were only written down at a later date. The cadence of poetry has two major advantages in such a setting. It sounds better, and the rhythm makes it easier to memorize.

What was all this poetry about, though? It may have all been in verse, but there were several different genres. Epics like *Beowulf* told stories about heroes facing monsters. Pieces like the *Battle of Maldon* took inspiration from real-life events, in this case, turning a military defeat into something heroic. Medieval romances contained tales of knights, chivalry, magic, damsels in distress, and love. The dream vision genre, like Chaucer's *Book of the Duchess*, had the narrator relating a dream that helped them to deal with a difficult event, such as the death of a loved one. There were also simply tales, such as Chaucer's *The Canterbury Tales*, most of which are written in verse with a few in prose. Fables told moral tales of anthropomorphic animals. Medieval England may not have had novels, but the people still had quite a bit of variety in their stories.

Drama also existed at this time, although it was nothing like what Shakespeare would write in the Elizabethan era. There were three types, and they were all religious. Mystery plays depicted important events from the Bible, such as creation. Miracle plays focused on the lives of saints, both real and fictitious. Morality plays were allegorical plays designed to teach a particular life lesson. The characters in morality plays were personifications of abstract concepts like death and charity. Together, all of these types of plays were designed to instruct the populace on proper godly living.

There was also nonfiction, which made up a large portion of medieval literature. Some of the surviving nonfiction works have become extremely important resources for what we know about the Middle Ages. Historians still quote and use books like the Domesday Book, the *Anglo-Saxon Chronicle*, and the *Ecclesiastical History of the English People*. Still, these historical pieces can also be quite frustrating because they sometimes seem to value telling a good story more than being accurate. Myths were often used to fill in the gaps in a historical account, with fact and fiction blending in a way that would make most writers today quite uncomfortable. For instance, Geoffrey of Monmouth's *The History of the Kings of Britain*, which contains the Arthurian legend, is written as though it was history even though it is mostly imagined.

Far more prominent than the historical writings were the religious works. Most of the people who were able to write were either monks or clergy, so theology was a very popular subject. For instance, Anselm, who was the archbishop of Canterbury from 1093 to 1109, wrote more than a dozen books on theology. Besides treatises, which were philosophical works examining and developing theology, there were also works written about the lives of saints and a large variety of hymns.

All in all, there was much variety in the literature of medieval England. There were romances, fables, epics, histories, allegories, philosophy, and more. Still, however much variety there was, the overwhelming majority of writing produced was religious in some way. While this may seem strange to us, we must remember that few people in the Middle Ages were educated, and the majority of those who were educated had received that education from the church. The amount of religious work, therefore, makes sense. When the majority of the writers are either monks or clergy, it is only natural that the majority of what they write would have a religious bent.

Architecture

Speaking of the church, medieval architecture in church buildings is one place where the full artistic capability of medieval England is on display. Medieval architecture may conjure up images of thatched roofs and blocky stone castles, but the buildings of this period could be truly magnificent. England saw the influence of several different architectural styles during the Middle Ages and also managed to develop some uniquely English styles. The evolution of architecture can most easily be traced in the churches of the medieval period, which was where elaborate techniques and designs were most often used.

The dominant architectural style of the Middle Ages was the Norman style. The Norman style was a type of Romanesque architecture that developed in areas controlled by the Normans. The key characteristic of Norman and Romanesque architecture is the semicircular arch. Such arches were used on windows and doors and also to connect columns. Columns, or cylindrical pillars, were another common feature of Norman architecture. The Norman style created huge sweeping spaces filled with pillars and tiers of rounded arches.

The Norman style, with its focus on pillars and arches, left plenty of room for decoration. These large spaces often had plenty of wall space, which were often decorated with murals. Even the pillars and arches themselves were sometimes painted, adding a colorful and ornate feel to the style. Unfortunately, paint tends to not last nearly as long as the stone, so we have very few surviving examples of Norman architecture that was decorated in this way. We have far more of another kind of embellishment that took off around the 12th century. The rounded arches themselves were carved with geometric shapes or figures, and the pillars, too, were often carved at their head in patterns.

Many buildings constructed using the Norman style have since been destroyed or altered, which means little remains of the original architectural style. There are, however, some surviving examples. Durham Cathedral is one such surviving building. The cathedral was built sometime in the late 11th or 12th century. Not only does the cathedral use the characteristic round arches and pillars of Norman architecture, but it also has a stone vault ceiling. The stone vault ceiling of Durham Cathedral is an architectural milestone. Many buildings in England at this time continued to use wood roofs because of the difficulty of creating stone roofs that would support themselves. The large stone vaulted ceiling of Durham Cathedral was a sign of increased architectural know-how and foreshadowed the emergence of the medieval period's other famous architectural style: Gothic.

Gothic architecture began to emerge around the end of the 12th century. It also uses the grand sweeping style of Norman architecture, but the easiest way to spot the difference between the Norman and Gothic architecture styles is the shape of the arches. Norman architecture uses round arches, while Gothic architecture uses pointed arches. Gothic architecture was also a product of increased engineering ability. The style focuses on creating enormous open spaces. This goal created many of the Gothic style's other defining features, such as rib vaults, flying buttresses, and pointed arches, all of which helped to support those tall structures and large high ceilings.

A Gothic-style building

While the Norman style began with painting and then adding carvings to embellish its buildings, the Gothic style is known for the tracery that embellishes its basic forms. Tracery uses bars and ribs of stone across openings, especially windows, or even overlaid on walls (known as blind tracery) to create a decorative effect. Tracery looks a bit like lace made of stone, and it is a large part of why the Gothic style feels so ornate.

With the rise of the Gothic style, many abbeys and churches originally built in the Norman style had Gothic elements added or used the new style when making additions or rebuilding. Although the Gothic style did not quite reach its peak in England as it did in France, there are many stunning examples of Gothic architecture left in England, such as the ruins of Whitby Abbey and the famous octagonal lantern of Ely Cathedral.

As it progressed, the Gothic style in many places got more ornate and flamboyant. England, however, had its own spin on things and developed the perpendicular style in the last two centuries of the Middle Ages. The perpendicular style was uniquely English, and, as the name suggests, it was characterized by an emphasis on vertical lines. Perpendicular churches were tall and filled with light. They included enormous windows that only used narrow tracery to allow in as much light as possible. Many of them also contained angel roofs. Angel roofs were a type of hammerbeam roof, which is where the beams that hold up the roof are stacked so that they support each other without the need for additional support. In angel roofs, these beams are then carved into the figures of angels. Angel roofs are intricately carved, but they sadly get little appreciation today because they are so hard to see. They are found in these tall perpendicular churches, which makes the rich detail and mastery behind them impossible to see with the naked eye.

The angel roofs and perpendicular churches that housed them were the height of English architecture in the Middle Ages. They were incredibly expensive to build and often overly lavish. Villages would build perpendicular churches larger than what the local population needed as a demonstration of piety. The construction of churches was not just about filling a practical need but also, maybe even more so, about displaying religious zeal and devotion. This helps to explain why so much of the medieval period's best architecture is found in religious establishments.

Visual Art

We have seen what the medieval period produced in both books and buildings, but what about what we usually think of when we hear the word art? What about paintings and sculptures and the type of stuff that gets hung in museums? The medieval period had these things but not in the way we picture when we hear the words fine art.

As we mentioned in the introduction to this chapter, art and function were closely tied. The angel roofs of English churches are a prime example of this. These angels are incredible sculptures carved by a master hand, but they are not sitting on a pedestal for everyone to admire. They are carved into the necessary supporting beams that hold the roof of the church. The same can be seen in the murals that decorated many Norman-style churches. These murals were undoubtedly fine pieces of art, but they were also completed with a specific purpose, decorating the empty spaces of the church. Medieval artists did create pieces of great beauty and skill but often with a specific purpose or commission in mind.

Take, for example, the Bayeux Tapestry, which is one of the most famous pieces of medieval English art that has been preserved to this day. The Bayeux Tapestry is a seventy-meter-long piece of embroidery that tells the story of the Norman Conquest. There are over seventy scenes depicting the events of the Conquest, as well as decorative borders showing fables. It was created sometime in the 11th century, and it is believed that it was commissioned by Bishop Odo, the half-brother of William the Conqueror. The Bayeux Tapestry is wonderful enough as a piece of art, but it is also more than that. It is a historical record. Since it has a clear bias toward the Norman version of events, it could also be a piece of political propaganda. Even something as decorative as a tapestry has a purpose that goes beyond simply looking pretty.

A section of the Bayeux Tapestry

The Bayeux Tapestry also shows us how the medium of visual art has changed over time. Wall hangings and tapestries were a major form of art in the medieval period, but they are practically unheard of today. Another form of art that was also widespread in the Middle Ages but has since declined is the illuminated manuscript. Illuminated manuscripts were originally created by monasteries. The name comes from the use of gold and silver to embellish the letters, which literally gives the pages an illuminated look. As the practice evolved, it came to refer to any manuscript that was decorated with bright colors and designs.

While illuminated manuscripts often included illustrations, their decorative features went beyond this. Illuminating a manuscript was not about adding pictures but about decorating the text itself. This included decorative borders, miniature pictures within the text itself, and highly ornate letters, especially capital letters at the beginning of a section. With the invention of the printing press in the 15th century, illuminated manuscripts fell out of style, but these hand-written and hand-decorated books were one of the main sources of visual art in the medieval period.

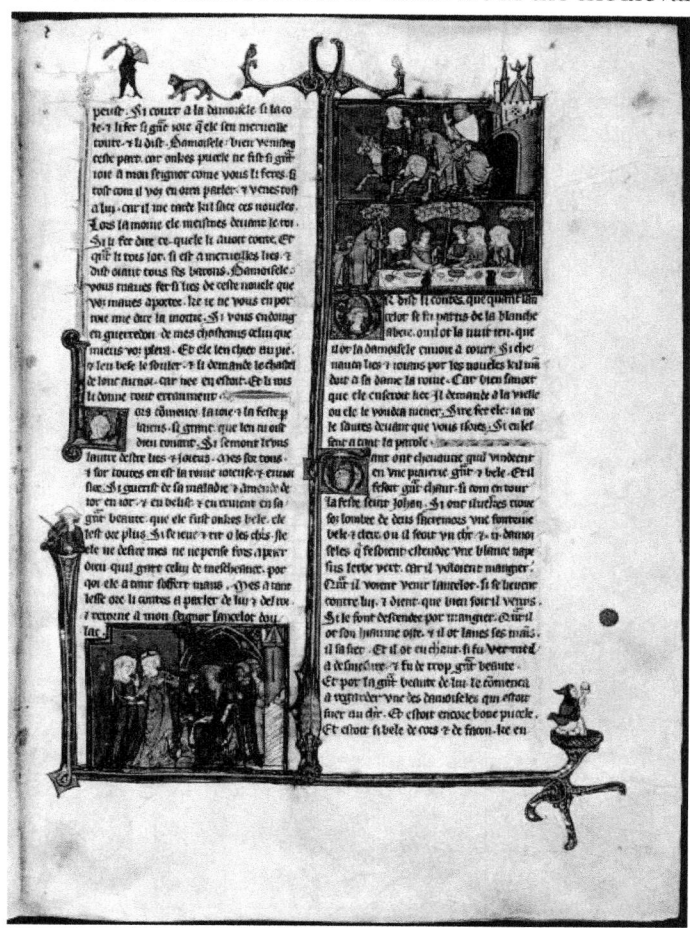

Page of an illuminated manuscript

https://commons.wikimedia.org/wiki/File:Page_from_the_Arthurian_Romances_illuminated_manuscript.jpg

For all their frills, illuminated manuscripts, like other medieval art, still maintain that connection to function. These were not isolated paintings but books. And based on what we have already learned about literature and architecture, you can probably guess that most illuminated manuscripts were religious books. Bibles and psalters (the Book of Psalms) were some of the most common and popular illuminated manuscripts. Like the building of expensive churches, creating ornate religious books was a way to show piety.

In the Anglo-Saxon period, art existed in the decorations used to embellish everyday objects like brooches and buckles. As we move through the Middle Ages to angel roofs and illuminated manuscripts, we begin to see art becoming less and less tied to practicality but still revolving around some kind of function, usually the display of religious devotion. In some ways, religion was responsible for much of the artistic growth of the medieval period because it provided a space in which pouring massive amounts of time and resources into making something beautiful was appropriate. It would have been a waste of time for a man to carve angels in his cottage, but to do it in his church was an act of faith.

Chapter 9: Royalty throughout the Middle Ages

Throughout this book, we have talked a lot about the various kings that held sway over England throughout the Middle Ages. While it is wrong to act as though these powerful men were the only ones steering the course of England during this time, it is equally wrong to underestimate the importance of the monarchy in the medieval period. These men wielded absolute power over the government of England, and their decisions, both the good and bad, made a large impact on the nation.

While today it is tempting to think of an absolute monarchy as a relatively simple and stagnant form of government, the place and power of royalty did undergo some changes throughout the Middle Ages.

In theory, the royalty works on a very simple hereditary system. The next king is the eldest son of the current king. However, in the Middle Ages, things often did not go this smoothly. Several of England's kings were kings by conquest rather than by blood, and in an era with shorter lifespans and higher mortality rates, England often found itself without a direct heir to claim the throne. Even when there was a direct heir, there were sometimes still problems with passing the scepter from one king to the next. In other words, who got to be king was often determined by factors other than lineage.

The Development of Kingship

Although we often picture a monarchy as being the default type of government, kings were something that had to develop in England. When the Anglo-Saxon tribes first arrived, they may have called their heads kings, but it would be a while before they resembled what we think of when we hear the word king.

The early Anglo-Saxon kings were essentially the chiefs of their tribes. The bigger their tribe was, the more power a king had, and to gain power, a king needed to excel at warfare. War was how a tribe could gain excess goods that would allow the royalty to amass their wealth and increase their status. A king could also gain wealth from his people directly through the use of tribute. To pay for the protection a powerful monarch offered, his subjects would pay tribute at an appointed place on a certain day. Royalty at this stage was tied closely to particular people rather than to an entire area.

As towns developed, the royalty began to see another and more efficient way for them to accumulate wealth. By taking control of towns and their trade centers and imposing fees, kings could amass far more riches and power without resorting to warfare. It was at this point that many kings started to set up around population centers.

Throughout the Early Middle Ages, the various Anglo-Saxon kings vied for power amongst themselves. More powerful kings forced their less powerful neighbors to pay them tribute, but they often stopped there instead of fully folding conquered territories into their own kingdoms. It wasn't until the coming of the Vikings that the Anglo-Saxons were forced to unify for the sake of defense, which allowed a king to control the entire English area.

The Wessex Dynasty

The Wessex kings were the first kings of all England. They rose to power when Æthelstan's grandfather, King Alfred the Great, beat the Vikings, causing Wessex to become the dominant Anglo-Saxon kingdom. Æthelstan was the first to officially have control over the entire English area. The House of Wessex ruled England uninterrupted from 927 to 1016 and then was restored from 1042 to 1066. Despite only ruling England for a total of 113 years, the Wessex dynasty included nine kings. Of the nine Wessex kings, five ruled for less than a decade, and only two ruled for more than twenty years.

- Æthelstan (r. 927–939)
- Edmund I (r. 939–946)
- Eadred (r. 946–955)
- Eadwig (r. 955–959)
- Edgar (r. 959–975)
- Edward (r. 975–978)
- Æthelred the Unready (r. 978–1013; 1014–1016)
- Edmund Ironside (r. 1016–1016)
- Edward the Confessor (r. 1042–1066)

The relatively short rules of many of these kings are a prime example of why royalty could get messy in the Middle Ages. Life could be brutal, and many kings, just like many of their people, died fairly young. There are only two instances in the Wessex dynasty where the throne passed directly from father to son (Edgar to Edward and Æthelred to Edmund Ironside). In most cases, the throne went from brother to brother rather than from father to son. If you add Æthelred being deposed briefly in 1013 and the rule of the House of Denmark, which interrupted Wessex rule from 1016 to 1042, you can get a glimpse of how complex the royalty of this period was. If a family wanted to keep the throne, they needed two things: heirs and military prowess. Unfortunately, it was a lot harder to stay alive in the medieval period, so having and keeping heirs was often difficult. Even if you did have heirs, there was also the risk of someone seizing the throne by force.

The House of Denmark

The House of Denmark seized control of England briefly from 1016 to 1042. Their twenty-six years of rule saw three different kings rule England:

- Cnut (r. 1016–1035)
- Harold Harefoot (r. 1035–1040)
- Harthacnut (r. 1040–1042)

Although they did not hold control for long, the House of Denmark shows just how important military might was to the rulers of England. Although Cnut was a conquering king, his nineteen-year reign was a time of peace and prosperity for England. Ironically, kings by conquest are often remembered by English history as being good kings. Taking a kingdom through military conflict put kings in a powerful position, which allowed them to easily handle any opposition to their rule. This often resulted in an overall more stable government. Whether the populace liked the conquering king or not, the purges and crushing of opposition that came with seizing a throne by force typically caused a pause to infighting for several years.

The Norman Dynasty

Although the Wessex dynasty was restored with Edward the Confessor in 1042, it was not to last. William the Conqueror, Duke of Normandy, became king in 1066 after defeating Harold Godwinson at the Battle of Hastings.

As we discussed in earlier chapters, William I was able to make a lot of changes in the English system, including giving titles and lands to his Norman supporters and instituting the feudal system. Although it is certain that many of the Anglo-Saxons did not like William I, especially those who lost their lands and positions, his rule, like Cnut's, was relatively stable. Royalty was thus highly tied to military conflict. The rulers who proved their might on the battlefield held more secure positions than those who inherited their titles.

The Normans ruled England for sixty-nine years but only had three kings.

- William I (William the Conqueror) (r. 1066–1087)
- William II (r. 1087–1100)
- Henry I (r. 1100–1135)

As stable as the Norman dynasty was in its military strength, it fell after only three kings due to the other crucial aspect of maintaining power: heirs. Thanks to the tragic sinking of the *White Ship*, Henry I died without any male heirs.

The House of Blois

Throughout this chapter, you may have been wondering why we keep referring specifically to the kings of England. After all, we know that England had queens. Some of England's most famous and long-reigning monarchs have been queens (Queen Elizabeth I, Queen Victoria, and Queen Elizabeth II). While England may have been ruled successfully by queens in the Tudor period and beyond, this was not the case in the Middle Ages. As we saw in Chapter 6, women were not well-respected in the medieval period, and throughout the medieval age, England was never ruled by a queen. This did not mean that queens did not exist. The wife of the king was the queen, but no woman was the practical ruler of England in her own right, although several (Eleanor of Aquitaine, Isabella of France, and Margaret of Anjou) did wield a good deal of power.

Technically speaking, there was no law saying a woman couldn't rule England, unlike some other European countries at this time, but the overall sexism of the day meant it was not considered even if it was legally possible. The closest a woman ever came to being the monarch of England was after the death of Henry I. When his male heir died, Henry I named his daughter, Empress Matilda, as his heir. However, after Henry I's death, his nephew and Matilda's cousin, Stephen of Blois, took the throne.

Although Matilda fought Stephen for nearly twenty years in the civil war known as the Anarchy, she never successfully seized the throne of England. She did control areas of England at different times, but the fight between her and Stephen only resulted in a stalemate, so although Matilda came close, she was never technically the queen of England.

The Plantagenets

While Matilda never got to be queen, her son managed to make a deal with Stephen of Blois, and in 1154, Henry II became the first of the Plantagenet kings. Ruling from 1154 to 1485, the Plantagenets are by far the longest-lasting royal dynasty of the English Middle Ages. As such, their ranks contain some of the best and worst English kings. The fourteen kings of the Plantagenet dynasty are:

- Henry II (r. 1154–1189)
- Richard I (Richard the Lionheart) (r. 1189–1199)
- John (r. 1199–1216)
- Henry III (r. 1216–1272)
- Edward I (Edward Longshanks) (r. 1272–1307)
- Edward II (Edward the Leopard) (r. 1307–1327)
- Edward III (r. 1327–1377)
- Richard II (r. 1377–1399)
- Henry IV (r. 1399–1413)
- Henry V (r. 1413–1422)
- Henry VI (r. 1422–1461; 1470–1471)

- Edward IV (r. 1461–1470; 1471–1483)
- Edward V (r. 1483)
- Richard III (r. 1483–1485)

Compared to the other English royal dynasties of the Middle Ages, the Plantagenets were rather prolific when it came to heirs. Henry II and Eleanor of Aquitaine had eight children, five of whom were sons. From John to Edward III, the throne managed to pass in a direct line from father to son, which, as demonstrated by the Wessex dynasty, was not as common as one might have thought in the Middle Ages. Edward III also had five sons who survived into adulthood. Their ability to produce surviving male heirs may have been a large part of why the Plantagenet dynasty was able to hold the English throne for so much longer than their predecessors.

However, if not having children had proved to be a problem for English kings in the past, the Plantagenets proved that having too many children could also be a problem. Henry II had to deal with revolts led by some of his sons and his wife, but it was Edward III and his five sons who proved to be the downfall of the Plantagenets.

You might not recognize the names of Edward III's surviving sons (Edward the Black Prince, Lionel of Antwerp, John of Gaunt, Edmund of Langley, and Thomas of Woodstock), but you will recognize the two houses that descended from them: York and Lancaster. The House of Lancaster traces its lineage back to John of Gaunt, and the House of York comes from both Lionel of Antwerp and Edmund of Langley. Thanks to Edward III's five sons, by the time you get to the reign of Henry VI, there were multiple people who could claim royal descent. The result was a very bloody and chaotic time known as the Wars of the Roses. That's not to say that Edward III's multiple children were the sole cause of the Wars of the Roses. There was a lot else that went wrong there, but the multiple claimants certainly contributed to how long and bloody the war became.

So, the Plantagenets had more than enough heirs to secure their royal dynasty, but they ended up killing each other off in a bloody civil war that made way for the Tudors. However, they still managed to keep the English throne for 330 years, and during that time, a lot changed in the way the English understood kingship. This was the time of the two Barons' Wars, the Magna Carta, and the Peasants' Revolt. If the Wessex, Dutch, and Norman dynasties had sought to establish the power of the king, the Plantagenet dynasty saw multiple challenges and a redefining of that power.

We often think of medieval kings as wielding absolute power, but it was during the medieval period that Parliament was established and met for the first time in 1215 in an effort to check the king's power. Parliament in these days was made up of nobles, so we are nowhere near a government controlled by the people. Still, it is important to recognize that Parliament did have some real power. Starting in 1362, Parliament had to approve any taxation the king wished to implement. This would prove to be a significant check on royal authority since kings could not wage war without gaining funds through taxation. By gaining control over the purse strings, Parliament had an effective check on the king's power. The king was still very much the one running the country, but he now needed the approval of England's most powerful men to do certain things.

The Problem with Royalty in the Middle Ages

Revolts against the king and the creation of the Magna Carta and Parliament show how mixed up our understanding of kingship can be today. Royalty in the Middle Ages did not command absolute power, nor were they necessarily respected as divinely appointed sovereigns. The idea that kings possessed a divine and sovereign right to rule absolutely, a theory known as the divine right of kings, was more prevalent in 17th-century England than it was in the Middle Ages.

That probably sounds backward. How is it that kings came to have a higher status later? It has to do with the large underlying problem that many medieval English kings faced. They were just men.

Whether they were fighting rebels in their own country or foreign forces, English kings had to spend a lot of time demonstrating that they could hold the throne, and it seems like for every king that managed this, there was another one that didn't. Powerful kings conquered and ruled firmly only to have their son or grandson lose all they had gained, and there was no guaranteed way for a family to keep a secure grasp on the throne. In 1135, England faced the Anarchy as a result of King Henry I dying without an heir. In 1455, England again bled under massive internal conflict with the Wars of the Roses, but this conflict stemmed from too many claimants with royal blood. So, not having an heir and having too many heirs led to chaos in this period. Then there was also the fact that simply taking the throne by force was an option. Both Cnut and William the Conqueror were foreigners who seized the English throne. Richard I forced his father to name him heir, Edward II was deposed by his wife, Henry IV ousted his cousin Richard II, and Richard III did away with his nephews to seize the throne.

English royalty in the medieval period had a lot of power, but that power could be taken or at least conflicted if the king lacked the character to hold it. In many ways, medieval kings had to stand on their own merits if they wanted to keep the peace more than some later royalty would.

Overall, the English throne in the Middle Ages was never as stable as we might think, and as the monarchy moved into the era after the Middle Ages, more emphasis was placed on the ultimate sovereignty of the monarch. Throughout the Renaissance and beyond, English royalty came to be wrapped in more pageantry. To create a more secure throne and dynasty, kings could no longer be just men. They had to be seen as something more so that they would maintain a natural right to their position. It was one thing to overthrow a powerful man or family. It was another to overthrow a divinely appointed sovereign. Of course, this understanding of royalty also led to many issues, but that was a problem for the 17th century.

Chapter 10: Law and Order

Medieval England could be chaotic at times, but there was still a relatively stable system of law and order that kept the peace throughout the land. The medieval English law system is in some ways incredibly bizarre, and in other ways, it resembles what still exists today.

The Courts

Throughout the medieval period, the English law system saw a lot of changes, and one of the best ways to see that is in the number of different types of courts that were established.

The Anglo-Saxon period had two major types of courts: the hundred and the shire. The hundred was a division of the larger shire and heard minor cases, while the shire courts heard the larger cases. The Norman Conquest and the feudal system added another type of court: the manorial court. Manorial courts were held by landlords for their tenants. They dealt with things like buying and selling land and minor criminal offenses. The manorial courts were restricted to their particular lord's jurisdiction. The fines these courts collected were part of a lord's income.

If that's not complicated enough, there were also church courts. The jurisdiction between the secular (royal courts) and church courts was often a point of conflict. For a long time, clerics had the right to be tried by church courts exclusively, and when Henry II tried to change this rule, it resulted in the famous Becket controversy.

Henry II was responsible for some other major changes in the English law system. In 1166, in response to the extreme lawlessness that abounded after the Anarchy period, Henry II issued the Assize of Clarendon. This was a series of laws that reformed the judicial system, and one major change it instituted was to establish traveling judges. Judges appointed by the king were to travel circuits around England hearing cases. It was the duty of a grand jury, which consisted of twelve men, to report serious crimes to these judges. Under this system, those accused of serious crimes had to be tried before the king's men, consolidating the authority of the law under the central government (the king).

So, medieval England had both local courts that heard the majority of cases and higher courts that heard more serious offenses and appeals. The exact jurisdiction of the various courts overlapped and could be terribly unclear, but the basic structure of a multi-tiered court system was there. In other words, the judicial system had been complicated for a very long time.

Punishment

Before we talk about how medieval people determined if someone was guilty (they did that in some pretty bizarre ways), let's talk about what happened if you were found guilty. If you did happen to get caught breaking the law in the medieval period, what type of punishment could you expect?

Like today's crime and punishment, medieval punishment varied a lot depending on the crime. The medieval law system was harsh and even gruesome, but they didn't chop off the hand of anyone who broke any law. Medieval punishments ranged from paying a fine to being drawn, hanged, and quartered. Here are some of the punishments unique to the period:

- **Stocks and Pillory:** The stocks and pillory were both a form of shaming punishment. In stocks, the guilty person had their ankles trapped in a board, while in a pillory, the person's head and arms were trapped. The pillory was a bit worse than the stocks, but both punishments were for minor crimes like vagrancy and drunkenness. The trapped person could be taunted by crowds and have things like rotting vegetables thrown at them. However, sometimes people had flowers thrown at them if they were well-liked in the community. There were even rules against throwing hard things (so no rocks) at people in the stocks or pillory.

- **Flogging:** For more severe crimes, many villages and towns had more than just stocks and pillories. They also had a whipping post. Flogging is exactly what it sounds like, and like many other medieval punishments, it was done in public. This element of shame was added to many medieval punishments.

- **Mutilation:** Chopping off a hand was a punishment for stealing in the medieval period. The punishment did vary based on what was stolen. You probably wouldn't lose a hand for stealing an apple, but you could lose a hand depending on what you stole and whom you stole from. Losing a foot was another potential punishment.

- **Hanging:** Although they did have some far bloodier methods of execution, the primary method of execution in medieval England was hanging. However, the long drop method of hanging, which ensured that the person's neck snapped, was not put into practice until the 1800s. Hanging in the Middle Ages was a much slower death by strangulation. Depending on their crime, some criminals' bodies were left hanging on the gibbet as a public display. The body might also be mutilated after death. These practices served as a warning to others and were part of the medieval period's attempt at crime prevention.

- **Burning at the Stake:** Being burned at the stake is just as horrible as it sounds—probably even more so. It's impossible to imagine the agony of being burned alive. What crime would cause you to receive such a horrific punishment? Religious heresy, including witchcraft, was the crime that merited burning at the stake. The practice of burning those accused of heresy continued past the Middle Ages. Bloody Mary, who was the queen of England from 1553 to 1558, earned that nickname for her persecution of Protestants, which included burning over three hundred people. Burning at the stake was also used as a punishment for women guilty of treason and for a few other crimes as well.

- **Drawing, Hanging, and Quartering:** The medieval punishment reserved for the worst of the worst was drawing, hanging, and quartering. This punishment was for those guilty of high treason. Drawing involved dragging the criminal to the gallows. They were then hung, after which they were taken down and quartered. Quartered referred specifically to removing the limbs, but they were often mutilated in other ways as well, such as beheading and disemboweling. The various body parts were then displayed publicly. If that doesn't sound gruesome enough, the really horrible part is that the person was taken down from the gallows before they were quite dead, so they were still alive at the beginning of the next step. Often, their entrails were removed before their own eyes and then burned before they were quartered and sometimes beheaded. Drawing, hanging, and quartering remained the punishment for treason until the 19th century. The last time it was used was in 1867, and it was abolished in 1870.

What might be even more shocking than the punishments is the fact that many of these harsher punishments, such as burning at the stake and drawing, hanging, and quartering, developed in the later Middle Ages (around the 11th and 12th centuries) and persisted into the 18th and even 19th centuries. We may like to think that these punishments were the product of some sort of dark age, but the medieval period was not alone in dishing out gruesome punishments.

But why exactly were the punishments so harsh? Were medieval people just overly cruel? There was a logic behind these methods. Medieval law and order was a system based on prevention through fear. There were no police. There was no jail. Jails of the time were not for holding prisoners as punishment but rather for holding people until their trial. There was no system for stopping crimes as they happened, and there was no system for keeping criminals separate from the rest of society. The medieval system instead relied on these harsh punishments to dissuade people from committing crimes.

Compurgation

Now that we know what happened if you were found guilty of a crime in medieval England, let's talk about how your guilt was determined. Without forensic science or even police to investigate crimes, they had a very different system for conducting trials. One of the main ways of conducting a trial was through compurgation, which was also called the wager of law.

Compurgation was more of a method designed for proving one's innocence rather than for establishing guilt. Keep in mind that this was long before the doctrine of "innocent until proven guilty" came around.

Those suspected of crimes in the Middle Ages had to prove themselves to be innocent, and compurgation was perhaps the most used method for doing that.

Compurgation was a system that centered on oath-taking. The accused would swear an oath declaring their innocence. Their oath would be believed if they could find enough people to also swear an oath to their innocence. This process typically required the accused to get twelve people to swear to their innocence. These people were not swearing that they knew that the accused had not performed the crime. Rather, they were swearing that they believed the accused's words. They functioned a bit like character witnesses.

Oaths were given precise monetary values, and the value of a person's oath also depended on their societal status. The word of a nobleman was worth more than that of a peasant. In some cases, to prove their innocence, the accused had to acquire oaths that added up to a total value.

Under this system, it seems like everyone should be able to prove their innocence to any crime, but that was hardly the case. Oath-making was a very serious business in the Middle Ages. It had religious and legal implications. Swearing an oath for someone with a bad reputation could get you into trouble, so people who appeared guilty or who had few friends would have a hard time meeting the requirements of compurgation.

Trial by Ordeal

One of the most puzzling aspects of medieval law to our modern understanding of law and order was the trial by ordeal. There were three larger types of trials by ordeal: trial by divination, trial by physical ordeal, and trial by combat. Of the three, trial by physical ordeal, which is usually simply called trial by ordeal, was the most common.

So, what was the trial by ordeal? It doesn't sound pleasant, and it definitely wasn't. Trial by ordeal was a way of determining a person's guilt that relied on God's judgment. A suspected person was subjected to a particular physical test with the belief that God would determine the outcome. If they passed, they were innocent. If they failed, they were guilty.

What were the actual physical tests, though? In medieval England, there were two versions of the trial by ordeal: the trial by cold water and the trial by hot iron. The trial of cold water involved tying the accused with ropes and tossing them into a body of water. If they sank, they were innocent. If they floated, they were guilty. This was based on water's connection with baptism. It was believed that the water would not accept a guilty person and thus would not sink. The trial by hot iron was perhaps even more unpleasant. A piece of iron was heated in a fire, and then the accused had to walk a certain distance holding it. Their guilt was not determined by whether they were burned at all but by how well the wound healed. Their hand was wrapped for a few days, and if it appeared unburned or if the wound did not appear diseased when it was unwrapped, they were innocent. Both trials were overseen by a priest, who would conduct the necessary rituals to prepare and conduct the trial.

When you first learn about the trial by ordeals, there are two understandable responses. Both "That's barbaric!" and "That's stupid!" may come to mind. Nearly drowning people and forcing them to hold hot metal seems both cruel and a terrible way to determine guilt, and that is true. It was both cruel and wildly inaccurate, yet for all that, there is more nuance to the trial by ordeal than there appears to be.

First of all, when was trial by ordeal used? Not everyone who was accused of a crime had to undergo one of these trials. Trial by ordeal was reserved for the king's court, which only heard serious crimes, so you wouldn't be facing trial by ordeal just for stealing an apple. Even in the cases that did go to the king's court, if you could satisfactorily prove your innocence, you did not have to face a trial by ordeal. The trial was meant to appeal to God's judgment when human judgment failed. We would expect it then to be used in cases where there was great uncertainty, but it was also used in cases where the accused was highly suspect. Trial by ordeal was frequently used on people who were considered untrustworthy or who could not find people to prove their innocence by compurgation. Trial by ordeal could be used both when there was uncertainty and also when a person appeared to be guilty.

The fact that the guilty were often subjected to trial by ordeal is evident from the cases where the person passed the trial. Even after passing the trial, some people were still ordered to leave England. God said you were innocent, yet you were still banished. This seems to suggest that in some cases, the people who underwent these trials were still believed to be guilty. So, what was the purpose of the trial?

To understand this, we have to realize something important about trials by ordeal. The fact was that most people passed the trials. The majority of people who underwent the trial of cold water sank, proving their innocence, and even more strangely, the majority of people who endured the trial of hot iron were also found innocent. This meant that if you were subjected to a trial by ordeal, chances were good that you would be proved innocent.

Think about what this means for guilty parties. Medieval punishment was harsh. If the crime was serious enough to warrant a trial by ordeal, then chances were the punishment if found guilty was far worse than the trial. You were probably facing death or mutilation. The trials were extremely unpleasant, but they were better than that. The trial by ordeal then could be a way for the guilty to escape much harsher punishment.

Of course, there was still a chance that you would fail the trial and then have to face the punishment for the crime on top of that, and there can be no doubt that innocent people were also forced to endure the trial at times. The practice did not make for a fair judicial system, but it may strangely have afforded mercy to more than we realize. Still, medieval society seemed to be aware of the faults with this. Trials by ordeal were outlawed by the church in 1215, and since priests were central to the trials, the trial by ordeal quickly disappeared after 1215.

Trials by combat were far less common, but they also existed in medieval times. These trials were usually only practiced by noblemen. Trials by combat also required that there be some sort of accuser for the suspect to face, so they were not practical in many cases. Like the trial by physical ordeal, the assumption was that God would be with the man in the right. If the accused lost the fight and survived, they would then have to face whatever punishment their crime dictated.

Trial by Jury

While many of the practices of medieval law and order seem either cruel and bizarre to us, this period also saw the start of something that has become central to many modern legal systems: trial by jury.

Trials by jury have a long history in England. They were not established by a single law but rather developed over time. The exact origins of the first jury trials are unclear. The Anglo-Saxon tribes may have already had the start of jury trials, but the practice might have been brought over by the Normans after the Conquest. The Assize of Clarendon in 1166 established the use of a grand jury to determine which cases came before the king's judges on their circuit. After the church abolished trials by ordeal in 1215, jury trials became more prominent since trials by ordeal were no longer an option.

Also, in 1215, the Magna Carta stated, "No free man shall be taken or imprisoned, or disseised, or outlawed, or exiled or anyways destroyed; nor will we go upon him, nor will we send upon him, unless by the lawful judgment of his peers, or by the law of the land." The "lawful judgment of his peers" shows clearly that trial by jury was a known concept at the time of the Magna Carta, and the fact that it was included in the Magna Carta shows that some importance was attached to the practice as well.

So, were medieval trials by jury the same as a jury trial today? In medieval practice, the jury was closer to what we would call witnesses. The jury was made up of men from the community who decided the case based on what they knew. There were no lawyers laying out evidence. The jury decided things based on whatever they happened to know about the case and the suspect.

The jury system was unique to medieval England. It spread to other areas with British colonialism and appeared in France after the French Revolution, but in the Middle Ages, juries were only found in England.

Medieval law often conjures up images of brutal executions and corruption, and while those things existed, there was more to the overall system than that. The period's introduction of trials by a jury has been one of the most lasting impacts of the English Middle Ages.

Chapter 11: Faith and Religious Identity

In the grand timeline of human history, atheism and even agnosticism are recent inventions. For most of the past, everyone at least professed to be religious or to believe in some deity. In medieval England, Christianity was the overwhelmingly dominant religion. It wouldn't be entirely inaccurate to say that at some point, everyone in medieval England was a Christian, at least in some sense. How is that possible?

Religion in the Middle Ages differed a lot from what we experience today. Remember that the American Bill of Rights with its freedom of religion amendment wasn't passed until 1791. Before that, religion was determined by the government. You were a Christian because your king had determined that you were a Christian. That didn't mean that everyone believed in the same things, but it did mean that officially everyone was of the same religion. And in the Middle Ages, that religion was Christianity.

Effects of Christianity

We have already discussed the conversion of the Anglo-Saxons in Chapter 4, so now let's look closer at what effect Christianity had on England and its people.

As we mentioned briefly when discussing the conversion of the Anglo-Saxons, one of the most important things that Christianity brought to England was literacy. We are not talking about bringing literacy to the general population but simply the fact that monks and priests could read and write. Many of the enormously important historical sources we now have, such as the Venerable Bede's *Ecclesiastical History of the English People*, were written by monks and other members of the clergy. Having a group that could write things down also meant that it was much easier to create a more unified law system and to keep track of things like births, deaths, and marriages. Christianity was thus instrumental in creating larger, more organized Anglo-Saxon kingdoms, which eventually led to one English nation.

As you probably realized in the chapter on art and architecture, Christianity also had a large impact on the culture of the period. Most works of art, literature, and architecture had religious motivations. Besides Christian art, the laws and customs of the time were also deeply tied to the dominant religion. There were church courts and laws that prohibited things like usury because they were prohibited in the Bible. You could be arrested for being a heretic in the same way that you could be arrested for robbery or murder.

The truth is that the influence of Christianity was so widespread in the Middle Ages that it is difficult to describe. Christianity was in the culture and the laws. It permeated the very rhythm of medieval life. It seeped into the background and context so much that it makes it very difficult for us today to discern how seriously people took their faith and religious identity in this period. Everyone was a Christian, but how Christian were they? Perhaps the best way to answer this question is to look at the other religious beliefs in medieval England.

Remnants of Paganism

The first thing we want to remember here is that the truly native beliefs of the Britons had already taken a severe hit before the arrival of the Anglo-Saxons. The Romans did not like the Druids, so much of the original organized religion of the native Britons had already been lost when Britain became a Roman colony. When the Anglo-Saxons then converted to Christianity, the organized religion of England gradually and fully shifted to Christianity. What persisted for much longer was not organized pagan religions but rather the folk beliefs and practices that went along with those religions.

Peasants in medieval England called and believed themselves to be Christians. However, at the same time, they continued to believe in things like fairies and spirits. The same people who attended Mass every Sunday would also perform spells and wear charms to protect themselves from these supernatural beings. These folk beliefs not only existed alongside the Christian church but were also sometimes mixed with it. For example, one explanation for the existence of fairies was that they were fallen angels that had become trapped on Earth after God shut the gates to heaven and hell. Another example is the feast days. While the feast days were organized by the church and related to saints, many of them had pagan origins. Easter, for example, appears to have taken its name from the goddess of spring, Eostre. Dancing around the maypole in spring is a pagan tradition, and even things like decorating trees on Christmas have pagan roots. Even though these holidays were now celebrated for reasons tied to Christianity, the celebrations themselves often continued practices tied to pagan beliefs. Christianity was the dominant religion, but the traditional beliefs persisted in a strange mixture with Christianity.

How were people okay with believing in both fairies and God? You don't need to know much about the Bible to know that official Christian doctrine does not support this mixing of folk beliefs and Christianity. Does this mean that the peasants hadn't bought into Christianity?

Remember that the average person in this day was illiterate, so they couldn't read the Bible. Adding to that, Mass was said in Latin. So, while everyone was Christian, most people didn't know exactly what that entailed. They could easily believe in fairies and still be Christian because they didn't realize that those things were contradictory.

The church as an organization did try to stamp out these things to some degree, but the spread of information and enforcement of rules was much slower and more difficult in the Middle Ages. Whatever the pope might have thought about things had little effect on what a peasant in rural England did. The church was much more effective in establishing "orthodox" Christianity in cities and towns than in rural villages.

Besides the remnants of paganism, there were also those who more fully rejected Christianity. The most famous counter-religious movement in the Middle Ages was the Cathars. The Cathars were a group based in southern France that idolized Sophia, the goddess of wisdom. Cathars swore to serve Sophia much in the way that knights in courtly love poems swore to protect their ladies. The connection runs so deep that some people believe that the courtly love genre of this period was a product of the Cathars attempting to spread their beliefs.

The church did not look kindly on the Cathars or other religious heretics. The Cathars were wiped out in the Albigensian Crusade, and the church's inquisition dealt severely with anyone else they deemed to be heretical. So, even if you did not agree with the Christian faith in the Middle Ages, it was best not to advertise it.

Daily Life and the Church

So, does that mean that people weren't Christian but were just too scared of the church to act otherwise? Not exactly. As we already mentioned, Christianity had an enormous influence on everyone in medieval England, from the king to a tenant farmer. The people of medieval England were not just Christian in name. Christianity was a large part of everyone's lives.

We have already discussed the many feast days spread throughout the year, but to reiterate, there were a *lot* of feast days (between forty to sixty). Besides those days off, Sundays were also days dedicated to rest or rather dedicated to worship. Religion, therefore, determined the cycle of rest and work for everyone, and in such a labor-focused society, that was equivalent to determining the very rhythm of life.

Religion was an essential part of the greater cycle of life as well. Babies were baptized shortly after birth. The church was the authority that married you. It was also the institution that buried you. The church was there for all of life's most important events, which meant that its presence was constantly felt.

Besides setting the calendar and playing a key role in the important events of a person's life, Christianity also influenced people's lives through a practice that became incredibly widespread throughout the Middle Ages: pilgrimages.

Pilgrimages

The idea of a religious pilgrimage is far from unique to medieval Christianity. Before Christianity, Jews traveled to Jerusalem and the Temple for important religious events. Today, Muslims still perform the Hajj, a pilgrimage to Mecca. However, in medieval England, the practice of pilgrimages was specifically linked with Christianity.

This itself is a bit strange because Christianity, unlike Judaism and Islam, does not specifically emphasize particular locations as holy. There is nothing in Christian doctrine that requires or even encourages taking a physical journey as an act of religious piety. If anything, the emphasis on Christian pilgrimages in the Middle Ages shows how tangled, or maybe rather influenced, medieval Christianity was by other beliefs and practices.

So, if Christian pilgrims weren't following some religious ordinance, why did they make pilgrimages? There were numerous reasons. Some people traveled to particular locations in hopes of finding miraculous healing. Other people made pilgrimages as a form of penance for their sins. There were also those whose pilgrimages were a mixture of faith and tourism. Early Christians traveled to the Holy Land to see the places where Christ and the apostles had walked. The resting places of saints became popular pilgrimage destinations as well. Many pilgrims would take pilgrimages tours, visiting several sites in a single trip. This desire to see things associated with their faith gave rise to the popularity of relics.

Relics are one of the more infamous things about religion in the Middle Ages. Sites claiming to have things like the bones of various saints, pieces of the cross, and even the Holy Grail (which was the cup Christ used at the Last Supper) attracted many visitors. Not only did people travel to see relics, but these religious objects also created quite the market. Pilgrims traveling to holy sites could purchase relics, both as a memento of their journey and for the powers these objects were said to possess. Visitors to Canterbury Cathedral, for instance, often bought vials of what was said to be Thomas Becket's blood diluted with water. The concoction was believed to have miraculous healing abilities.

When you learn about relics today, it's hard not to roll your eyes. It seems like an excellent system for tricking gullible travelers into buying random scraps of wood and animal bones. However, the people in the Middle Ages were aware of this downside to relics. Chaucer's *The Canterbury Tales*, which is a story about a group of people going on a pilgrimage to Canterbury, includes a character who sells fake relics. Relics were a big business in this period, but it's unclear how seriously people took it.

We might think of pilgrims as being a few isolated religious fanatics, but the practice was fairly widespread in this period. It was so prominent that there was a booming business surrounding pilgrimages. Inns cropped up along well-known travel routes to popular destinations, and pilgrims often bought distinctive badges, staves, and garments that marked them as pilgrims, not to mention the relics. To pay for these things, pilgrims had to carry all of their funds for the trip on their person, which made them an easy target for robbers. The Knights Templar were originally created to protect these pilgrims. Pilgrimages were so common that infrastructure rose around this activity.

Speaking of the Knights Templar, there was another type of pilgrimage that has become almost synonymous with the Middle Ages: the Crusades. Wait a second! The Crusades weren't pilgrimages. They were religious wars where European Christians attempted to retake the Holy Land from the Muslims and halt the spread of Islam. That's true, but the Crusades were, in a way, a type of pilgrimage. Like traveling to a particular holy site, participating in a crusade was an act of faith and was often viewed as a means of penance and redemption. Crusades were journeys with religious purposes, so they were pilgrimages, albeit violent ones.

Between crusaders and other pilgrims just wanting to see the sites, the Holy Land was a popular pilgrimage destination. Rome was another since it was the home of the church. England, however, was home to one of the most popular pilgrimage destinations: Canterbury. Canterbury was the site of the martyrdom of St. Thomas Becket in 1170, after which it became one of the most visited pilgrimage sites. Other pilgrimage sites included St. Albans, Westminster Abbey, York, Walsingham, and others. Most sites were visited largely by people within a local area, but the more venerated a site was, the farther people would travel to see it.

Other Religions of the Middle Ages

Although Christianity certainly dominated Europe, it was not the only major organized religion of this time. Judaism and Islam were the other two major faiths of the period.

As you can probably tell from the existence of the Crusades, Muslims and Christians did not get along in the Middle Ages. Remember, this was the period of history when the church was burning heretics at the stake, so the idea of religious tolerance was nonexistent. As Islam continued to expand in the Middle East, Christian Europe felt that it had to stop that advance and take back the Holy Land, hence the Crusades.

The exact history of the Crusades is messy. There were a lot of them, and they involved a lot of different groups. The Christian crusaders did not manage to drive the Muslims out of the Holy Land. With its position as an isolated island, England was not greatly affected by this religious conflict, although Richard the Lionheart did spend more time crusading than he did in England. England did, however, have a much more involved and rockier relationship with a different religious group: the Jews.

Since Rome had sacked Jerusalem and destroyed the Temple in 70 CE, the Jews had been without a homeland. They thus lived amongst various other nations, including England. Remember that religious tolerance was not a virtue in those days, so it can hardly be said that the Jews in England were well-liked. Antisemitism was rampant, yet somehow the presence of a small Jewish population was tolerated. Why?

It came down to money. In the Middle Ages, the church had laws against usury. While that would later come to mean lending money with exploitative interest rates, in the medieval period, it meant lending money with any interest. Christians were not allowed to lend money to make money, which made it very hard to acquire capital with which to fund larger projects and investments. Since the Jews were not members of the church, they did not have to follow such rules, so Jewish moneylenders were an important source of capital. Of course, that also meant that people often owed Jews money, which did not help antisemitic feelings.

While many wealthy English thus despised the Jews because they were indebted to them, the most powerful man in England had a very different relationship with the Jews. The king made quite a bit of money from his Jewish subjects. The Crown was allowed to confiscate all of the property of any usurer upon their death, although this privilege was not used as much as you might think. Instead, the Crown would allow the Jews to keep their wealth so that he might tax and fine them heavily.

In the 13th century, this forced partnership between the Jews and the Crown deteriorated. The Jews became increasingly poorer due to the heavy taxation from the Crown and were soon no longer a source of significant income for the king. Without the funds they provided, all pretense of tolerance ended. In 1290, Edward I issued the Edict of Expulsion, expelling all the Jews from England. This decision stood for more than 360 years. Jews were not legally allowed back in England until 1657.

If you have been wondering why Christianity was so dominant in the Middle Ages, you have probably realized by now that it's largely because other religions were not tolerated. Heretics were burned, pagans were wiped out, and Jews were expelled. Still, like most things in the Middle Ages, there is more to medieval Christianity than that. Churches were the center of community life, and faith and piety were the motivation behind many of the period's greatest artistic achievements.

In the next chapter, we will take a closer look at the role of the church as an institution.

Chapter 12: Role of the Church: Church and State

It can be hard for us in the modern day to truly grasp just how central the church was in not only medieval England but all of Europe in the Middle Ages. The medieval Catholic Church was by far the most powerful institution in the Middle Ages. Kings sought the church's approval before invading other countries.

Organization of the Church

One of the things that made the church so effective in maintaining and growing its power was its organization. The church's hierarchical system allowed it to effectively wield power over an enormous area.

The organization of the medieval Catholic Church is very straightforward. At the highest level, you had the pope. Under him were the cardinals, who were the administrative heads of the church. Then come the archbishops and bishops, who exercised control over a particular cathedral and region. At the lowest level, you had priests who looked over smaller parishes and villages.

Looking at England specifically, the top of the church hierarchy was the two archbishops, the one for York and the one for Canterbury. The archbishop of Canterbury was actually above the archbishop of York on the church ladder, though, and was the head of the English church in the Middle Ages.

Besides the clear structure of the clergy, medieval England also had quite a few monastic institutions. These existed alongside the normal church order. They were run by abbots or abbesses. Since they were fairly self-contained and independent organizations, there weren't significant issues between the power and structure of the church and the monasteries.

Now, we said that one of the things that gave the church so much power in the Middle Ages was its organization, but how can that be? What was so special about this tiered structure? More than you might think. William the Conqueror tried to institute a very similar structure in the feudal system to strengthen the power of the king. The multiple levels, which all ultimately tie back to a central authority—in the church's case, that was the pope, who got his authority directly from God—both served to strictly unify and yet extend the reach of the church's power.

The lower levels of the hierarchy (the priests) ensured that the church had widespread influence. The higher levels of the hierarchy ensured that all of the different parts were on the same page. Instead of a world in where every church in every village was doing its own thing, everyone was doing the same thing

In medieval times, this level of bureaucracy was revolutionary. Remember that one of the reasons the Anglo-Saxon kings converted to Christianity was because they saw how such a system could extend the reach of their practical power. The church itself did this better than anyone. At its peak, the church was by far the most powerful institution in the Western world. Let's take a closer look at what powers the church had.

The Power of the Church

Perhaps the most extreme method that the church used to guide the medieval world was excommunication. Excommunication meant being kicked out of the church, but it was far more serious than it initially sounds. To be removed from the church would mean losing all fellowship with other church members, which in this time was everyone. The average person who was excommunicated would face severe social isolation, but that wasn't the worst of it. The church was God's authority on Earth. To be kicked out of the church also meant losing your place in God's kingdom. You would be condemning your eternal soul to hell, and that was something few people were willing to risk.

Excommunication was even used to keep kings in line. In 1208, King John was excommunicated for refusing to accept the pope's appointee to the office of archbishop of Canterbury. John held out for five years, but he gave in in 1213. Excommunication did not always push kings into doing what the church wanted, but it was one way that the church and state battled things out in this period.

The church's power also had a far more worldly source: money. Between both tithes and gifts that the church received, it was a very wealthy institution, and in the Middle Ages, just like today, money was power. Wealthy priests and bishops enjoyed lavish lifestyles and enormous influence, and the fact that they could excommunicate people meant it was practically impossible to call out even the most corrupt ones.

The church also had a level of jurisdiction in what we would now consider secular affairs. The legality of things like marriage and divorce was handled by the church rather than the state. Remember that it was priests who oversaw trials by ordeal, and those trials disappeared from use because the church outlawed them. So respected was the church's authority when it came to matters of law that people who committed major crimes, such as murder, could claim sanctuary in a church to escape punishment, at least temporarily. There were also church courts where you could bring disputes rather than going before a government court.

So, the power of the church in this day was very real, and the church also saw no problem with intervening in matters that we today would consider to be strictly secular. Such a situation naturally produced conflict.

The Becket Controversy

The church and state were quite entangled in this period. They both acted as governing authorities over the people of medieval England, and that was sure to lead to conflict. Kings often tried to fill church positions with their own men to reduce this conflict and strengthen their power. Perhaps nothing better illustrates the conflict between the state and church than the Becket controversy of the 12th century.

Thomas Becket began as a close friend of King Henry II. He was such a close friend that in 1155, Henry II appointed him to the highest position in England under the king: the chancellor of England. Then, seven years after that, in 1162, Henry II saw an opportunity to put his close friend in an even greater position. Thomas Becket was made the archbishop of Canterbury.

Becket's appointment as archbishop of Canterbury shows much of what had gone wrong in the medieval church. Becket was not a clergyman. He was a layman and a government official. The archbishop of Canterbury should have been elected, but instead, he had been appointed by the king. At the time of his appointment, Becket was also still the chancellor of England, so he now held both the most powerful church position and a powerful government position. It was clear that the king wanted those loyal to him in positions of power, regardless of whether those positions were ecclesiastical or political. The separation of church and state was nonexistent.

That is only the beginning of the story of Henry II and Thomas Becket, though. Henry II's plan of putting his close friend in a high church position backfired unexpectedly. Shortly after becoming the archbishop of Canterbury, Thomas Becket resigned his position as the chancellor of England. It was a clear sign that Becket was leaning toward the church's side of things rather than the king's, and it didn't stop there. Becket began to oppose Henry II, arguing that the king had overstepped his authority in interfering in ecclesiastical matters.

The irony of this situation is hard to miss. Thomas Becket, who had received his appointment as archbishop of Canterbury because the king interfered in church matters, was now telling his once close friend that the king needed to keep his nose out of the church's business. We can only imagine Henry II's outrage. As for why exactly Becket underwent such a dramatic change, we don't know. In a matter of such personal transformation, we lack any historical evidence to explain this matter. All we know is that Becket was very serious about his new stance.

The dispute that caused the great eruption between Henry II and Becket was criminous clerks. The clergy had the right to be tried exclusively by church courts rather than royal courts, regardless of the crime. A priest convicted of murder could essentially escape the king's justice by transferring his case to a church court, where he would receive a lesser punishment. Even if a man was convicted of something like rape or murder, church courts would likely only strip him of his office. Henry II saw this as a major problem, and it was more of a problem than we may first realize. Although there were not that many priests in England, there were a good many people who fell under the category of the clergy, even though they were not ordained—around one in six men, in fact. As part of his effort to establish stricter law and order after the Anarchy period (the civil war between Stephen and Matilda), Henry II wanted clergy convicted of serious crimes in church courts to be handed over to the royal courts for punishment.

To us today, this may seem reasonable, but not to the bishops of England and not to Thomas Becket. Turning over criminous clergy to the royal courts for punishment would destroy the base of clerical immunity from the secular courts. It would destabilize the church's freedom from the authority of the king. After much conflict, Henry II presented the bishops of England and Becket with the Constitutions of Clarendon, which included sixteen clauses that they would have to swear that the church would obey, among which was Henry II's idea for dealing with criminous clerks. Outright refusing to agree to it would have been bad enough, but Becket went a step further. Despite their reluctance, Becket convinced all of the other bishops to sign the Constitutions of Clarendon along with himself. Becket changed his mind a few days later and took back his oath.

Henry II was livid, but now instead of going after the entire church, he was after Thomas Becket. Henry II created charges to condemn Becket, but Becket refused to even hear the verdict of the king's council because he was a member of the clergy; they had no right to judge him. Becket then fled the country, seeking safety in France.

Becket lived in exile from 1165 to 1170, during which there were several attempts to get the archbishop of Canterbury and the king of England to reconcile. Ultimately, it was a matter of pride that brought Becket back to England. In 1170, Henry II had Becket's rival, the archbishop of York, crown his son Henry the Younger. It was a direct insult to Becket's office, and Becket finally agreed to return to England where he would re-crown Henry the Younger.

After returning from exile to a country where he was still fairly unpopular with the government, you might have expected Thomas Becket to lay low for a while, but Becket appeared to enjoy doing the unexpected. Immediately after returning to England, Becket excommunicated some of the members of the English clergy, including the archbishop of York. In a fit of anger at this news, Henry II said something that four of his knights took a bit too literally. The accounts of exactly what Henry said vary. Some say that the king asked, "Will no one rid me of this troublesome priest?" or "Will no one rid me of this turbulent priest?" Other accounts say that Henry II said, "What miserable drones and traitors have I nurtured and promoted in my household who let their lord be treated with such shameful contempt by a low-born clerk!"

Whatever he said, it was enough for four of the knights present. They rode to Canterbury Cathedral and attempted to arrest Becket. When he refused, things got out of hand. Becket was murdered in the cathedral. Murdering an archbishop in a church is not a good publicity move. Whatever people might have thought about Becket's actions in life, his death quickly turned him into a saint and a martyr. Canterbury Cathedral became one of the most popular pilgrimage destinations not just in England but in all of Europe, and Becket's remains, particularly his blood, were said to have miraculous healing properties. Henry II even visited the site of his old friend's murder and had to demonstrate penance for his involvement in it.

Depiction of Henry II and Thomas Becket
https://en.wikipedia.org/wiki/Thomas_Becket#/media/File:Jindrich2_Beckett.jpg

The story of Thomas Becket and Henry II has quite a lot of drama and even some unexpected twists, but what we care about for our purposes is how this shows the strain between the church and state in the medieval period. The church was essentially a political entity, and having two political governing bodies acting within a single sphere is bound to cause problems. Questions of ecclesiastical versus royal authority would eventually cause England to leave the Catholic Church and establish the Church of England, wherein the head of state (the monarch) was also the head of the church.

Church Critics

Kings were not the only ones to have issues with the medieval Catholic Church. Even though the Protestant Reformation wouldn't get underway until the 1500s, there were already those who questioned how the church acted.

The king was upset because the church was interfering with his authority, but why did the average citizen have problems with the church? To put it simply, corruption was rampant. The power and wealth the church afforded made church positions very attractive. They were so attractive that people were willing to buy their way into them. This act, known as simony, was officially condemned but quite common. Another significant issue was nepotism, which was when church officials gave their kin prominent positions.

It doesn't stop there! The church was also heavily criticized for selling indulgences. Indulgences were payments a person could make to lessen their or a loved one's time in purgatory. It was a very lucrative business. People would pay quite a lot of money to get into heaven. Indulgences technically didn't start as a "pay your way" to heaven plan. The first indulgence appeared with the Crusades, as you could pay for your sins by participating in the holy war. Unfortunately, it didn't take long for corrupt church officials to see the dollar signs, and indulgences quickly became a money-making business.

England produced one of the medieval church's most famous critics before Martin Luther: John Wycliffe. Wycliffe, like many people, was opposed to the immense wealth the church controlled and continued to gain through practices like indulgences. He argued that the church should give up all its possessions. Wycliffe's ideas piqued the interest of some statesmen, particularly John of Gaunt, who was unhappy with the immense wealth and power of the church.

Wycliffe's opposition to the church became even more pronounced and vehement as time went on. He argued against the right of sanctuary, which, in his view, prevented justice from being served. He also heavily attacked the doctrine of transubstantiation, believed strongly in predestination, and was one of the first to promote an English translation of the Bible, all of which would later become key aspects of the Protestant

Reformation. It is safe to say then that discontent with not only the church's power but also some of its doctrine did not begin with Luther. Many people in the medieval era were aware of the church's corruption. Kings like Henry II were not the only ones who thought that the power of the church had gone too far.

If this was the case, why did it take until the 1500s for all of this to boil over in the Reformation? We have to remember that there weren't any alternatives to the Catholic Church then. If you disagreed with the church, you couldn't just go down the street to a church you did agree with. And if you tried to break away, you would either be excommunicated or burned at the stake as a heretic. People took the idea of heaven and, even more so, hell very seriously. You weren't going to risk an eternity of punishment by disagreeing with the church. Even kings could be excommunicated. With this in mind, it's almost more surprising that people criticized the church at all.

By the end of the medieval period, the church's corruption had hit an all-time high, and it wouldn't be long before Martin Luther nailed his *Ninety-five Theses* to a door in 1517. It also wasn't long before the English government would have enough of the Catholic Church's interference. Henry VIII would break with Rome in 1534, creating the Church of England, with the English monarch as its head. This new system would attempt to solve the conflict between the church and state by more closely merging the two.

For all its problems, the medieval Catholic Church wielded enormous influence for a long time. Its organization and wealth made it a structure that even kings could not match. It could be argued that in medieval times, it was the church rather than the government that truly had the most influence on people's lives.

Chapter 13: Key Battles That Shaped Medieval History

As we have already seen, medieval history was full of plenty of violence and battles. We have made passing mention to many of these battles throughout this book, but which battles stand out as key moments in English history?

There are far more important battles that occurred in the English Middle Ages than we have time to cover, so we will take a look at just five battles that truly shaped medieval history. These are the engagements whose results would be felt down through the years in England. They are significant for their contribution to both English and military history.

The Battle of Edington (878)

You may be surprised to find that we are not starting with the Norman Conquest and the Battle of Hastings. While the Battle of Hastings does snag the second spot on our list of key battles, we couldn't forgive ourselves if we didn't include at least one battle from the Anglo-Saxon period. The Anglo-Saxons, after all, were pretty good at the whole warfare thing, and their success in this particular battle had huge repercussions for England.

The Battle of Edington took place in 878 between the forces of King Alfred of Wessex and the Vikings led by King Guthrum. The Vikings had invaded in large numbers in 865, and in the thirteen years between then and the Battle of Edington, they had managed to conquer almost all of

England. Mercia and Wessex were the last Anglo-Saxon kingdoms to fall to the Vikings. As the story goes, King Alfred was driven out of his kingdom and took refuge in a swamp. Luckily for England, Alfred was about to make a major comeback.

After hiding in the marshes for several months, Alfred gathered a force to challenge the Vikings in the spring of 878. The two sides clashed sometime in May near the fortress of Chippenham, which was where Alfred had been defeated and forced to flee several months earlier. In the battle itself, the Anglo-Saxons used a shield wall formation against the Danes, and over a long day of fighting, they wore down the Vikings and routed them. The Anglo-Saxons had won a great and what proved to be a decisive victory.

The peace agreement that shortly followed the battle, called the Peace of Wedmore, had Guthrum converting to Christianity. The Danes agreed to retreat into the northeast and east of England, essentially leaving Wessex. This was the establishment of the Danelaw. While Alfred was not able to finish the job of driving the Vikings entirely out of England, the Battle of Edington was a reversal of the Viking takeover that had begun in 865 with the arrival of the *mycel hæþen here* (Great Heathen Army).

Without Alfred's victory at the Battle of Edington, England as a nation might have never come to be. Not only did this battle halt and lead to the eventual reversal of the Viking conquest, but it also gave the Wessex dynasty its start. Since Alfred was the only king able to drive back the Vikings, he paved the way for Wessex to dominate. His grandson, Æthelstan, became the first king of the English. That's more than enough to call the Battle of Edington a key battle in English history.

The Battle of Hastings (1066)

Sometimes the most significant battles in a nation's history are the losses. The Battle of Hastings in 1066 was a loss for the English, and it would end up being a huge turning point in the history of the Middle Ages.

To recap a bit from what we discussed in early chapters, in 1066, England's ruler, Edward the Confessor, died with no children, creating a succession crisis. Harold Godwinson took the throne, but he would have to fight for it, as multiple people saw Edward the Confessor's childlessness as an opportunity to claim the English throne.

Harold was successful in fending off his first rivals: his own brother Tostig and the king of Norway, Harald Hardrada. Harold's forces defeated them near York at the Battle of Stamford Bridge. We bring this up because the Battle of Stamford Bridge had a significant impact on the more famous Battle of Hastings. William of Normandy would land in England only three days after Harold's victory at Stamford Bridge, and the Battle of Hastings took place around nineteen days after Stamford Bridge. Furthermore, the Battle of Stamford Bridge took place near York in the north, while the Battle of Hastings took place in the far south near, big surprise, Hastings. Harold's forces had to march first from London to aid the northern earls in York with the Battle of Stamford Bridge. Then they had to turn around and march back south to engage William's forces. Thus, Harold's forces were far from fresh at the Battle of Hastings, and many historians consider Harold's decision to engage William's forces so soon as a fatal blunder.

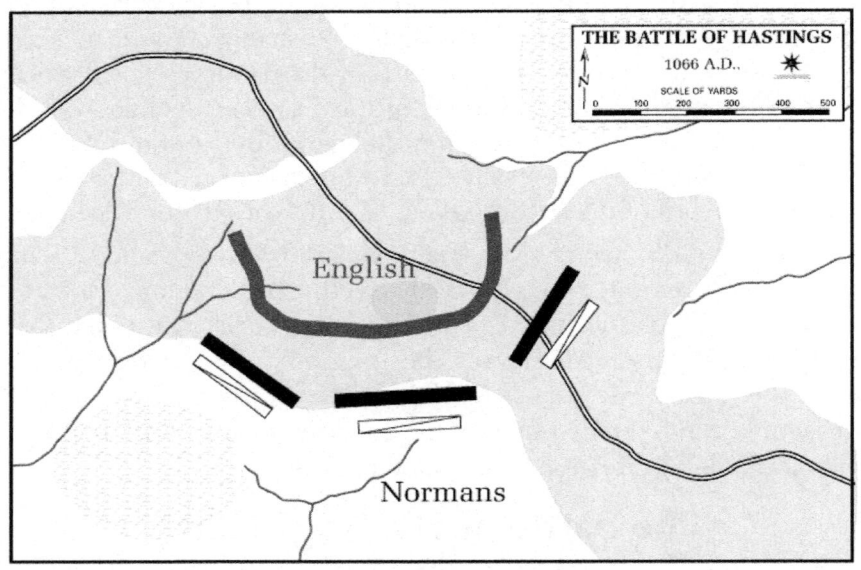

A basic layout of the Battle of Hastings
https://commons.wikimedia.org/wiki/File:Battle_of_Hastings,_1066.png

However, at the start of the actual engagement, it was not at all clear that the Normans would carry the day. Harold's forces held a position at the top of a ridge. For the Normans to win, they needed to charge and break the English line. For the English to win, they needed to hold the line until the Normans were exhausted and retreated. At first, the shield wall of the English was able to repulse the Norman cavalry, but their only real chance was if the Normans gave up. They didn't. Over time, the defensive position of the English was worn down by the repeated Norman assaults. At some point, Harold was killed, as were his two brothers. Leaderless, the English forces scattered as night fell.

After the Battle of Hastings, William faced no serious opposition to his invasion. He was crowned William I in London on December 25th. The story of the Battle of Hastings was told over and over again. The famous Bayeux Tapestry even has a pictorial depiction of this famous battle, showing things like the English axmen facing the Norman cavalry. Unfortunately, all of this retelling also means that there are several contradicting versions that historians are forced to sift through. We don't know all the details, like how exactly Harold died, but we do know that the Battle of Hastings was the key to the Norman Conquest, and there can be no doubt that Norman rule went on to cause some significant changes for England.

The Battle of Bannockburn (1314)

The kingdoms of Scotland and England were joined together under a single king in 1603 when James VI of Scotland became James I of England. The nations, however, remained two separate states with a single monarch until the Acts of Union of 1707, which officially united them. What does this have to do with medieval history? Well, Scotland and England might have been united a lot sooner were it not for the Battle of Bannockburn.

The Battle of Bannockburn was the final decisive battle in a conflict between Scotland and England known as the Wars of Scottish Independence. Edward I, known as the Hammer of the Scots, had begun the process of trying to take over Scotland in 1296, and he did a pretty good job. Although, largely because of the movie *Braveheart*, we remember William Wallace as the great figure who led the Scots to victory at the Battle of Stirling Bridge in 1297. Within a year, Edward I had defeated Wallace at the Battle of Falkirk. For the next six years, England and Scotland fought bitterly, but by 1304, due to diplomatic maneuvering rather than conflicts, Edward I had essentially triumphed. The English controlled Scotland.

The English might have kept their hold on Scotland were it not for the fact that Edward I died in 1307. After his death, the rebel Scots, led by Robert the Bruce, began making serious progress, winning battle after battle and taking back Scotland by force. Things came to a head in 1314 at Bannockburn.

Edward I's son, Edward II, could not simply sit by while Robert the Bruce took back Scotland. In 1314, he invaded Scotland and faced the Bruce's forces. The purpose of the invasion was to bring relief to Stirling Castle, which was the only remaining English stronghold in Scotland that had not surrendered to Robert the Bruce. When Edward II's forces arrived, though, the Scots were waiting for them.

The fighting lasted for two days, with both sides stopping for the night. As the English had a much larger force, the battle was a horrendous defeat for the English and a stunning victory for the Scots. The Scottish infantry had bested the English cavalry. The Battle of Bannockburn was the practical end to the Scottish Wars of Independence, although Scottish independence was not formally recognized by England until 1328.

Besides its importance in both Scottish and English history, the Battle of Bannockburn also has significance for its contribution to military history. The success of the infantry here helped to alter medieval warfare so that the infantry rather than the cavalry began to have more importance on the battlefield. This was the beginning of the end of the age of mounted knights, and our next battle, which occurred around one hundred years later, would only hasten that demise.

The Battle of Agincourt (1415)

Obviously, this chapter focuses on battles that shaped English medieval history, and while the Battle of Agincourt certainly fits the criteria, Agincourt also has a lot of significance in military history in general. The Battle of Bannockburn had shown the power of the infantry, but it was the events of this battle that sounded the death keel of the medieval knight in shining armor.

If you know anything about the Battle of Agincourt, you probably know that it was an astonishing victory for the English, so much so that it's almost taken on a mythical quality in English history. The Battle of Agincourt is the great climax to Shakespeare's play *Henry V.* During World War II, that play and the Battle of Agincourt were depicted on film, with the famous actor Laurence Olivier in the lead role, as part of an effort to maintain British morale. Over five hundred years after it happened, Agincourt had remained a battle that swelled English pride. It was their great triumph. However, no one prior to the battle would have guessed that that would be the outcome.

The Battle of Agincourt took place in France during one of Henry V's campaigns of the Hundred Years' War. The campaign began when Henry V landed in Normandy in August of 1415. Henry V then laid siege to the city of Harfleur. Although he succeeded in capturing the city, the siege had taken longer and been far more costly than Henry V had hoped. In October, Henry V and his forces made for Calais, a port held by the English, where he could set sail back for England. Unfortunately for them, the English were unable to cross the River Somme and reach Calais before they were intercepted by the French forces. The odds were decidedly not in their favor. Although the exact numbers are up for debate, the French had a sure numerical advantage over the English at Agincourt. Henry V's army was around five thousand and six thousand men, and the French army was said to have been somewhere between twenty thousand and thirty thousand. While this may be an exaggeration, even the most skeptical scholars place the French army at around twelve thousand—twice the number of the English. Besides their numerical disadvantage, the English were also exhausted. They had fought a six-week siege at Harfleur and then marched hard to make it to Calais. Things did not look good.

To meet the French, Henry V placed his army on a field bounded on either side by forests. The archers were positioned in wedges on either side of the other soldiers. This formation was crucial since it worked to offset the French numerical advantage. The narrow front limited how many men the French could effectively throw at the English at a time and made it impossible for the French to surround them. The English were also helped by the weather. The rainy weather had turned the field to mud, which slowed the advance of the French knights, giving the English archers far more time to pick them off.

The first wave of French knights was unable to overwhelm and scatter the English archers as they needed to, partially because the English archers had come up with the idea of driving sharpened stakes at angles into the ground to protect themselves from the charge of the French knights. When the second wave of knights then arrived, they did more harm than good for the French effort. The French became too tightly packed to maneuver, and the battle began to highly favor the English. By the time the third wave of French arrived, between the corpses and churned mud, everything was too messy for them to charge at all or to escape the rain of English arrows. The English finished the battle quickly. Reports say that, in all, the Battle of Agincourt only lasted between half an hour to three hours.

Agincourt significantly weakened the French military position. Henry V was able to follow up on his victory with more successes, and by 1420, he was engaged to the French princess, Catherine, and had been named heir to the French throne.

Besides being an important English victory in the Hundred Years' War, Agincourt had also been a victory for the English archer over the mounted knight. Warfare tactics had already begun to evolve, as we saw with the Battle of Bannockburn, and Agincourt pushed them even further. The medieval knight would soon be a figure found in fairy tales and romances rather than on the battlefield.

The Battle of Bosworth (1485)

Speaking in terms of the monarchy and government of the Middle Ages, the Battle of Bosworth was the conflict that capped off the medieval period and started England down a new path.

The final engagement in the infamous Wars of the Roses, the Battle of Bosworth, was a battle between the forces of Richard III and Henry Tudor. The forces of Richard and Henry clashed on August 22nd, 1485. Like many of the battles on this list, it was the side that initially seemed to be at a disadvantage that ultimately carried the day. The forces of Henry Tudor were outnumbered and led by a young man inexperienced in battle. Richard III not only had superior numbers but was also a battle-hardened veteran of the Wars of the Roses. If the two monarchs were actually to meet on the battlefield, there was little doubt who would walk away from the encounter.

Fortunately for Henry Tudor, Richard III never reached him, so no hand-to-hand combat between the two took place. Despite his superior numbers, Richard III's army was defeated, and Richard himself was killed in battle. Henry's victory was at least in part thanks to the forces of the Stanley brothers. These two English lords had pledged their forces to both Henry and Richard. Thomas Stanley's forces remained neutral throughout the entire battle, but William Stanley finally threw his lot in with Henry at a key moment, swinging the battle in the future Tudor king's favor. While many see the actions of the Stanleys as evidence of Richard III's tyrannical nature, it also shows just how bloody and unstable the Wars of the Roses had made England. Men were reluctant to join either side in this clash of kings until a winner became clear because picking the wrong one was often a fatal mistake.

And the Battle of Bosworth truly was a clash between kings. Although they did not face each other directly, both Richard III and Henry Tudor had styled the battle as a sort of trial by combat. Whichever side came away the victor was the one that God favored. They would have the divine right to the throne. It was a battle that everyone seemed to understand would be decisive before it even began.

With these stakes, it is no wonder that after losing the Battle of Bosworth, Richard III has gone down in history as one of the most infamous kings in English history. Even so, history also records that Richard III fought bravely at Bosworth. In context, that famous line from Shakespeare, "My horse! My horse! My kingdom for a horse!" is not Richard seeking to run away but rather his desire to charge back into battle. Richard III had staked everything on the Battle of Bosworth, and when he lost, he lost not only his life but also his legacy.

Richard III was the last English monarch to be killed in battle, a fact that shows a lot about why this battle was so significant. The death of Richard III was the end of the Plantagenet dynasty, a line whose greatness had, in many ways, been tied to their martial abilities. The greats of the Plantagenets were mighty warriors: Richard the Lionheart, Edward the Hammer of the Scots, and Henry V, the hero of Agincourt. The bad Plantagenet kings were those who failed to win battles: King John, Edward II, and Henry VI.

When Richard III died at Bosworth, that legacy ended. The Tudor monarchs would not define themselves by warfare in the same way that the Plantagenets had. The Battle of Bosworth ironically would begin to push England down a less war-centered path. It was both a culmination of and an end to the warfare of the Middle Ages.

Chapter 14: Medieval Myth

When you hear the word myth, what do you think about? Do you picture the many gods and goddesses of the Greco-Roman world? Do you think about stories of heroes embarking on daring quests? Do you think about tales from folklore with their many versions and clear morals?

What is a myth? That is a harder question to answer than one might initially think. We associate a lot of different things with that little word. Is a myth a religious belief, or is it simply a story? Is it a way that people explain the world around them, or is it simply entertainment? How old does a story have to be to be considered a myth? There are a lot of questions that get in the way of our definition of a myth.

However, that is a debate for a more academically focused book. What we care about for this book is that myths can cover a wide range of things. So, we won't just be talking about gods in this chapter. We will be looking at the legends, epics, tales, and stories that made up the world of medieval English myth.

The Arthurian Legend

Before we look at some of the overarching themes and realities that influenced medieval myth, let's start with the most famous myth from medieval England: the Arthurian legend. If any medieval English myth has survived through the ages, it is the legend of King Arthur. Like most myths, there are a lot of different variations and stories surrounding King Arthur. Besides King Arthur himself, the Arthurian legend also contains plenty of other famous mythic elements and characters like the wizard

Merlin, the sword Excalibur, the Knights of the Round Table, the Lady of the Lake, and so much more. The Arthurian legend is the most famous surviving British myth, and it is one of the few legends that we associate specifically with Britain. However, this story, while it is British, isn't actually English.

King Arthur was originally a Celtic hero, and he may have been a real person. As we learned at the very beginning of this book, when the Romans left Britain, the Anglo-Saxons invaded. The Celtic inhabitants of the island were pushed out. However, historical records do tell of one incredible Celtic victory over the Anglo-Saxon invaders: the Battle of Badon. The earliest texts that mention Badon do not name Arthur, but in the 9th century, the *Historia Brittonum* by Nennius names Arthur as the Celtic leader and attributes the victory to him. This appears to be the earliest mention of Arthur, although another text from around this time, the *Annales Cambriae*, also mentions Arthur. The legend only grew from there, thanks largely to the writing of Geoffrey of Monmouth in the 12th century, who would come to be known as the father of the Arthurian tradition.

Arthur leading the charge at Mount Badon (an illustration for Tennyson's "Lancelot and Guinevere")

So, does that mean that Arthur existed? It's far from certain. Although both Nennius and Geoffrey of Monmouth claimed to be writing histories, both works clearly value the narrative more than historical accuracy. Also, the Battle of Badon took place sometime around 450, and Nennius, who was again the first to name Arthur, didn't write his account until around four centuries later. We aren't even certain that the battle itself took place. What we do know is that whether he began as a real person or not, King Arthur quickly moved beyond that.

Stories featuring Arthur abounded in oral traditions of the Middle Ages, and eventually, some medieval writers put the legend to paper. Chrétien de Troyes (a French writer) added tales of chivalry and romance to the legend, but the person we have to thank for most of our modern ideas of King Arthur is Sir Thomas Malory, who wrote *The Death of Arthur* (*Le Morte d'Arthur*), a book compiling many of the tales into a single story, in 1485.

The legend of King Arthur is thus a myth that is truly medieval in terms of its time of development. Even though the Battle of Badon took place slightly before the medieval period, stories about Arthur were first told and then written down in the Middle Ages, and the setting of the stories was altered to fit the period in which they were told rather than the period in which Arthur might have lived.

The fact that we think of Arthur as being so quintessentially British when he was originally celebrated for beating the Anglo-Saxons shows us something that made British and English myths in the Middle Ages unique. There was a lot of mixing. The small island of Britain had been conquered and settled by so many different people that it was host to Celtic, Christian, and Germanic myths all at the same time. Arthur is a Celtic myth. Now, let's turn our attention to the most famous Anglo-Saxon myth from this period.

Beowulf

Coming in just slightly behind Arthur in terms of notoriety is the epic Old English poem, *Beowulf*, which tells the tale of its titular hero. The story of Beowulf appears to take place around the 6th century. However, we are not sure when the poem was first written down. There is a surviving manuscript from around the year 1000, but some scholars believe it may have been put to paper as much as two hundred years earlier. Like other poetry and tales of its day, *Beowulf* likely existed in the oral tradition long before it was officially composed by an unknown author.

Beowulf is famous for being one of the earliest works of literature in Old English, and it also happens to be the earliest European epic that we know of. However, while it is famous for being written down for the first time in Old English, *Beowulf*, like the Arthurian legend, isn't exactly English. It is a Scandinavian tale. In the first half of the poem, Beowulf helps Hrothgar, the king of Denmark, by killing two monsters that have been terrorizing the Danes. In the second half, Beowulf becomes the king of Geatland, which was an area in what is now southern Sweden.

Beowulf is then part of a more Germanic culture that came to England with the Anglo-Saxons at the beginning of the Middle Ages. In the story, we can also see the influence of Christianity. Unlike the heroes of ancient epics like the *Odyssey*, *Iliad*, and *Aeneid*, Beowulf spends all of his time fighting monsters, pure incarnations of evil, rather than men. Even then, the tone of *Beowulf* feels far more somber. The story ends with an aged Beowulf becoming mortally wounded in his fight with a dragon. The classic warrior hero is there, but *Beowulf* also carries a sense of melancholy that is not present in other ancient epics. It reflects the tensions of a culture that glorified warfare while also valuing the doctrines of Christianity.

With both Celtic and Germanic influences, as well as the ever-present influence of Christianity, myth in medieval England came from a variety of sources. There are few stories from this period that are pure "English." However, there is a collection of tales that were written in the Late Middle Ages that do hold that title.

The Canterbury Tales

The Canterbury Tales was a book written by Geoffrey Chaucer near the end of the 14th century. It follows the journey of thirty pilgrims on their way to visit Thomas Becket's shrine at Canterbury Cathedral. On the way, they engage in a storytelling contest, and the book is mostly a collection of the various tales the pilgrims tell. There are twenty-four tales, but the book is uncompleted. Chaucer had plans for many more stories.

The Canterbury Tales may be closer to literature than a myth. Unlike the Arthurian legend and *Beowulf*, *The Canterbury Tales* was written first rather than starting as a popular story that was only later written down. However, many of the tales included are at least partially taken from other sources, so although Chaucer altered and wrote them in the 14th century, some of the stories were much older.

Another reason *The Canterbury Tales* is an important example of English myth is because of the sheer variety. The collection includes a large variety of stories, from crude humor to piety, tragedy, and fables. One reason it has so much variety is that Chaucer included so many different classes of people in his story. There is a knight, a nun, a monk, a miller, a physician, a sailor, and many more that make up the group of thirty pilgrims, and they all tell a tale that fits with their position. The book is thus an excellent example of many different types of medieval stories. You can read *The Canterbury Tales* and have a general idea of what types of stories people told in this period.

The Canterbury Tales is also important in the history of English culture. After the Norman Conquest, French became the preferred language of the powerful, and English (they were using Middle English at this time) was reduced to being seen as a lesser language used by peasants. Chaucer, however, wrote *The Canterbury Tales* in Middle English, not French, and it was one of the earliest works of truly English literature because of it. Between *Beowulf* and *The Canterbury Tales*, the medieval period is hugely important for how it turned English myths and stories into literature. This is the period when written stories first began gaining popularity, though it would be a long time yet before they surpassed the oral tradition.

Medieval Folklore

Speaking of the oral tradition, most people in the medieval period were illiterate, so telling stories aloud was how most myths and tales got passed around. Medieval folklore refers specifically to European stories that were popular between around 500 and 1500.

There is an immense variety of tales that fall under the category of medieval folklore, and there is a long history of scholars who have tried to sort through and categorize it. The main reason for the difficulty is the oral nature of folklore. While the Arthurian legend, Beowulf, and *The Canterbury Tales* all have famous pieces of literature associated with them, folk tales were not extensively written down until around the 19th century. Because they were purely oral, the tales varied from location to location and even from telling to telling. Telling a folk tale was not just a matter of recitation. It was a performance. Tellers would alter the basic formula for particular audiences and settings. All of that makes for a lot of different stories and different versions of the same story.

To try to make sense of all the variety, folklorists have developed different categories to describe some of the general types of tales from this period. Here are some of the kinds of stories you might have heard from the Middle Ages:

- Animal Tales - Remember Aesop's fables? Stories with animals acting like humans have been around for a long time, and these fables typically taught moral lessons.

- Anecdotes and Jokes - Just like today, medieval people enjoyed a good joke. There were lots of stories about cheating wives and stupid husbands.

- Tales of the Stupid Ogre - These were stories about supernatural beings that get outsmarted by the protagonist of the story.

- Religious and Realistic Tales - These tales often had contemporary settings and strong Christian morals.

- Magic Tales - As the name suggests, these tales have magic and include many popular fairy tales that have survived today, such as Cinderella and Rapunzel. The medieval version of most of these tales is much darker than the family-friendly versions that Disney made.

These varieties give you an idea of just how many different types of stories there were, and they still don't cover everything. *The Canterbury Tales* has good examples of many of the different kinds.

So far in this chapter, we have focused a lot on different stories that compromised medieval myth, but another aspect of medieval myths is the fantastical creatures that often appeared in the stories and which, for many people in the Middle Ages, might also be lurking around a corner in the real world.

Fairies and Monsters

We mentioned briefly in the chapter on religion that many people in England believed strongly in the existence of fairies and other spirits. However, these were not the cute tiny creatures that wear clothes made out of leaves and spread fairy dust. Medieval fairies were a different breed. They were malevolent beings that you needed to please, or they would play nasty tricks on you.

Take Puck or Robin Goodfellow, for example. In Shakespeare's *A Midsummer Night's Dream*, Puck is a mischievous and playful figure, but

Shakespeare wrote it during the Renaissance. In the medieval era, though, "puck" could mean devil. A puck was not a fun-loving being but an evil spirit. Fairies were believed to be devils. After the spread of Christianity, one explanation said that fairies were said to be fallen angels that had become trapped on earth. They were eternally damned and malevolent creatures, and the people of medieval England took them very seriously. People didn't even like to say the word fairies and so often referred to them as the little people.

There were many different types of fairies. One type was a will-o'-the-wisp, which took the form of a glowing light that led people astray. They could get you lost or even lead you to your death in a marsh. Another type was brownies, which would do housework if you were nice to them. Banshees were foretellers of doom, and goblins were never good news. To the medieval mind, the English countryside was filled with magical beings.

The belief in the little people in England was so strong that it has not completely died out. There were reports of fairy sightings as late as the 20th century. In the British Isles, the little people are more than just stories. They are a part of the culture of the region.

Besides fairies and spirits, medieval stories and literature also had quite a lot of fantastic monsters. Bestiaries from the period were books filled with pictures of various animals, some real and some mythical. Even the real animals sometimes looked mythical since people in England tried to depict animals from far-away lands that they had never seen. Dolphins had human faces but with their mouths on their torso area. Here are some of the most well-known and also some of the most bizarre creatures of the period:

- Pegasus - The pegasus is a winged horse originally from Greek and Roman mythology.
- Dragon - The dragon is the ultimate beast. It is connected with serpents and thus also with the devil. Dragons in medieval mythology are purely evil.
- Manticore - A manticore is a beast with the body of a lion, the head of a man, and the tail of a scorpion. They were said to come from the area around India and Persia.
- Merknight - You have heard of mermaids, but the medieval period also had merknights and mermen, which are exactly what they sound like. Their bottom half is a fish, and the top half is an armored man.

- Sea Monk - These strange creatures were said to have the body of a fish and a head like a monk, with a shaved head and a ring of hair. This may have been describing seals.

- Onocentaur - A creature with the head of a donkey and the body of a man. It seems Shakespeare was not the one to make up that bizarre creation in *A Midsummer Night's Dream* after all.

- Blemmyae - A monster with the body of a man but with no head and its face on its chest.

These are just a few examples of the many varied beasts of medieval myth. They range from the classics that still appear in stories today to the downright bizarre. Since medieval people knew very little about the world beyond their local area, it was very easy for them to believe that these creatures existed somewhere. That may sound crazy, but when you think about it, a giraffe and an elephant can sound mythical to someone who has never seen one.

So, English myth in the Middle Ages was full of lots of creatures and magic, which is what we generally picture when we think of medieval tales. However, not every story saw Beowulf fighting a dragon or Arthur receiving the sword from the Lady in the Lake. There were fables, jokes, religious stories, and more. Also, medieval myths continue to have an impact today. While we may not be as concerned about offending the little people anymore, many of the fairy tales that we tell our children today are versions of stories that originated in the Middle Ages. A lot has changed, but we still enjoy many of the same stories that medieval people did.

Chapter 15: Medieval Medicine

Many people are guilty of over-romanticizing not just the Middle Ages but almost any past era in history. We probably do this because we are so aware of our problems in the present day. However, if there is one societal advancement that not even the most old-fashioned person wants to give up, it has to be modern medicine. Not dying is something that everyone can get behind, and thanks to things like vaccinations, anesthesia, the discovery of germs, antibiotics, and many more advancements, your chances of recovering from an illness today are significantly improved.

So, what was the world like before modern medicine? The first vaccine, which was for smallpox, wasn't developed until 1796. The first antibiotic was penicillin, and that wasn't discovered until 1928. We didn't even know that germs caused illness until 1861. A lot of the things that we consider to be hallmarks of medicine were still hundreds of years away in the Middle Ages, so what did they do instead? How did they understand health, and what did they do if someone got sick?

The Humors

A lot of medieval ideas about human health came from the ancient Greek and Roman societies. One of the big ideas from Greek medicine that had a large influence on medieval medicine was the four humors.

This was a theory developed by Hippocrates. It said that the human body consisted of four humors (fluids), which were yellow bile, phlegm, black bile, and blood. These four humors were controlled by the four elements: fire, water, earth, and air. Illness was believed to be the result of an imbalance of these four fluids. Having too much black bile made you melancholic, phlegm made you phlegmatic, yellow bile made you choleric, and blood made you sanguine.

Bloodletting was thus a common medicinal treatment because it was believed that purging the body of excess blood would restore balance. This procedure was often done through cuts, but blood could also be drained using leeches. If blood wasn't the problem, physicians might also suggest particular foods to restore the body's humor balance.

The humors went beyond just keeping you healthy. They were also believed to affect personality and were categorized based on heat and moisture.

- Black Bile: Cold and Dry
- Phlegm: Cold and Moist
- Yellow Bile: Hot and Dry
- Blood: Hot and Moist

The balance of humors in a person's body changed with their age, seasons of the year, and even their gender. For example, youths were considered to be hot and moist and thus had more blood, while older people were thought to be cold and dry, having more black bile. The balance of humors in a person could have a great impact on their temperament. It was believed that yellow bile made a person courageous, but too much phlegm made people cowardly.

Belief and reliance on the idea of the four humors persisted well past the Middle Ages. Emphasis on the humors' impact on a person's emotions and personalities became even more pronounced in the Renaissance. The theory of the humors did not fall out of favor until it was replaced by germ theory in the 19th century.

Diagnosis and Treatment

Medieval doctors may have been incorrect about the causes of illness, but they did take observing the symptoms of their patients very seriously. Medieval physicians were experts in diagnosis. They determined a person's ailment by listening to their patients, observing, feeling the pulse, and taking urine samples.

Urine samples were perhaps the most common method of diagnosis, so much so that the urine flask was the symbol of the medieval doctor. While medieval doctors could not run lab tests on urine like today, they did visually examine it to determine a diagnosis.

A medical practitioner examining a urine flask—painting from the 17th century
https://commons.wikimedia.org/wiki/File:A_medical_practitioner_examining_a_urine_flask._Oil_p
ainting_Wellcome_V0017268.jpg

Once they had made a diagnosis, how did medieval doctors treat their patients? While some procedures like bloodletting were used, the main form of treatment was herbal medicine. You could get these medicines from a physician or monks at a monastery, but in rural areas, you often went to a local herbalist.

Like the theory of the four humors, much of what medieval people knew about medicinal plants came from the ancients. The *De materia medica,* written by Dioscorides, a Greek, was a highly influential book that described the use of hundreds of plants.

Medieval people did not solely rely on what they learned from the ancients, however. Monasteries housed gardens that grew important medicinal plants. Besides growing them, the monks would also experiment to learn more about the uses of these plants. However, while they were interested in what uses particular plants had, the monks were not as keen on discovering why exactly certain plants were able to cure particular ailments. They were content with the explanation that God had made it so.

Like many aspects of medieval life, there was a divide in the medical treatment of the rich and the poor. Only the rich had access to trained physicians. Peasants had to make do with whatever local wise woman or herbalist lived near them. These rural practitioners relied on their experience and folk knowledge that was passed down, which often included the uses of various herbs as well as other more surreptitious methods like charms.

That didn't mean that a peasant with a serious illness was completely out of luck, though. There were hospitals in the Middle Ages, thanks in large part to the church. Hospitals were often attached to large monasteries, and it was the monks and nuns who lived there who would treat the sick and dying. It is unclear exactly how much the average monk or nun knew about medicine, but monasteries were one of the largest sources of medicinal herbs, so it is safe to say that they probably knew more than the layperson.

Surgeries and Procedures

If medicinal herbs were not enough to deal with an illness, then other things could be used to treat a patient. As we have already mentioned, bloodletting was a common treatment, but there were also far more involved procedures. However, surgeries were not performed by doctors. In the Middle Ages, the doctor and surgeon professions were separate. Procedures were typically carried out not by doctors but by barber-surgeons.

The name of this profession may sound strange, but it is appropriate, for the barber-surgeons of the medieval era both cut hair and cut off limbs. A barber-surgeon did a variety of tasks, such as setting bones, bloodletting, pulling teeth, performing amputations, and, of course, cutting hair. They were especially valuable on the battlefield, where amputations and other emergency medical needs were quite frequent. However, overall, barber-surgeons were held in much lower esteem than physicians.

That lack of esteem might have been because no one wanted to undergo surgery if they could help it. Surgery was a horrific experience that might kill you rather than save you, and that was not because of a lack of skill on the part of medieval surgeons. The main problem was the lack of anesthesia. Imagine undergoing any type of surgery without being put to sleep first, and you'll have a pretty good understanding of why surgery was not the go-to solution for medical problems in the Middle Ages. Opiates, herbs, and alcohol were used to try to dull the pain, but it could only dull it. No matter what, surgery was sure to be an excruciating experience.

The pain was not the only problem. The other was infection. There is a reason that doctors today perform surgeries with masks on in a completely sterilized room. Even if the surgery is effective, if the wound from the procedure becomes infected, then the patient might end up in worse shape than when they started. In the Middle Ages, they lacked the disinfectants and sterilization techniques that we use now. To prevent infection, wounds were typically cauterized, which refers to the practice of burning a wound to stop the infection and halt the bleeding.

Because of these problems, surgeries in the Middle Ages tended to be on more external parts of the body. Without anesthesia, medieval surgeons could not reach a person's vital organs, like the heart, without a very high risk of killing them in the process. However, they were able to perform procedures like removing cataracts and even trepanning, which involved drilling a hole in the skull.

Perhaps the most shocking thing about medieval surgery, though, is how successful it often was. Thanks to the constant warfare, surgeons became quite skilled at setting bones and patching up traumatic wounds. They could not perform open-heart surgery, but they could mend broken skulls, amputate limbs, and more. Surgery was gory, painful, and quite dangerous, but it existed because it did get results.

Medieval Illnesses

What exactly were medieval doctors treating their patients for? We will talk extensively about the most famous illness of the period—the plague—in the next chapter, but that was far from the only disease that existed at the time. Here are some of the diseases other than the Black Death that plagued people in medieval England:

- Leprosy - While leprosy is a particular disease, in the Middle Ages, any skin condition that was disfiguring enough would have been referred to as leprosy. One of the main reasons for the prominence of leprosy was the lack of personal hygiene, which made it much easier for people to develop infections. The disease destroys the outside of the body, resulting not only in open sores but also in the loss of fingers, toes, and, in some cases, a person's nose. Leprosy was considered to be highly contagious, and lepers were typically isolated from society to protect others. They even had to ring a bell to warn people of their approach.

- St. Anthony's Fire - This disease is so named because it causes redness and burning in a person's hands and feet. Unfortunately, it doesn't stop there. The redness spreads, becoming gangrene that could cause the loss of entire limbs. St. Anthony's Fire was caused by ingesting rye that had been tainted by a particular fungus.

- Sweating Sickness - This was a fast-acting illness that appeared at the end of the Middle Ages. Symptoms progressed rapidly from a headache and prostration to severe sweating and delusions. A person was often dead within hours of the first sign of the disease, but if they managed to make it through the first day, then they often survived. Even today, we are not exactly sure what the sweating sickness was, but it virtually disappeared sometime after the last major outbreak in 1551.

- Smallpox - Until the vaccination was developed in 1796, smallpox was a devastating disease, especially for children. Those who survived often had scars from the pockmarks, but people were immune to a second infection.

- Tuberculosis - Another disease that was present in the Middle Ages that, like smallpox, lasted for a long time was tuberculosis. This illness causes masses in the lungs, which can cause people to cough up blood. Unlike almost all the other major diseases of the Middle Ages, tuberculosis is still a major disease. It spreads most rapidly in dense populations, so the impact of tuberculosis worsened after the Middle Ages when industrialization caused rapid city growth.

These illnesses were just some of the things that could afflict a person in medieval England. There were also issues like arthritis and, for women, the danger of childbirth. Infant mortality rates were especially high. It was not an easy time to stay healthy, no matter the person's class.

Religion and Medicine

Today, we may find it easy to sneer at the ignorance of medieval people, but without a knowledge of germs, the origins of various illnesses and ailments are quite mysterious. The four humors were one way that illness was explained, but like almost everything in this period, disease and medicine were also tied to religion.

In the Gospel of Luke in the Bible, there is a moment where Jesus and his disciples encounter a blind man. The disciples ask Jesus whose sin has caused the man's blindness, his own or his parents. This small moment is a perfect example of how the medieval church often thought of illness. All grief and destruction in the world were due to sin. Therefore, disease and illness must be the result of sin. This remains true in Christian doctrine today, but what Jesus's disciples implied with their question and how the medieval church viewed the relationship between sin and illness is different. It is not just that sin generally is the source of all bad things but that an individual's sin is the cause of their individual illness. If you fell ill, it was because you had sinned, and God was punishing you.

Now, if you keep reading that story in the Gospel of Luke, you will discover that Jesus specifically told his disciples that that was not the case. It was no individual sin that caused the man's blindness. However, the general population of medieval England could not read, nor did they even own a Bible. Everything they knew of their religious beliefs came from what the church told them, so the idea that illness was the result of a person's sin was blindly accepted. You can start to see why the translation of the Bible into English had such a large impact on the Protestant Reformation and the ultimate break with the Roman Catholic Church.

Understanding this view of disease and sickness being tied to sin is crucial for us to understand why so many people sought religious cures for physical ailments. Pilgrimages to shrines like Canterbury were common for those seeking healing, and particular shrines were appealed to for particular illnesses. Canterbury appears to have been especially important for people suffering from bleeding disorders. Besides traveling to particular holy sites, people could also pray to certain saints and seek blessings from their local clergy.

The tie between religion and treatments could get much more physical, though. For instance, one reason for trepanning, which was the practice of drilling a hole in a person's skull, might have been to relieve a person of an evil spirit. There was also a common belief called the doctrine of signatures, which said that plants that resembled certain body parts could be used in healing those body parts. This philosophy had its roots in antiquity, much like the humors, but in the medieval period, it was ascribed to God's will.

So, a lot of medieval medicine was influenced by religion, specifically Christianity. There was a general faith in providence that meant that people did not probe too deeply into the causes or the cures of various illnesses. We might declare such an attitude to be naive, but in a world without advanced medical technology, the attitude that things were so because God made them so may have been comforting. It gave reason to ailments that at the time seemed horrific and unreasonable.

Medieval Medical Blunders

Throughout this chapter, you have probably noticed several things that don't seem like the best idea for treating illnesses. Drilling holes in a person's skull is not a way to stop odd behavior, and the four humors are not the cause of disease. Considering what they had to work with, medieval medicine wasn't all bad, but they were very wrong about a lot of things.

Perhaps the most common blunder that medieval people made in terms of medical treatments was bloodletting. Because of the belief in the need for the balance of the four humors, bloodletting and leeches were very common treatments for a variety of ailments. However, in reality, you kind of need your blood. If you lost too much during the process, then the treatment would kill you faster than the disease. And even if it didn't kill you, the blood loss could leave you weakened, and the wound might become infected. Besides that, in most cases, bloodletting had no effect whatsoever on the diseases it was supposed to treat.

Why in most cases? Bloodletting may have been practiced so extensively because it did appear to help at times. A patient suffering from high blood pressure and other heart problems might experience a temporary recovery from bloodletting, but it did not fix the problem or cure the patient. It has also been suggested that bloodletting might have worked in some cases because it killed bacteria that needed the iron available in the blood to survive, but even if that's true, it's still a double-edged sword because the human body also needs iron. Even if bloodletting might have had some positive side effects, it was still dangerous and harmful and used widely for all sorts of illnesses.

The other serious health blunder of the Middle Ages went beyond medical treatments to medieval life in general, and that blunder was hygiene or rather a lack thereof. Smelling bad and being dirty are unpleasant enough, but it is the unseen things that make personal hygiene so important. Germs can easily spread like wildfire in a society where no one uses soap, and the chances of any type of infection are significantly higher.

The lack of self-cleaning wasn't the only problem, though. Society as a whole had some hygiene issues. Waste was not properly disposed of and could easily contaminate rivers and other sources of drinking water. Drinking water was so likely to make a person sick that most people in medieval England drank ale as their regular drink instead.

With no knowledge of germs, medieval people did not understand the need for sanitation. Although germ theory would not enter the scene until the 19th century, the people of medieval England started to clean up their act sooner thanks to one of the most infamous diseases to ever exist: the Black Death.

Chapter 16: The Black Death

As we come to the end of our walk through medieval England, we have to close with something that both helped to make the Middle Ages infamous and helped to end them. The Black Death swept through and ravaged Europe from 1347 to 1351. Since England was an island and thus more isolated, it did take longer for the plague to reach it, but by 1350, it had reached even the northern end of the British Isles.

The Black Death vs. Plague

Before we dive into the details of the spread, cause, and impact of the Black Death, we need to clarify some terms that can be quite confusing. What is the difference between the Black Death and the plague?

Plague does not refer to an outbreak of any deadly disease. The term plague refers specifically to the disease caused by the bacterium *Yersinia pestis*. It is a disease that exists primarily in rodents and is passed to humans through contact with fleas that have bitten infected rodents. Plague still exists today, especially in areas with large rodent populations that harbor the disease. There have been outbreaks of plague as late as the 20th century, but thanks to modern medicine, especially antibiotics, plague is no longer a serious threat to human life.

The Black Death, on the other hand, refers to a specific outbreak of plague in Europe from 1347 to 1351. This was not the only outbreak of the plague to occur. It is the second recorded pandemic of the plague, but it was by far the deadliest. Plague is the disease, while the Black Death is a particular plague pandemic of the 14th century.

Spread

The Black Death came to Europe from Asia, and its spread is considered by many to be the first and also most devastating act of biological warfare. The Mongol army under Kipchak khan Janibeg laid siege to Kaffa (which is modern-day Feodosiya) in Crimea in 1346. Because the city of Kaffa (also spelled Caffa) had sea access, the Mongol army found it very difficult to force the city to surrender, although conditions in the city deteriorated quickly because of the siege.

The long siege kept the Mongol army in place for a long period, and the plague, which the army already carried, spread throughout the army. After around a year, the siege was far from the Mongols' biggest worry. The plague was wiping out the army, but Janibeg thought of one way to turn the situation to his advantage. The Mongol army used catapults to fling the corpses of those who had died from the plague into the city of Kaffa. In the cramped and dirty conditions of a besieged city, the result was inevitable. Kaffa, like the Mongol army on its doorstep, was brought to its knees by the disease. Tradition says that four boats attempted to flee Kaffa and sailed for Italy, and it was from these four boats that the plague spread to Europe.

This is a pretty dramatic version of events, but how accurate is it? This understanding of the plague's origins comes from a manuscript written by Gabriele de' Mussi of Piacenza. It was written only a year or two after the events it describes, and although de' Mussi may not have seen the events himself, he likely had access to eyewitnesses. Thus, it seems likely that we can trust his account.

However, there are a few things that may not be entirely accurate about this version of events, and it is surprisingly not the invention of biological warfare. That is entirely plausible. What we are less sure of is the idea that the plague spread to Europe entirely through the survivors of the siege of Kaffa. There were several other routes that probably had a hand in taking the disease from Asia to Europe as well. There were both overland and sea trade routes between the infected areas and Europe that likely also contributed to the spread.

What we do know is that the plague hit Italy first and then spread northward. England managed to escape infestation for around a year, but sometime in the summer of 1348, a ship carrying the disease landed at Melcombe Regis in Dorset. It didn't take long to spread, and London was facing the pandemic before the end of the year. By 1350, the plague had reached even the northernmost part of Scotland.

This rapid spread is a large part of just what made the plague so destructive. It ran through the continent in an unstoppable march that left massive amounts of death in its wake. How exactly did it spread, though?

By now, the story of the rats and the fleas is almost legendary. Rats infected with the plague moved from location to location aboard ships. These infested rats were then bitten by fleas, and the fleas then bit people; thus, the Black Death swept through Europe.

That much is true, but the rats and fleas may not have been the only way the plague spread. Once humans became infected, it might have also passed more directly from person to person or from person to flea without the need for the rat hosts. The story of the catapulted corpses at Kaffa certainly confirms that the plague could be spread without the need for rats, but the rats did play a large role.

Cause

So, we know how the Black Death spread, but what caused it in the first place? At the time, there were a lot of theories. Some said that the plague was a punishment from God. Others believed that the plague was spread through bad smells. However, the most harmful belief for the cause of the plague was that the Jews were responsible.

Jews were thought to be less affected by the plague than Christians, and this might have been partially true because Jews often practiced better hygiene than medieval Christians due to their religious rituals. The idea spread that Jews had poisoned wells in major cities, making them the source of the plague. Jews were massacred, particularly in German-speaking areas. England did not participate in this antisemitic violence, but that was only because all the Jews had been expelled from England fifty years early with Edward I's Edict of Expulsion.

Needless to say, the plague was not caused by Jews, nor by bad smells, so what did cause it? Today, we know that the Black Death was caused by the bacterium *Yersinia pestis*, which can still cause plague today. *Yersinia pestis* is carried by resistant rats, which carry the plague but are not killed by it, and then passed to other species, including people, by fleas. The overall lack of hygiene in the Middle Ages meant that both rats and fleas were in abundance pretty much everywhere, so there was little they could do to halt the plague's spread.

Symptoms and Types of Plague

We have talked about how it started and what caused it, but what was the Black Death like? It's a very dramatic name, but did the sickness live up to it? In truth, the name does not even begin to cover how horrible the plague was.

You may have heard the plague also referred to as the bubonic plague, and that is because there are three forms that the plague could take, depending on the strain of *Y. pestis* that caused it. Bubonic plague was by far the most common, but all three were present during the Black Death, and they caused different symptoms.

- Bubonic Plague - This was the most common form of plague. It caused massive swelling of the lymph nodes. The swellings were known as buboes, and they occurred around the neck, groin, and armpits. They were around the size of eggs, oozed pus, and were incredibly painful. The buboes were not the only symptom of the plague. There was also a high fever, nausea, aching joints, and just generally feeling awful. Most people who contracted bubonic plague were dead within a week, and it is believed to have had around a 70 percent mortality rate. What makes matters worse is that bubonic plague was the least deadly form the plague took.

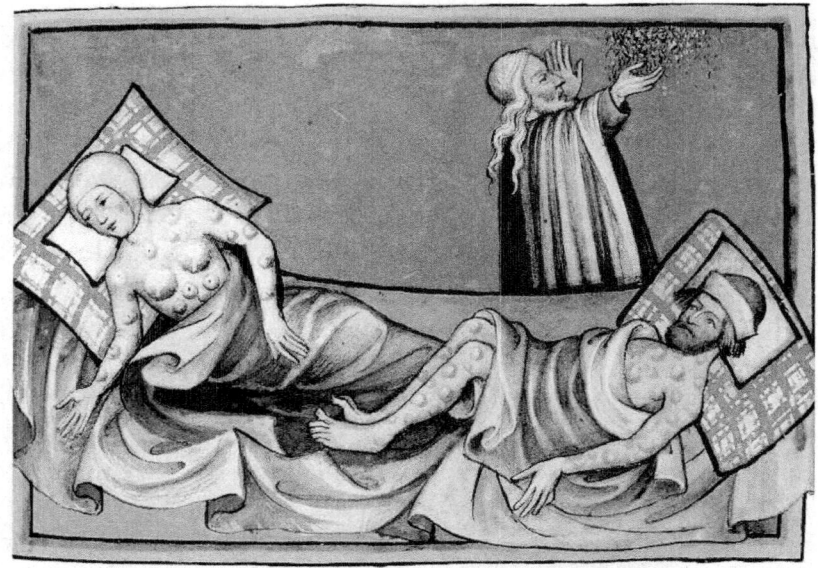

Image of people with bubonic plague

- Pneumatic Plague - At some point, another strain of the disease appeared, and this version was airborne. It attacked the lungs first, and the survival rate was virtually nonexistent. The more positive estimates place the mortality rate of pneumatic plague at around 90 percent to 95 percent. Today, the pneumatic plague is considered to be the most dangerous because it can be spread easily from person to person.

- Septicaemic Plague - You might have thought things couldn't get worse, but the plague had one final form that was even more deadly in the Middle Ages. Septicaemic plague infects the bloodstream and is spread through the bite of an infected insect. It can occur on its own or develop due to bubonic plague. Because it is in the blood, it spreads the plague throughout the entire body, causing skin and other tissue to die and turn black. Some believe that this may be where the name Black Death originated, but we don't know for sure. Body parts like fingers and toes could even fall off. It was essentially blood poisoning, and in the Middle Ages, it killed everyone who got it. The mortality rate was 100 percent, maybe 99 percent if you want to be positive. Luckily, this was the rarest form of plague.

Whatever form of plague you got, your chances of survival ranged from practically nonexistent to extremely low. Your only real hope was to avoid contracting the disease.

The plague was an indiscriminate killer. It didn't care if you were rich or poor. Even royalty was not safe. In 1348, Joan, the daughter of Edward III, contracted the plague and died at the age of thirteen. Still, those who could afford to were able to lock themselves away in rural estates where they did have a better chance of avoiding the disease.

Treatment

So, was there anything that could be done for those suffering from the plague? Doctors did attempt to treat patients, but there was simply no cure, and it was highly dangerous for the doctors themselves. The gear doctors wore to protect themselves has since become an easily recognizable costume. Plague doctors wore a mask with a long beak that resembled a bird and glass holes for their eyes. The beak held things like flowers and herbs because it was believed that the disease spread through smell. Doctors also wore long coats and gloves and used a cane to examine patients to protect themselves. The outfit was completed with a brimmed hat that was the sign of their profession. Plague doctors got their start during the Black Death, but the iconic outfit as we know it today probably wasn't completely developed until later outbreaks of the plague.

Plague doctor

The lack of an actual cure did not stop people from trying several bizarre things. One method was to pluck a live chicken and place the chicken against the buboes of the infected person. The idea was that the chicken would draw the sickness out of the person and into itself. Another method was eating or drinking crushed emeralds. There were several different potions and mixtures that claimed to cure the plague, and people even drank urine. Some sought more spiritual cures. There was the standard prayer and fasting, but people also practiced public flagellation (whipping themselves) because they believed that the plague was the result of God's wrath.

The only treatments that might have been somewhat successful were running away and quarantine. Those who fled the town and cities stood a chance of avoiding the plague altogether, but they also often succeeded in spreading it. Quarantine might have put a halt to the plague's rapid spread, but it was impossible to enforce. People did not understand what was causing the plague, so their attempts to treat it were focused on incorrect assumptions and information.

Death Toll

We know that the Black Death was horrible, but just how bad was it? Over four years, the plague killed twenty-five million people in Europe, which was around 40 percent of the entire population (although some estimates go as low as 30 and as high as 60 percent). England itself faced a similar death rate, with between 30 to 40 percent of people dying. That's just looking at Europe, though. The plague started in Asia and also spread to Africa, where the death rates were similar.

To put things in perspective, let's look at some more recent tragedies in human history. World War II was the deadliest military conflict in history, with anywhere from thirty million to sixty million deaths caused by the war worldwide. The Black Death killed about twenty-five million in Europe alone, which is close to the lower estimate for World War II. Still, comparing the numbers directly like this doesn't offer a full comparison of how deadly the two events were. Remember that the total population in the 1940s was far greater than it was in the 14th century. Percentages tell a clearer story. In World War II, the countries hit the hardest lost around 20 percent of their population, with most countries losing far less than that. The Black Death's impact was double that at around 40 percent and spread far more evenly across all of Europe.

Another way to understand just how bad the Black Death was is to compare it to other epidemics. The Spanish influenza pandemic of 1918 killed around fifty million people across the globe. If we include Asia and Africa, the Black Death may have had a similar or higher death count. However, again, percentages paint a clearer picture. Spanish influenza killed close to 3 percent of the world population. The Black Death killed 40 percent; even the lower estimate of 5 percent (which seems unlikely) is higher. In terms of deadliness, almost nothing else comes close.

If you want to understand the deadliness of the plague, you also need to remember that the Black Death refers to only a single outbreak of the plague from around 1347 to 1351. That single outbreak killed between a third and a half of the population of an entire continent. It's hard to find a catastrophe that even comes close to the Black Death.

Impact

Death on such a massive scale has far-reaching consequences, and the Black Death's impact was subsequently enormous.

The first impact was on medical knowledge. Medieval doctors had relied on ancient knowledge with ideas about the humors and the importance of the positions of the planets, but the Black Death shattered many of those conceptions. The plague refused to retreat with any of the treatments that medieval physicians tried, and the need for more medical knowledge became clear. The Black Death was thus a push to begin expanding medical knowledge, which was a big change in mindset from the traditionally medieval "people are sick because God wills it" approach.

The Black Death impacted religious attitudes beyond that as well. The plague was understandably viewed by many as possibly heralding the end of the world. Half of the people living in some cities and even entire villages were wiped out. Under such circumstances, an increase in religious piety and interest is only natural. At the same time, the Catholic Church was weakened by the loss of so many of its clergy. People were more interested in religion, while the church in Rome had less of a death grip. More colleges and universities sprang up but with stronger national rather than papal ties. This was the beginning of a process that would eventually lead to the Reformation. The absolute power and unity of the medieval church were at an end.

The Black Death also had an impact on the societal structure. With almost half the population suddenly gone, there were no longer enough workers. Large areas of previously cultivated lands fell into disuse, which was a serious blow to the wealthy landowners who owned them. The labor shortage gave the peasants who had not died leverage they had never had before. The demand for workers was higher than the supply, and for the first time, landowners were offering better wages and conditions to try to entice workers. The feudal system was seriously shaken.

The feudal system and overall social hierarchy of medieval England were also struck by the plague in another way. Since the plague killed both the elites and peasants alike, everyone was suddenly on a more equal footing. If the Black Death was God's wrath, then His wrath had descended on everyone. Peasants began to have a new awareness of their rights and dignity.

Peasants who survived the plague also began to experience better living. Not only were they being paid more, but taxes also went down. The destruction of 40 percent of the population also created a surplus of goods, which drove down the prices of everything. So, peasants had more money, and everything was cheaper. People were able to buy things that they had never been able to afford before and enjoy a new standard of living.

The changes in the lives of the lower classes are hard to overstate. It was only around thirty years after the Black Death that England experienced its first popular uprising: the Peasants' Revolt of 1381. The Black Death effectively broke the iconic feudal system of the Middle Ages, and for that reason, many people consider it to be the event that ended the medieval period.

Conclusion

That's the basic story of medieval England. The Black Death was the event that started the ball rolling toward the end by destroying the basic structure of medieval life, and we use the Battle of Bosworth and the end of the Plantagenet dynasty as a more distinct line in the sand for the end of medieval England. However, placing history into eras like this, while it certainly makes studying them more convenient, does create a sense of separation that doesn't exist in reality. The medieval period is not strictly confined between the borders of 600 and 1485. While it may feel like ancient history, things that happened in medieval England were crucial in shaping the world as we know it today.

We think of the Middle Ages and feudalism as a highly oppressive time, where the rich exploited the poor and where human rights were virtually nonexistent. This is, to a large degree, true, but medieval England was also the place where much of our understanding of human rights got started. The Magna Carta of 1212 is one of the most important documents in the history of democracy, for it was there for the first time that rules were set out to protect people from their own government. Around 150 years after the Magna Carta, England saw its first popular uprising in the Peasants' Revolt of 1381. What the barons had realized in their fights against the king, the general population now understood. They could make demands. They were human beings with dignity that should not be ignored by those above them. It was thus *during* the Middle Ages that people first began to get a real sense of their basic rights and to fight for them. The Renaissance often gets credit for developing the ideas that became central to our modern world, but it was in the Middle Ages that the necessary shifts in attitude began. Who knows where human rights and democracy would be today if not for the changes in mindset that took place in the medieval period?

That is far from the only way in which the medieval period has shaped our world. The wars and battles of the Middle Ages formed nations and governments. The Viking invasions pushed England into a unified nation. The Scottish Wars of Independence assured the independence of Scotland for another four hundred years, which would prove to have an enormous impact on English and Scottish history. King John's losses put an end to England's claim to lands that would become France. The map of England and Europe that we know today was in many ways drawn in the blood spilled in the Middle Ages.

Perhaps the most subtle impact of the Middle Ages has been in culture. Stories from the Middle Ages like the Arthurian legend, Beowulf, and a myriad of fairy tales continue to be told and retold in the present day. Buildings, especially churches, from the period still stand and are even used today. Games like chess and backgammon were introduced to the West in this era.

Finally, we cannot end the book without looking at how the medieval church has shaped our modern world. Whether you are a Christian or not, if you live in the Western world, you have been greatly affected by Christianity. It's hard to talk about almost any aspect of the Middle Ages without mentioning the church. It influenced everything from art, architecture, and literature to philosophy, law, and the very rhythm of life. The holidays we celebrate, the fact that we tend not to work on Sunday, hospitals, schools, and so many more aspects of daily life got started by the medieval church. The medieval church produced scholars and poets, started universities, and preserved manuscripts from the ancient world. Love it or hate it, Western civilization owes much of what it is to the medieval church.

There's a lot that people get wrong about medieval England. As we said at the very beginning of this journey, medieval England was neither as glamorous nor as horrendous as we often paint it. However, perhaps the thing we get most wrong is the idea that it was an entirely separate time. The modern world would not exist without the changes and developments that took place in the Middle Ages. The people who lived then may not have been as different from us as we think.

If you enjoyed this book, a review on Amazon would be greatly appreciated because it would mean a lot to hear from you.

To leave a review:

1. Open your camera app.
2. Point your mobile device at the QR code.
3. The review page will appear in your web browser.

Thanks for your support!

Here's another book by Enthralling History that you might like

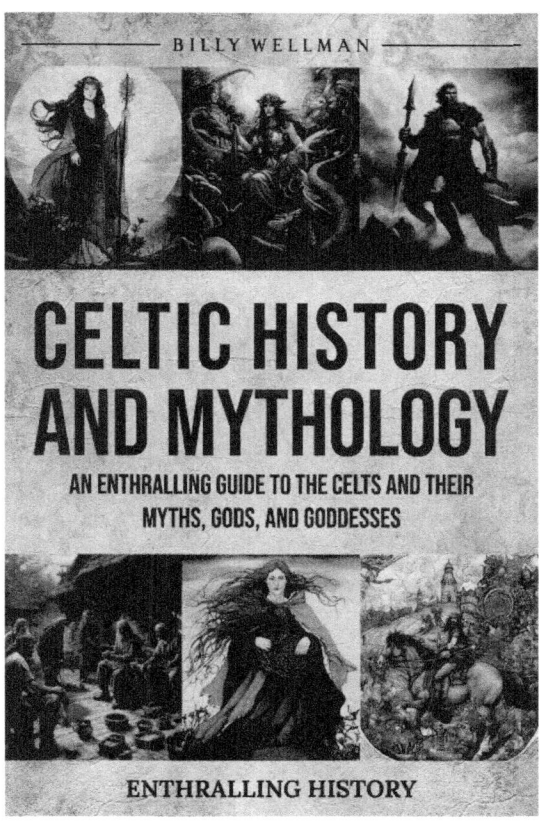

Free limited time bonus

Stop for a moment. We have a free bonus set up for you. The problem is this: we forget 90% of everything that we read after 7 days. Crazy fact, right? Here's the solution: we've created a printable, 1-page pdf summary for this book that you're reading now. All you have to do to get your free pdf summary is to go to the following website:

https://livetolearn.lpages.co/enthrallinghistory/

Or, Scan the QR code!

Once you do, it will be intuitive. Enjoy, and thank you!

Sources

Brown, M. P., & Farr, C. A. (Eds.). (2005). *Mercia: An Anglo-Saxon Kingdom in Europe*. Bloomsbury Publishing.

Brown, R. A. (1969). *The Normans and the Norman conquest / R. Allen Brown*. (1. publ.). Constable.

Chaney, W. A. (1960). "Paganism to Christianity in Anglo-Saxon England." *The Harvard Theological Review, 53*(3), 197–217. http://www.jstor.org/stable/1508400

Esposito, G. (2021). "The Viking Invasions of England." In *Armies of the Vikings, AD 793-1066*. Pen & Sword Books Limited.

Gebhardt, T. R. (2017). "From Bretwalda to Basileus: Imperial Concepts in Late Anglo-Saxon England?" In T. R. Gebhardt, C. Scholl, & J. Clauß (Eds.), *Transcultural Approaches to the Concept of Imperial Rule in the Middle Ages* (pp. 157–184). Peter Lang AG. http://www.jstor.org/stable/j.ctv6zdbwx.9

Higham, N. J., & Ryan, M. J. (2013). *The Anglo-Saxon world / Nicholas J. Higham and Martin J. Ryan*. Yale University Press. https://doi.org/10.12987/9780300195378

Hindley, G. (2013). *A brief history of the Anglo-Saxons*. Hachette UK.

Keynes, S. (1986). "A Tale of Two Kings: Alfred the Great and Æthelred the Unready." *Transactions of the Royal Historical Society, 36*, 195–217. https://doi.org/10.2307/3679065

Leyser, H. (2019). *A short history of the Anglo-Saxons / Henrietta Leyser*. (First edition.). I.B. Tauris and Company, Limited. https://doi.org/10.5040/9781350985148

Reynolds, S. (1985). "What Do We Mean by 'Anglo-Saxon' and 'Anglo-Saxons'?" *Journal of British Studies, 24*(4), 395–414. http://www.jstor.org/stable/175473

Williams, A. (2003). *Athelred the Unready: The Ill-Counselled King.* A&C Black.

"A Brief History of Capital Punishment in Britain." HistoryExtra, December 15, 2021. https://www.historyextra.com/period/modern/a-brief-history-of-capital-punishment-in-britain

"An Introduction to Early Medieval England." English Heritage. Accessed December 6, 2021.
 https://www.english-heritage.org.uk/learn/story-of-england/early-medieval

"Anglo-Saxons: A Brief History." The Historical Association. Accessed December 6, 2021
. https://www.history.org.uk/primary/resource/3865/anglo-saxons-a-brief-history

"Athelstan." Encyclopedia Britannica. Encyclopedia Britannica, inc. Accessed December 6, 2021. https://www.britannica.com/biography/Athelstan

"Battle of Agincourt." Encyclopedia Britannica. Encyclopedia Britannica, inc. Accessed
December 10, 2021. https://www.britannica.com/event/Battle-of-Agincourt

"Battle of Bannockburn." Encyclopedia Britannica. Encyclopedia Britannica, inc. Accessed
December 10, 2021. https://www.britannica.com/event/Battle-of-Bannockburn

"Battle of Bosworth Field." Encyclopedia Britannica. Encyclopedia Britannica, inc. Accessed
December 10, 2021. https://www.britannica.com/event/Battle-of-Bosworth-Field

"Battle of Edington." Encyclopedia Britannica. Encyclopedia Britannica, inc. Accessed December 10, 2021. https://www.britannica.com/topic/Battle-of-Edington

"Battle of Hastings." Encyclopedia Britannica. Encyclopedia Britannica, inc. Accessed December
6, 2021. https://www.britannica.com/event/Battle-of-Hastings

"Beowulf." British Library. Accessed January 25, 2022.
 https://www.bl.uk/collection-items/beowulf

"Bria 16 1 b the Murder of an Archbishop." Constitutional Rights Foundation. Accessed January 17,2022.
https://www.crf-usa.org/bill-of-rights-in-action/bria-16-1-b-the-murder-of-an-archbishop

"Crime and Medieval Punishment." History, December 2, 2021.

https://www.historyonthenet.com/medieval-life-crime-and-medieval-punishment

"Danelaw." Encyclopedia Britannica. Encyclopedia Britannica, inc. Accessed December 6, 2021. https://www.britannica.com/place/Danelaw

"Divine Right of Kings." Divine Right of Kings - New World Encyclopedia. Accessed December 29, 2021. https://www.newworldencyclopedia.org/entry/Divine_Right_of_Kings

"Durham Cathedral - an Overview." Durham Cathedral Durham World Heritage Site. Accessed

December 29, 2021. https://www.durhamworldheritagesite.com/learn/architecture/cathedral

"Four Humors - and There's the Humor of It: Shakespeare and the Four Humors." U.S. National

Library of Medicine. National Institutes of Health, September 19, 2013

. https://www.nlm.nih.gov/exhibition/shakespeare/fourhumors.html

"Gothic Architecture." Encyclopedia Britannica. Encyclopedia Britannica, inc. Accessed December 29, 2021. https://www.britannica.com/art/Gothic-architecture

"Harthacnut." Hardicanute, or Harthacnut, King of England and Denmark. Accessed December 6, 2021. https://www.englishmonarchs.co.uk/vikings_4.htm

"King Athelstan." Athelstan Museum, February 27, 2020. https://www.athelstanmuseum.org.uk/malmesbury-history/people/king-athelstan

"King Canute." Canute or Cnut the Great, son of Sweyn Forkbeard. Accessed December 6, 2021. https://www.englishmonarchs.co.uk/vikings_2.htm

"King Edward I of England." BBC Bitesize. BBC, December 6, 2019. https://www.bbc.co.uk/bitesize/topics/z8g86sg/articles/z77dbdm

"List of 5 Most Significant Battles of the Hundred Years' War." List of 5 Most Significant Battles of the Hundred Years' War - History Lists. Accessed December 6, 2021. https://historylists.org/events/list-of-5-most-significant-battles-of-the-hundred-years-war.html

"List of English Monarchs." Wikipedia. Wikimedia Foundation, December 5, 2021. https://en.wikipedia.org/wiki/List_of_English_monarchs

"Magna Carta (1215) to Henry IV (1399) - UK Parliament." parliament.uk. Accessed December 29, 2021. https://www.parliament.uk/about/living-heritage/evolutionofparliament/originsofparliament/birthofparliament/keydates/1215to1399

"Medieval Architecture." English Heritage. Accessed December 29, 2021. https://www.english-heritage.org.uk/learn/story-of-england/medieval/architecture

"Medieval Religion." English Heritage. Accessed January 17, 2022. https://www.english-heritage.org.uk/learn/story-of-england/medieval/religion

"Monsters, Marvels, and Mythical Beasts: Medieval Monsters." Research Guides. Accessed January 25, 2022. https://guides.library.uab.edu/c.php?g=1014328&p=7346799

"Old English Language." Encyclopedia Britannica. Encyclopedia Britannica, inc. Accessed December 6, 2021. https://www.britannica.com/topic/Old-English-language

"Plague - Symptoms." Centers for Disease Control and Prevention. Centers for Disease Control and Prevention, November 15, 2021. https://www.cdc.gov/plague/symptoms/index.html

"Robert the Bruce." BBC Bitesize. BBC, December 6, 2019. https://www.bbc.co.uk/bitesize/topics/z8g86sg/articles/zm2747h

"The Anglo-Saxon Tribal Kingdoms." The Anglo-Saxon Tribal Kingdoms - The Heptarchy. Accessed December 6, 2021. https://www.englishmonarchs.co.uk/saxon_25.html

"The Battle of Edington." The Battle of Edington. Accessed December 10, 2021. https://www.englishmonarchs.co.uk/vikings_16.html

"The Canterbury Tales by Geoffrey Chaucer." British Library. Accessed January 25, 2022. https://www.bl.uk/collection-items/the-canterbury-tales-by-geoffrey-chaucer

"The Celts of England." Celtic Life International - Celebrating the Celtic Life for over 30 years. Accessed December 6, 2021. https://celticlifeintl.com/the-celts-of-england

"The English Invasion of Wales." Historic UK. Accessed December 6, 2021. https://www.historic-uk.com/HistoryUK/HistoryofWales/The-English-conquest-of-Wales

"The First Battle of St Albans." Historic UK. Accessed December 6, 2021. https://www.historic-uk.com/HistoryMagazine/DestinationsUK/The-First-Battle-of-St-Albans

"The Great Famine." The great famine. Accessed December 6, 2021. http://www.halinaking.co.uk/Location/Yorkshire/Frames/History/1315%20Great%20Famine/Great%20Famine.htm

"The History of the English Longbow." Historic UK. Accessed December 10, 2021.

https://www.historic-uk.com/HistoryUK/HistoryofEngland/The-Longbow

"The Medieval Marvel Few People Know." BBC Travel. BBC. Accessed December 29, 2021. https://www.bbc.com/travel/article/20170427-the-extraordinary-angel-roofs-of-england

"The Period of the Scandinavian Invasions." Encyclopedia Britannica. Encyclopedia Britannica, inc. Accessed December 6, 2021. https://www.britannica.com/place/United-Kingdom/The-period-of-the-Scandinavian-invasions#ref482644

"The Plague, 1331-1770." The Black Death. Accessed January 27, 2022. http://hosted.lib.uiowa.edu/histmed/plague

"Trial by Ordeal." Oxford Reference. Accessed 1 Jan. 2022. https://www.oxfordreference.com/view/10.1093/oi/authority.20110803105644353

"Romanesque Architecture." Encyclopedia Britannica. Encyclopedia Britannica, inc. Accessed December 29, 2021. https://www.britannica.com/art/Romanesque-architecture

"Scotland's History - the Wars of Independence." BBC. BBC. Accessed December 10, 2021. https://www.bbc.co.uk/scotland/history/articles/the_wars_of_independence

"St Hild of Whitby." English Heritage. Accessed December 29, 2021. https://www.english-heritage.org.uk/visit/places/whitby-abbey/history-and-stories/st-hild

"Viking Ships." Royal Museums Greenwich. Accessed December 6, 2021. https://www.rmg.co.uk/stories/topics/viking-ships

"Wars of the Roses." Historic UK. Accessed December 6, 2021. https://www.historic-uk.com/HistoryUK/HistoryofEngland/The-Wars-of-the-Roses

"Wat Tyler and the Peasants Revolt." Historic UK. Accessed December 6, 2021. https://www.historic-uk.com/HistoryUK/HistoryofEngland/Wat-Tyler-the-Peasants-Revolt

"What Happened to Britain after the Romans Left?" The Great Courses Daily, July 29, 2020. https://www.thegreatcoursesdaily.com/britain-after-the-romans-left

"Women Get the Vote." UK Parliament. Accessed December 13, 2021. https://www.parliament.uk/about/living-heritage/transformingsociety/electionsvoting/womenvote/overview/thevote

Abbott, G. "Burning at the Stake." Encyclopedia Britannica, July 5, 2019. https://www.britannica.com/topic/burning-at-the-stake.

Barker, Juliet. *1381: The Year of the Peasants' Revolt.* Cambridge: The Belknap Press of Harvard University Press, 2014.

Barlow, Frank. *The Feudal Kingdom of England 1042-1216.* 5th ed. London: Longman, 1999.

Bell, Bethan. "A Ghoulish Tour of Medieval Punishments." BBC News. BBC, July 2, 2016.
https://www.bbc.com/news/uk-england-36641921

Bovey, Alixe. "The Medieval Church: from Dedication to Dissent." British Library, April 30,
2015. https://www.bl.uk/the-middle-ages/articles/church-in-the-middle-ages-from-dedication-to-dissent

Bovey, Alixe. "The Medieval Diet." British Library. Accessed January 4, 2022.
https://www.bl.uk/the-middle-ages/articles/the-medieval-diet

Bovey, Alixe. "Medieval Monsters." British Library, April 30, 2015.
https://www.bl.uk/the-middle-ages/articles/medieval-monsters-from-the-mystical-to-the-demonic

Bovey, Alixe. "Women in Medieval Society." British Library, April 30, 2015.
https://www.bl.uk/the-middle-ages/articles/women-in-medieval-society

Boyer, Sam. "The Battle of Mount Badon." The Battle of Mount Badon | Robbins Library Digital
Projects, 2004. https://d.lib.rochester.edu/camelot/text/boyer-battle-of-mt-badon-overview

Bremner, Ian. "History - British History in Depth: Wales: English Conquest of Wales C.1200 –
1415." BBC. BBC, February 17, 2011.
https://www.bbc.co.uk/history/british/middle_ages/wales_conquest_01.shtml

Britannica, T. Editors of Encyclopedia. "Arthurian legend." Encyclopedia Britannica, May 27,
2021. https://www.britannica.com/topic/Arthurian-legend.

Britannica, T. Editors of Encyclopedia. "Assize of Clarendon." Encyclopedia Britannica,
September 6, 2007. https://www.britannica.com/event/Assize-of-Clarendon.

Britannica, T. Editors of Encyclopedia. "Bayeux Tapestry." Encyclopedia Britannica, May 30,
2021. https://www.britannica.com/topic/Bayeux-Tapestry.

Britannica, T. Editors of Encyclopedia. "Beowulf." Encyclopedia Britannica, August 20, 2021. https://www.britannica.com/topic/Beowulf.

Britannica, T. Editors of Encyclopedia. "Black Death." Encyclopedia Britannica, August 27, 2021.

https://www.britannica.com/event/Black-Death.

Britannica, T. Editors of Encyclopedia. "Compurgation." Encyclopedia Britannica, November 22, 2011.
https://www.britannica.com/topic/compurgation.

Britannica, T. Editors of Encyclopedia. "Drawing and Quartering." Encyclopedia Britannica, July

5, 2019. https://www.britannica.com/topic/drawing-and-quartering.

Britannica, T. Editors of Encyclopedia. "Illuminated Manuscript." Encyclopedia Britannica, July

15, 2021. https://www.britannica.com/art/illuminated-manuscript.

Britannica, T. Editors of Encyclopedia. "Manorial Court." Encyclopedia Britannica, February 15,

2007. https://www.britannica.com/topic/manorial-court.

Britannica, T. Editors of Encyclopedia. "Miracle Play." Encyclopedia Britannica, February 6,

2019. https://www.britannica.com/art/miracle-play.

Britannica, T. Editors of Encyclopedia. "Morality Play." Encyclopedia Britannica, January 16,

2014. https://www.britannica.com/art/morality-play-dramatic-genre.

Britannica, T. Editors of Encyclopedia. "Ordeal." Encyclopedia Britannica, April 13, 2018.

https://www.britannica.com/topic/ordeal.

Britannica, T. Editors of Encyclopedia. "Plague." Encyclopedia Britannica, August 6, 2020.

https://www.britannica.com/science/plague.

Britannica, T. Editors of Encyclopedia. "Templar." Encyclopedia Britannica, April 28, 2020.

https://www.britannica.com/topic/Templars.

Britannica, T. Editors of Encyclopedia. "The Canterbury Tales." Encyclopedia Britannica, May

14, 2020. https://www.britannica.com/topic/The-Canterbury-Tales.

Britannica, T. Editors of Encyclopedia. "Tuberculosis." Encyclopedia Britannica, July 29, 2021.

https://www.britannica.com/science/tuberculosis.

Britannica, T. Editors of Encyclopedia. "Sweating Sickness." Encyclopedia Britannica, February

15, 2019. https://www.britannica.com/science/sweating-sickness.

Brooke, John. "The Black Death and Its Aftermath." Origins, June 2020. https://origins.osu.edu/connecting-history/covid-black-death-plague-lessons?language_content_entity=en

Buis, Alena. "The Romanesque in Normandy and England." Art and Visual Culture Prehistory to

Renaissance. Accessed December 29, 2021. https://pressbooks.bccampus.ca/cavestocathedrals/chapter/the-romanesque-in-normandy-and-england

Carpenter, David. *The Struggle for Mastery: Britain 1066-1284.* Oxford: Oxford University Press,

2003.

Cartwright, Mark. "Clothes in Medieval England." World History Encyclopedia. World History

Encyclopedia, June 28, 2018. https://www.worldhistory.org/article/1248/clothes-in-medieval-england

Cartwright, Mark. "Leisure in an English Medieval Castle." World History Encyclopedia. World

History Encyclopedia, May 31, 2018. https://www.worldhistory.org/article/1232/leisure-in-an-english-medieval-castle

Castelow, Ellen. "The Origins and History of Fairies." Historic UK. Accessed January 25, 2022

. https://www.historic-uk.com/CultureUK/The-Origins-of-Fairies

Cybulskie, Danièle. "Medieval Pilgrimages: It's All about the Journey." Medievalists.net, August

4, 2017. https://www.medievalists.net/2015/08/medieval-pilgrimages-its-all-about-the-journey

Daileader, Philip. "Henry II vs. the Church: The Murder of Thomas Becket." The Great Courses

Daily, November 4, 2020. https://www.thegreatcoursesdaily.com/henry-ii-vs-the-church-the-murder-of-thomas-becket

de Beer, Lloyd, and Naomi Speakman. "Thomas Becket: The Murder That Shook the Middle Ages - British Museum Blog." British Museum Blog - Explore stories from the Museum, May 27, 2021. https://blog.britishmuseum.org/thomas-becket-the-murder-that-shook-the-middle-ages

Duggan, L. G. "Indulgence." Encyclopedia Britannica, November 25, 2015.

https://www.britannica.com/topic/indulgence.

Fee, Christopher R. *Gods, Heroes, and Kings: The Battle for Mythic Britain.* Cary: Oxford

University Press, Incorporated, 2004. Accessed January 25, 2022. ProQuest eBook Central.

Flantzer, Susan. "Royal Deaths from Plague." Unofficial Royalty, January 9, 2022.

https://www.unofficialroyalty.com/royal-deaths-from-plague-4-23/.

Fleming, Robin. Britain After Rome: The Fall and Rise: 400 to 1070. New York: Penguin, 2011.

Goldiner, Sigrid. "Medicine in the Middle Ages." Metmuseum.org, January 1, 2012.

https://www.metmuseum.org/toah/hd/medm/hd_medm.htm.

Hajar, Rachel. "The Air of History (Part II) Medicine in the Middle Ages." Heart views: The

official journal of the Gulf Heart Association. Medknow Publications & Media Pvt Ltd, October

2012. https://www.ncbi.nlm.nih.gov/pmc/articles/PMC3573364/.

Harrison, Julian. "Who Were the Anglo-Saxons?" British Library. Accessed December 6, 2021.

https://www.bl.uk/anglo-saxons/articles/who-were-the-anglo-saxons.

Hannan, M. T. and Kranzberg, Melvin. "History of the Organization of Work." Encyclopedia

Britannica, November 1, 2021. https://www.britannica.com/topic/history-of-work-organization-648000.

Highman, Nicholas J., and Martin J. Ryan. *The Anglo-Saxon World.* New Haven: Yale University

Press, 2013.

Hitti, Miranda. "Bloodletting's Benefits." WebMD. WebMD, September 10, 2004.

https://www.webmd.com/men/news/20040910/bloodlettings-benefits

Hudson, Alison. "The Battle of Hastings: Fact and Fiction." British Library. Accessed December

6, 2021. https://www.bl.uk/anglo-saxons/articles/the-battle-of-hastings-fact-and-fiction

Ibeji, Mike. "Becket, the Church and Henry II." BBC. BBC, February 17, 2011.

https://www.bbc.co.uk/history/british/middle_ages/becket_01.shtml

Johnson, Ben. "Æthelflæd (Aethelflaed), Lady of the Mercians." Historic UK. Accessed December

29, 2021. https://www.historic-uk.com/HistoryUK/HistoryofEngland/Aethelflaed-Lady-of-the-Mercians

Johnson, Ben. "Norman and Medieval Fashion and Clothing." Historic UK. Accessed January 5,

2022. https://www.historic-uk.com/CultureUK/Medieval-Fashion

Jones, Dan. *The Wars of the Roses.* New York: Penguin, 2014.

Kemp, J. Arthur. "St. Anselm of Canterbury." *Encyclopedia Britannica,* September 20, 2021.

https://www.britannica.com/biography/Saint-Anselm-of-Canterbury

Kerr, Margaret H., Richard D. Forsyth, and Michael J. Plyley. "Cold Water and Hot Iron: Trial by

Ordeal in England." *The Journal of Interdisciplinary History* 22, no. 4 (1992): 573–95.

https://doi.org/10.2307/205237

Leyser, Henrietta. *The Anglo-Saxons.* London: I.B Tauris & Co., 2017.

Mark, Joshua J. "Medieval Cures for the Black Death." World History Encyclopedia. World

History Encyclopedia, April 15, 2020. https://www.worldhistory.org/article/1540/medieval-cures-for-the-black-death

Mark, Joshua J. "Medieval Folklore." World History Encyclopedia. World History Encyclopedia,

February 19, 2019. https://www.worldhistory.org/Medieval_Folklore

Mark, Joshua J. "Medieval Literature." World History Encyclopedia. World History

Encyclopedia, December 26, 2021. https://www.worldhistory.org/Medieval_Literature

Mark, Joshua J. "Religion in the Middle Ages." World History Encyclopedia. World History

 Encyclopedia, June 28, 2019. https://www.worldhistory.org/article/1411/religion-in-the-middle-ages

Mark, Joshua J. "The Medieval Church." World History Encyclopedia. World History

Encyclopedia, June 17, 2019. https://www.worldhistory.org/Medieval_Church

Mark, Joshua J. "Women in the Middle Ages." World History Encyclopedia. World History Encyclopedia, March 18, 2019.
https://www.worldhistory.org/article/1345/women-in-the-middle-ages

Masson, Victoria. "The Black Death." Historic UK. Accessed January 27, 2022. https://www.historic-uk.com/HistoryUK/HistoryofEngland/The-Black-Death

Palmer, Bill. "Our 1918 Pandemic – the Numbers Then and Now." marshallindependent.com, March 27, 2021. https://www.marshallindependent.com/opinion/local-columns/2021/03/our-1918-pandemic-the-numbers-then-and-now

Pernoud, R. "Eleanor of Aquitaine." *Encyclopedia Britannica*, May 31, 2021. https://www.britannica.com/biography/Eleanor-of-Aquitaine

Rhodes, P. and Bryant, John H. "Public Health." Encyclopedia Britannica, April 22, 2021. https://www.britannica.com/topic/public-health.

Ross, David. "Anglo-Saxon England - Culture and Society." Britain Express. Accessed December 9, 2021. https://www.britainexpress.com/History/anglo-saxon_life-kinship_and_lordship.htm

Ruben, Miri. The Hollow Crown: A History of Britain in the Late Middle Ages. New York: Penguin, 2005.

Shipman, Pat Lee. "The Bright Side of the Black Death." American Scientist, May 2, 2018 . https://www.americanscientist.org/article/the-bright-side-of-the-black-death

Simons, E. Norman. "Mary I." Encyclopedia Britannica, November 13, 2021. https://www.britannica.com/biography/Mary-I.

Singer, Sholom A. "The Expulsion of the Jews from England in 1290." *The Jewish Quarterly Review* 55, no. 2 (1964): 117–36. https://doi.org/10.2307/1453793

Sorabella, Jean. "Pilgrimage in Medieval England." Metmuseum.org, April 1, 2011. https://www.metmuseum.org/toah/hd/pilg/hd_pilg.htm

Stacey, J. "John Wycliffe." Encyclopedia Britannica, December 27, 2021. https://www.britannica.com/biography/John-Wycliffe.

Stephens, J.E.R. "The Growth of Trial by Jury in England." jstor.org. The Harvard Law Review Association. Accessed January 3, 2022. https://www.jstor.org/stable/pdf/1321755.pdf

Trueman, C N. "Food and Drink in Medieval England." History Learning Site. The History

Learning Site, March 5, 2015. https://www.historylearningsite.co.uk/medieval-england/food-and-drink-in-medieval-england

Ward, Jennifer. *Women in England in the Middle Ages.* London: Hambledon Continuum, 2006.

Webb, Diana. "Pilgrimage Destinations in England." The Becket Story. Accessed January 17, 2022. https://thebecketstory.org.uk/pilgrimage/destinations-england

Wheelis, Mark. "Biological Warfare at the 1346 Siege of Caffa." Emerging infectious diseases.

Centers for Disease Control and Prevention, September 2002. https://www.ncbi.nlm.nih.gov/pmc/articles/PMC2732530

Zeisel, H. and Kalven, Harry. "Jury." Encyclopedia Britannica, March 29, 2019. https://www.britannica.com/topic/jury.

Printed in Great Britain
by Amazon

50684689R00165